Violence and Sex Work

Violence and Sex Work in Britain

Hilary Kinnell

WILLAN
PUBLISHING

Published by

Willan Publishing
Culmcott House
Mill Street, Uffculme
Cullompton, Devon
EX15 3AT, UK
Tel: +44(0)1884 840337
Fax: +44(0)1884 840251
e-mail: info@willanpublishing.co.uk
website: www.willanpublishing.co.uk

Published simultaneously in the USA and Canada by

Willan Publishing
c/o ISBS, 920 NE 58th Ave, Suite 300,
Portland, Oregon 97213-3786, USA
Tel: +001(0)503 287 3093
Fax: +001(0)503 280 8832
e-mail: info@isbs.com
website: www.isbs.com

First published 2008

ISBN   978-1-84392-350-3 paperback
       978-1-84392-351-0 hardback

British Library Cataloguing-in-Publication Data

A catalogue record for this book is available from the British Library.

Project managed by Deer Park Productions, Tavistock, Devon
Typeset by GCS, Leighton Buzzard, Bedfordshire
Printed and bound by T.J. International Ltd, Padstow, Cornwall

Contents

Acknowledgements

To thank all the people who have helped me, directly and indirectly, in writing this book, would add significantly to its length: my children, friends and colleagues, academics and practitioners, have all been generous with their support, information, advice and tolerance, not only during the period it has taken me to write it, but over all the years of my involvement in the sex work field. Mostly importantly, though, I am indebted to all the working women whose lives have touched mine, especially those who worked with me in the early days of the outreach project in Birmingham: you know who you are – thank you!

Sex worker or prostitute?

'We call ourselves "working girls". When you say "prostitute" it's a dirty word.'

(Addley 2006)

I prefer the term 'sex worker' to 'prostitute' because of the negative associations of the latter, but I also use 'prostitute', particularly in historical contexts, because that was the term then in common usage. Women who sell sex share a perception of paid-for sex as 'work' in contrast to the 'real sex' of private relationships, a distinction which is lost in arguments about whether what they do should be seen as 'work' or 'abuse'. I do not think that sex work is 'a job like any other', it manifestly is not, but commercial sex is unquestionably an economic activity, so the term 'work' seems entirely appropriate. I also believe that understanding sex work as a form of labour helps to promote rights and protections for sex workers, such as the right to safe working conditions and protection from exploitation and violence.

Introduction

Who am I to talk?

I began working with sex workers in 1987, when I set up an HIV prevention outreach project for sex workers in Birmingham. I did not expect to become a campaigner about sex work in general nor violence in particular: my interest was in sexually transmitted infections, having joined the Public Health Medicine Department of the Central Birmingham Health Authority (CBHA) in a generic HIV prevention role in January 1987.[1] CBHA happened to cover the parts of the city which contained the major areas of street soliciting and most of the saunas,[2] so investigating the HIV prevention needs of sex workers was on their agenda from the start. Nobody knew anything about the number of sex workers, how many customers they had, whether they used condoms or injected drugs, nor about existing levels of HIV in that or any other subsection of the population. It was clearly the business of the Public Health Department to find out the epidemiological facts, and to develop such prevention programmes as seemed necessary. Thus it became my job to explore this area of human behaviour.

---

[1] In 1987 the Department was called the Community Medicine Department, but its name was soon changed to Public Health Medicine. The CBHA merged with South Birmingham Health Authority in 1993.

[2] Also known as massage parlours, but in Birmingham they were called saunas.

The attitudes of the sex workers towards the outreach project were almost universally positive, although some were suspicious of any overtures from 'officials' and 'social worker types'. Some resented the inference that they needed advice from 'straight people' about protecting their health or that they couldn't be trusted to buy their own condoms, but one objection which they never expressed in any form was abhorrence for policies to 'provide a clean supply of women for men's risk-free sexual gratification', a discourse which has been common currency among some feminists for over a century. I have always felt this objection to sexual health promotion demonstrates grotesque cruelty, implying as it does that nothing should be done to prevent women contracting HIV, syphilis, gonorrhoea, herpes and cervical cancer, in order to punish men for having sex with them. Twenty years ago, when Britain was in the grip of a national panic about the advent of HIV, only die-hard moralists like the Birmingham MP, Dame Jill Knight argued that trying to prevent it was morally offensive.[3] Sex workers, however, were mostly surprised and rather touched that 'officials' were trying to help them to protect themselves.

I, therefore, do not feel any need to apologise for my original sexual health perspective. There are some things we, as a society, know how to do: preventing sexually transmitted diseases is one of them; it's easy and it's cheap, in comparison with treatment or cure, if cure is possible. There are other things we do not know how to do: changing sexual behaviour is one of these. We can deplore and punish, but so far no kind of socially unacceptable sexual behaviour has proved noticeably amenable to reform. Neither do we seem much motivated to cure poverty or homelessness or drug addiction. This suggests to me that the drivers of the sex industry, both demand and supply, are beyond society's current ability to influence significantly, but harm reduction, including prevention of sexually transmitted diseases, is possible. My only anger in this context is for the craven way in which some public health authorities have neglected the health needs of sex workers for other less politically difficult 'target groups' in the years since.

However, at the time, it was immediately obvious that street sex workers had many pressing concerns besides sexual health, including

---

[3]Dame Jill Knight, MP for the Edgbaston constituency in Birmingham until 1997. '"Aids is a myth" say moral crusaders', *The Sunday Correspondent*, 20 January 1990; 'MP's fury at condom handout', *Birmingham Post*, 22 February 1995.

their vulnerability to violence. After meeting the formidable Australian contingent of sex worker activists at the 1989 International Conference on AIDS in Montreal, and learning about their 'Ugly Mugs' system for warning sex workers about violent individuals, we began issuing our own Ugly Mugs, and they proved as welcome as the free condoms. There were also some successful prosecutions, where police were able to identify attackers with the help of details on the Ugly Mugs. Then in September 1992, Birmingham City Council announced its intention of establishing a tolerance zone for street soliciting, on a disused factory site, remote from either houses, shops or services.[4] Not only were street workers to be forced to work there, but women working from houses and saunas were to be driven there too. Although this scheme never materialised, its prospect led us to do a quick survey of sex workers' experiences of violence, to find out if location of work materially affected their risk of violence. The results were stunningly conclusive: equal numbers of street and indoor workers were interviewed, but 84 per cent of all violent incidents reported had taken place when the victim was engaged in street work (Kinnell 1995).

Over the following two years, three sex workers known to us were murdered, as were ten others elsewhere in the country. We had numerous visits from police officers from different forces wanting to copy our Ugly Mugs file, or show us pictures of unidentified dead women, or check our contact records to say when we had last seen them. It was then that I began to collect information about sex worker murders, and have been doing so ever since. However, all possibility of serious consideration of methods to reduce sex workers' vulnerability was swept aside in the summer of 1994, when the people of Balsall Heath[5] decided the way to deal with sex workers was to drive them off the streets with baseball bats and dogs. None of the objectives of the outreach project – not sexual health, drug care, safety, support or even maintaining basic contact with sex workers – were considered remotely important, compared to the political mileage to be made out of support for the aggrieved residents (see Chapter 8).

I left Birmingham in March 1996, and afterwards became involved in Europap,[6] a European network of agencies and researchers

---

[4]'Vice girl factory site plan for Brum', *Evening Mail*, 11 September 1992.
[5]Balsall Heath: the main area of street soliciting in Birmingham at that time.
[6]Originally European Projects for AIDS Prevention in Prostitution, then renamed European Network for HIV/STD Prevention in Prostitution.

concerned with sex work and sexual health (Mak 1996). In 1998 I became national coordinator for Europap-UK, supporting and developing a network of agencies for sex workers throughout the country, which was reconstituted as the UK Network of Sex Work Projects (UKNSWP) in 2002. The UKNSWP aims to:

> promote the health, safety, civil and human rights of sex workers, including their rights to live free from violence, intimidation, coercion or exploitation, to engage in the work as safely as possible, and to receive high quality health and other services in conditions of trust and confidentiality, without discrimination on the grounds of gender, sexual orientation, disability, race, culture or religion. The UKNSWP recognises and supports the rights of individual sex workers to self-determination. This includes the right to remain in sex work or leave sex work.

I remained on the UKNSWP Executive Committee until March 2005, and continue to be an Associate Member. While I fully support its aims, the UKNSWP is not responsible for any opinions, conclusions or mistakes contained in this book.

Through Europap-UK and subsequently UKNSWP, national working groups were set up to address issues of particular concern to sex workers and to those providing services to them. One was the Safety, Violence and Policing Group, which first met in October 1999 and continued to meet until 2007. Work begun by this group culminated in the UKNSWP's Good Practice Guidance on running Ugly Mug and Dodgy Punter schemes (UKNSWP 2007). During my years as the national network coordinator, with input from numerous agencies working with sex workers, violence and its relationship to law enforcement strategies became my chief concern. I have written various contributions to books and journals on this subject, and now welcome the opportunity Willan Publishing has given me to explore the issues in far greater depth.

Why this book?

There is a mass of academic literature about prostitution. Numerous disciplines explore the subject from every possible angle: sociology,

---

This network was funded by the Europe Against AIDS programme of the European Commission.

criminology, jurisprudence, geography, theology, psychology, epidemiology, health promotion – no one could possibly keep abreast of all the theories, insights and evidence that cram libraries and wash around cyberspace, and I do not pretend to be aware of more than a small fraction of it. Even so, it seems to me that there is still considerable misunderstanding of the nature of violence in the sex industry and that public awareness of the issues is constrained by media representations, fictional stereotypes and widespread misinformation. After Steve Wright's conviction for the five Ipswich murders, Joan Smith (2008) and Fiona McTaggart MP misquoted British research on sex workers' risk of murder and applied figures for the USA to the UK, while Denis MacShane MP demanded compulsory DNA testing for clients who use brothels, claiming 'almost all the horrible murders of prostituted women are by men who have frequented them beforehand.' In fact only three sex workers were killed when working in a brothel in 17 years.[7] A few weeks earlier, Welsh Assembly Member Christine Chapman claimed 'over the last 10 years, about 60 prostitutes have been murdered in England and Wales, with just 16 arrests.'[8] This wildly inaccurate statement seems to be based on a poorly written paragraph in the Home Office document, *Paying the Price* (2004: para. 5.22), which is referenced to an article I wrote in 2001 but is now, naturally, out of date (Kinnell 2001).[9]

The belief that sex worker homicides are common, almost always committed by 'clients' and frequently unsolvable, contributes to visions of a dark and unknowable territory beyond the rule of law, and those who cultivate this view of the sex industry seem to have little interest in the facts, while government and police secretiveness make accurate information hard to get, allowing misconceptions to flourish. I hope to shed some light on the characteristics of both victims and perpetrators of violence in the sex industry, the circumstances in which it takes place, and the policies that fail to prevent it.

It is also apparent that there are some with extensive knowledge of the sex industry, whose experience is underrepresented in academic

---

[7]See page 175; 'Brothel users "should give DNA"', *BBC News*, 28 February 2008 (see http://news.bbc.co.uk/go/pr/fr/-/1/hi/uk_politics/7269531.stm).
[8]'Tragic reality of prostitution', *BBC News*, 6 February 2008 (see http://news.bbc.co.uk/go/pr/fr/-/1/hi/wales/7228949.stm).
[9]This article (Kinnell, 2001), refers to 51 homicides, 29 prosecutions and 16 known convictions (not arrests) for homicides committed between January 1990 and March 2001.

literature, who rarely feature in the Comment pages of *The Guardian* and whose voices are frequently disregarded in policy debates. These are people who work in outreach projects for sex workers: people who have spent years engaging with sex workers; who have met thousands of women and hundreds of their clients, partners, pimps, friends and families; who have negotiated with local residents, vigilantes, social workers, police officers and politicians; who have battled countless times to get women into refuges; spent weeks supporting women due to give evidence in court against rapists and pimps; who have identified dead bodies and organised funerals. No doubt there are epistemologists who have wise things to say about this kind of knowledge. I don't know, and I have rarely met a sex worker who would care, but I think it is the kind of knowledge that deserves a lot more attention than it gets. Just as sex workers are marginalised, regarded with suspicion if not distaste, their views discounted, so, frequently, are those who work with them, the inconvenient truths that their work reveals ignored, and sometimes suppressed by bullying and threats. This silencing of the most knowledgeable and most relevant voices in public discussions of prostitution is particularly evident in relation to sex workers' safety and vulnerability to violence, and is something I hope this book will redress.

I began writing this book in the immediate aftermath of the Ipswich murders of 2006. Despite its appalling tragedy, the enormity of the crimes committed in Suffolk led to an explosion of public debate about sex work policy, which gave me hope that, if only more people understood why sex workers are vulnerable to violence, about who commits it and why current policies have failed so miserably to prevent it, the tide of cruelty might begin to turn. I also hoped that those with direct influence over prostitution policy would recognise the lessons of Ipswich and refocus their attention on safety instead of repression. As the months have progressed since, it has become painfully obvious that the government intends to persist with its policies of repression, further criminalising sex workers and their clients, reintroducing imprisonment for street soliciting, doggedly ignoring all the lessons of the recent and more distant past. Since politicians' memories seem so short, perhaps it is worth mentioning that during all the years Peter Sutcliffe was killing women[10], sex workers were frequently sent to prison for months at a time. Neither the fear of imprisonment nor the fear of murder halted the street

---

[10] 1975–1980.

sex industry, at a time when crack was unheard of and other illegal drugs were of minor importance. The Sutcliffe era may have sparked enough shame and disquiet over the vulnerability of sex workers and the social attitudes that encouraged violence, to allow the removal of imprisonment as a penalty for soliciting and loitering.[11] Yet today, in the shadow of another serial killer, there is neither shame nor disquiet about the policies that have allowed this to happen again. The declared strategy of the Home Office towards prostitution is to eliminate it, its tools a ragbag of recycled instruments of repression and enforced reform, already tested and discredited by decades of failure to produce the desired result. Despite all evidence to the contrary, I do not believe this obstinacy arises out of stupidity or ignorance. The more I have studied violence against sex workers, the more convinced I become that prostitution policy is not designed to protect the vulnerable, nor to deter or restrain the violent, but to 'send messages' to a variety of moral and voting constituencies, whose views on the subject are much more important to policy-makers than the safety of a few thousand politically powerless and friendless unfortunates, and, of course, to facilitate other money-making, political and criminal justice agendas.

The government's stance is legitimated by a radical feminist ideology which asserts that sex work is intrinsically violent and that all men who pay for sex are violent misogynists. This ideology was both influenced by, and derived credibility from, the crimes of Peter Sutcliffe, the last significant case of serial sex worker murders before Ipswich. I have, therefore, opened this book with a re-examination of the case of Peter Sutcliffe, partly because of its enduring influence on common beliefs about murderous violence towards sex workers and the nature of sex workers' vulnerability, but also to explore various manifestations of feminist activism at that time, to assess how far radical feminists identified themselves with sex workers or addressed their interests.

I then offer an alternative definition of violence which reflects the ways in which sex workers themselves define and experience it, and includes activities which cause fear, humiliation, manhandling or exposure to danger. This approach not only encompasses criminal violence committed by individuals, only some of whom may be 'clients', but also legalised, institutional and societal violence. The rest of the book examines the nature and extent of this violence, the circumstances which facilitate it, and the people responsible for

---

[11]Criminal Justice Act 1982, s 71.

it, challenging assumptions that violence towards sex workers only occurs in interactions with clients, or from pimps and traffickers, and questioning whether these assumptions help to camouflage the way in which public abhorrence for sex work gives tacit consent to violence from many sectors of the community and interferes with measures that might prevent it.

As I write, the prospect of any change in the direction of government policy towards sex work seems remote. It seems as if, despite the numerous changes which British society has experienced in the past century, there are still powerful interest groups, perhaps powerful social instincts, which demand that there should still be a class of women who are designated as the recipients of violence and abuse, and for whom the law offers no protection and little redress. I began by hoping that my book might help to change this, but I am not optimistic. I can, nevertheless, document the nature of the violence which sex workers experience, and challenge the ideas and policies that allow these things to happen. This is my aim.

Chapter 1

Peter Sutcliffe: a long shadow

Between 1975 and 1980 Peter Sutcliffe, a lorry driver living in Bradford, West Yorkshire, attacked and murdered women, some of whom were sex workers. Most of his known crimes were committed in Yorkshire, hence the sobriquet he acquired long before his arrest – 'the Yorkshire Ripper'. The West Yorkshire police wrongly assumed that the culprit they sought was primarily motivated by hatred of prostitutes; when other, 'innocent women' were also attacked, intense fear and anger was felt by numerous women living in the area, and public disquiet with the failure of the police investigation became increasingly vociferous. The investigation was also seriously misdirected in the last three years by hoax letters and a tape made by someone with a strong 'Geordie' accent, who claimed to be the murderer, so convincing the police that the killer was from the North East.[1] Sutcliffe was eventually arrested in January 1981, subsequently confessing to killing 13 women and attempting to murder another eight. At trial he pleaded not guilty to murder on the grounds of diminished responsibility, claiming to have heard the voice of God directing him to kill prostitutes. Sutcliffe's defence claimed that he suffered from paranoid schizophrenia, genuinely believed he heard such 'voices' and was therefore insane, not guilty of murder. This defence was rejected by the jury, finding Sutcliffe guilty of murder, although psychiatrists later reiterated their diagnosis of paranoid

---

[1]The hoaxer was eventually identified as John Humble, who pleaded guilty to perverting justice in March 2006.

schizophrenia, whereupon he was transferred to Broadmoor, where he remains.

Revisiting the macabre Sutcliffe circus, I have used *Deliver Us from Evil* (Yallop 1981), which has the immediacy of a text written contemporaneously with the events described and covers much more than the appalling details of the crimes and stupefying ineptitude of the police investigation. Yallop also gives a vivid account of the street soliciting areas of West Yorkshire in the 1970s, the way policing of street prostitution changed, or did not change, as the toll of victims mounted, and the emergence of a new kind of feminist activism which sparked widespread protests about violence against women. Bilton's more recent account (*Wicked Beyond Belief* 2006) at times reads like a 600-page exoneration of the West Yorkshire police[2] but is undoubtedly comprehensive. I have also visited websites devoted to the subject[3] and read those parts of the report on the official review of the police investigation as have been made public (Byford 1981). My knowledge of the facts about the case is based on these sources. Also, in exploring the paths by which Sutcliffe's activities became incorporated into the version of radical feminist ideology which currently dominates debates on prostitution, I have examined a number of feminist texts which were written during or soon after the Ripper era. In this I am traversing territory already covered by Walkowitz (1992), but my focus is less on developments in feminist ideology, more on the actions of those who professed this ideology and the implications of their ideology for current policy towards sex work.

Sutcliffe's crimes continue to exert a profound influence on public perceptions of violence in the sex industry; they are frequently referenced in media reports of sex worker murders, while some rapists and murderers apparently seek to achieve notoriety by emulating his example.[4] Reverberations from the Sutcliffe era can also be discerned in contemporary policing of street prostitution, in today's debates about prostitution policy and in radical feminist constructions of

---

[2]David Peace points out deficiencies of the investigation which Bilton underplays, and high-profile miscarriages of justice in other investigations carried out by the West Yorkshire police concurrently with the Ripper case ('The night of the hunter', *New Statesman*, 24 March 2003).

[3]Ripper websites: I found http://www.execulink.com/~kbrannen/victim17.htm most helpful.

[4]For example, Adam Bowler (see page 195), Rizwan Yaqub and David Fairbanks (see page 153).

violence against sex workers. These aspects of the Sutcliffe story need to be understood; their impact on contemporary thought about and policy towards prostitution needs to be recognised, so I hope the survivors among Sutcliffe's victims and their relatives will forgive me for drawing attention to events which cannot but cause immense pain (McCann 2004).

Sutcliffe's victims

Sutcliffe is still regarded primarily as a prostitute-killer, despite the fact that many of his victims were not sex workers. Does it matter? I think it does, partly because characterisation of all Sutcliffe's victims as sex workers caused and must continue to cause distress to survivors who were not sex workers and to the families of non-sex workers who died. *The Telegraph* website referred to Sutcliffe murdering '13 prostitutes' in February 2008.[5] A 'true crime' television programme in January 2008[6] named some of Sutcliffe's non-sex worker victims, without making clear that they were not sex workers, while Wilson (2007) uses Sutcliffe as the paradigm of a serial killer who targets sex workers but profiles one of his non-sex worker victims without examining what made her also vulnerable. The 'Sutcliffe-as-prostitute-killer' myth also sustains present-day assumptions that people who kill sex workers do not present a danger to non-sex workers, and disguises the factors which did contribute to his victims' vulnerability.

Among Sutcliffe's victims the only uniting factors were that they were alone outside at night and they were female. Their ages ranged from 14 to 47; some – both sex workers and non-sex workers – had had a drink, some had had several, others were stone cold sober. Their occupations included schoolgirl, shop assistant, civil servant

---

[5]Stephen Adams, 'Britain's worst serial killers', *The Telegraph*, 23 February 2008, at: http://www.telegraph.co.uk/news/main.jhtml?xml=/news/2008/02/21/nsuffolk621.xml.

[6]*The Yorkshire Ripper: Peter Sutcliffe*, broadcast on the Crime and Investigation Network TV channel, on 5 and 6 January 2008. The mistakes of this programme are particularly inexcusable, since experts interviewed included two police officers who had worked on the Sutcliffe investigation, Andrew Laptew and Dick Holland, the author of *Wicked Beyond Belief*, Michael Bilton, and the criminologist David Canter. I was not able to discover when this programme was made, but Holland died in February 2007 so it must have been before then.

and postgraduate medical student; some were regular sex workers, but several of those categorised by police as sex workers had no convictions for soliciting, and in some cases the only evidence that the victims had been soliciting when they were attacked came from Sutcliffe himself.

Sutcliffe's first acknowledged victims were Anna Rogulskyj (July 1975, Keighley), Olive Smelt, (August 1975, Halifax) and Tracey Browne, a 14-year-old schoolgirl (August 1975, Silsden).[7] They all suffered terrible head injuries, but survived. None was a sex worker and none was in or near a 'red-light' district when attacked, but the pervasiveness of misrepresentations about Sutcliffe's victims and about police failures continue to this day: Harrison and Wilson (2008) compare the attacks on Rogulskyj and Smelt to Sutcliffe's earliest known attack on a sex worker (in 1969), indicating that they were also sex workers and in 'red-light' districts when attacked, while the television programme cited above also implied that these attacks happened in 'red light' districts and that the police ignored them because attacks on sex workers were so common. Rogulskyj and Smelt were not included as possible victims of the 'Ripper' until 1978, and Tracey Browne was never included, despite having provided a detailed description of her assailant and an accurate photofit of Sutcliffe. In later years, feminist writers claimed that police had not taken the deaths among sex workers seriously until non-sex workers were killed, but a more accurate criticism would be of their failure to link these three attacks or investigate them vigorously.[8]

Sutcliffe's first known murder victim was Wilma McCann (October 1975) in Leeds. She had no convictions for soliciting, but police described her as a 'good time girl' who sometimes had sex for money. The strongest evidence that she did comes from Bilton, who states that Wilma was not claiming Social Security benefits despite having four small children. She may have chosen to do without – many sex workers are proud to be independent of state hand-outs – but if she was *refused* benefits, as women routinely were, if they had men friends with whom they might be cohabiting, sex work may have been a choice of desperation. Even so, the only evidence that she expected money for sex came from Sutcliffe himself. The next murder victim, Emily Jackson (January 1976, Leeds) had sold sex for only a

---

[7]Sutcliffe pleaded guilty to the attacks on Rogulskyj and Smelt at his trial in 1981, and confessed in 1992 to the attack on Tracey Browne, although he has never been tried for it.

[8]'Prejudice in death', Julie Bindel, *The Guardian*, 21 October 2005.

month to pay off family debts and had no convictions for soliciting either, but her death was immediately connected to McCann's and a week later Detective Superintendent Dennis Hoban announced, 'We are quite certain the man we are looking for hates prostitution ... I am quite certain this stretches to women of rather loose morals who go into public houses and clubs, who are not necessarily prostitutes ...'[9]

In May 1976 Sutcliffe attacked Marcella Claxton, again in Leeds. She survived. Police described her as a prostitute, but she did not have any soliciting convictions and later denied that she asked Sutcliffe or anyone else for money for sex. Marcella was said to have learning difficulties, but she gave an accurate description of her attacker. The police, however, ruled this attack out of the series, insisting her assailant must have been a black man, perhaps because Marcella was black herself and had been drinking in a West Indian club earlier that night. It is also possible the police had an eye on the tense race relations in Leeds. Six months earlier, there had been a minor riot in Chapeltown:[10] a vice squad car was overturned by a gang of mainly black youths, injuring two officers. A year later, after three more murders, the Assistant Chief Constable, George Oldfield, went on a charm offensive to the black community of Chapeltown, begging for assistance in the enquiry and stating, 'So far, all the victims have been white' (Yallop 1981). Marcella's attack was not included in the series until Sutcliffe confessed to it.

Irene Richardson (February 1977, Leeds) had no convictions for soliciting either. She had been working as a cleaner and applying for jobs as a nanny, was homeless, recently abandoned by her boyfriend and had been sleeping in a toilet block. Although it was said that she *may* have sold sex for survival, on the night she died she told a friend she was going to look for her boyfriend. Again, there is only Sutcliffe's word for it that she asked him for money. She was killed yards from where Marcella Claxton had been attacked, but although police initially connected the two, reinterviewing Marcella and obtaining from her an accurate photofit of Sutcliffe, she was again deemed an unreliable witness. Patricia Atkinson (April 1977, Bradford) did have convictions for soliciting, but witnesses who saw her earlier that night place her getting uproariously drunk in various

---

[9]Wilson, however, accepts Bilton's assessment that the police attempted to put 'the best possible gloss on the women's lives' (Wilson, 2007).
[10]Chapeltown – the area of Leeds most closely associated with street prostitution at the time.

pubs, not soliciting: evidence that she expected money for sex comes from Sutcliffe.

When 16-year-old shop assistant Jayne MacDonald was murdered two months later (June 1977, Leeds), it was assumed that she had been 'mistaken for a prostitute' because she was in an area 'frequented by prostitutes'. ACC Oldfield emphasised that Jayne was 'an innocent victim', and while the police have since been pilloried for making this invidious distinction, their apparent attitudes precisely reflected those adopted in the press.[11] The police were also frustrated by the lack of public assistance in the enquiry into murders of prostitutes, and hoped Jayne's death would provoke more response. It did, as Byford commented:

> MacDonald's youth and the fact that she was not a prostitute produced rather more response from the public and media interest sharpened in consequence. Both the police and the press expressed the view that the killer might have made a mistake and wrongly identified MacDonald as a prostitute. The possibility that any unaccompanied woman was a potential Ripper victim was not considered at that time. (Byford Report 1981: para. 313)

At this stage police began checking earlier attacks on non-sex workers, but the attack on Marcella Claxton was still excluded from consideration. Only two weeks after the murder of Jayne MacDonald, Maureen Long was attacked: she survived. She was not a prostitute but was nevertheless described as 'acting as a prostitute' (Byford Report) because she accepted a lift from a stranger after a night out and because Sutcliffe claimed she seemed willing to have sex with him.

The next four known attacks were on sex workers. Three died: Jean Jordan (October 1977, Manchester) who had cautions for soliciting but no convictions; Yvonne Pearson (January 1978, Bradford), and Helen Rytka (January 1978, Huddersfield), who also had no convictions. The fourth was Marilyn Moore (December 1977, Leeds) who survived, and gave an accurate description of Sutcliffe. The resultant photofit

---

[11]To the present day, the fact that Jayne Macdonald was also a very pretty girl is adduced as a further reason for outrage at the tragedy of her death. In contrast, Bilton describes unfavourably the appearance of some of Sutcliffe's non-innocent victims (Bilton, 2006; Crime and Investigation Network TV, note 6 above).

was seen by Tracey Browne, attacked two years earlier. Tracey went back to the police insisting that she had been attacked by the same man, but she was not taken seriously. Unfortunately Moore's recollections about her attacker's car were less accurate, and it was the car description that the police followed up assiduously, regarding her description of the man as unreliable.

Vera Millward, who was 40, died in May 1978, in Manchester. Her most recent soliciting conviction was five years earlier, and it was believed she had only one regular client whom she may have expected to meet the night she died, but he did not turn up. Perhaps she solicited Sutcliffe, as he claimed, since her regular had let her down, but she was also a sick woman, suffering from chronic stomach pains, and Bilton suggests she was making her way to the casualty department of the very hospital in whose grounds she died when Sutcliffe offered her a lift. Vera was the last sex worker to die at Sutcliffe's hands, and possibly the last sex worker he attacked. After Vera, in the 19 months from May 1978 to his arrest in January 1981, *all* Sutcliffe's known victims were non-sex workers. Four died: Josephine Whitaker, 19 (Halifax, April 1979); Barbara Leach, 20 (Bradford, September 1979); Marguerite Walls, 47 (Pudsey near Leeds, August 1980); and Jacqueline Hill, 20 (Leeds, November 1980). Two survived: Uphadya Bandara, 34 (Leeds, September 1980), and Teresa Sykes 16 (Huddersfield, November 1980).

The Byford Report

While many police officers today were not born until after Sutcliffe was convicted, it seems likely that the institutional memory of that terrible debacle still resonates within the service. Referring to it in an article about unsolved sex worker murders in 1995, Bilton wrote:

> Few outside the police service can imagine the professional shock waves that resulted from this very public humiliation, not least the severe embarrassment and alarm felt among higher ranks when the then Home Secretary, Willie Whitelaw,[12] told MPs in January 1982 of the litany of serious errors of judgment made during the five year murder hunt. (Bilton 1995)

---

[12]Margaret Thatcher's Home Secretary, William Whitelaw.

Whitelaw's statement concerned the findings of Her Majesty's Inspector of Constabulary, Lawrence Byford, appointed to undertake a review of the Ripper investigation in May 1981, four days after Sutcliffe's trial ended. Byford presented his report to Whitelaw in December the same year, but despite calls by MPs for it to be made public, it was deemed so sensitive, so likely to cause catastrophic loss of public confidence in the police and to worsen the already damaged morale of the West Yorkshire force, it was not made public until 2006. Some parts of it are still not public.[13] Even more extraordinary, although stuffed with useful recommendations about the investigation of major serial offences, it was not made available to senior police officers, not even chief constables. At first Byford strenuously objected to this secrecy, but was assured that its recommendations would be addressed by the Home Office through training for senior officers and by provision for adequate computer support (Bilton 2006).

Byford's main criticisms related to the inadequacy of the information systems to deal with the deluge of paperwork generated by the massive enquiry, the lack of effective overall management, the casual attitudes of junior officers tasked with routine enquiries, some terrible blunders in handling the media and poor judgement in their reliance placed on the hoax letters and tape. However, Byford also stated:

> With the additional benefit of hindsight it can now be clearly established that had senior detectives of the West Yorkshire assembled the photofit impressions from *surviving victims of all hammer assaults or assaults involving serious head injuries on unaccompanied women*, they would have been left with an inescapable conclusion that the man involved was dark haired with a beard and moustache. (Byford Report 1981: para. 572, my emphasis.)

Although I regard Joan Smith's recent foam-flecked demands for the punishment of men who pay for sex as unhelpful and mistaken,[14] I

---

[13]The Home Office seems to have done its best to make it extremely difficult to read even now. There are 18 separate Adobe files, with non-sequential titles, and the web page does not point out which sections are still secret.
[14]Joan Smith, 'Hunt vicious men, not "vice girls"', *The Independent*, 17 December 2006; Joan Smith, 'Prostitutes are victims, not criminals', *The Independent*, 13 April 2007.

agree with her conclusion that the police investigation failed because their perception of the killer as someone who primarily targeted sex workers meant they excluded much valuable evidence arising from his many attacks on non-sex workers (Smith 1989). Byford made the same points, but in his 'Conclusions and Recommendations', he did not highlight the fact that most assaults which generated good descriptions of Sutcliffe, were excluded because the victim was not a prostitute. This is interesting, because he did make such a point in the still-censored section of his report on 'Description of Suspects, Photofits and Other Assaults' (Byford Report 1981: paras 170 to 197). Bilton has evidently had access to the whole report because he quotes a telling point from this section:

> The information from the survivors of assaults would have been equally effective in … (dispelling) the theory that Jayne MacDonald was the first non-prostitute victim. (Byford Report 1981, quoted in Bilton 2006)

Despite highlighting the importance of the attacks on non-sex workers in his book (Bilton 2006), commenting in the recent television documentary, Bilton nevertheless excused the police failure to recognise the similarities of the descriptions given by survivors, arguing that it was reasonable to mistrust the testimony of prostitutes: because they had so many clients each night, how would they remember which one attacked them? Bilton may be an expert on Sutcliffe, but he evidently has no experience of hearing sex workers recount the attacks they suffer. The documentary also claimed that 'descriptions of the killer varied wildly', while repeatedly showing collages of the photofits, which, as Byford stated, clearly demonstrated common features. The need to represent sex workers as unreliable witnesses, even today, seems to outweigh any obligation to present the actual facts of the case.[15]

Policing of prostitution during the Sutcliffe investigation

The Byford Report does not examine the policing of prostitution during the investigation, nor the difficulties that the criminalisation of street soliciting created for investigating officers, and neither does Wilson. Despite asserting that 'it is the state that has created the

---

[15]Crime and Investigation Network TV (see note 6 above).

circumstances in which serial killings take place' and identifying the creation of 'vulnerability through policing' as a prime cause of sex workers' victimisation, he considers only the 'policing' involved in the investigation, and not the policing of street prostitution itself (Wilson 2007). Yallop and Bilton, however, chronicle several initiatives by West Yorkshire police to improve their normally hostile relationships with sex workers, to overcome their unwillingness to help the enquiry and to increase their safety. They made repeated appeals for sex workers to volunteer information about violent clients, but the fluctuations in arresting policy towards street workers – at a time when women were routinely imprisoned for soliciting offences – militated against their cooperation.

After the murder of Jackson (January 1976) and the attack on Claxton (May 1976), both in Leeds, the numbers of sex workers in Chapeltown dropped dramatically, but by early 1977, there were at least as many as before. After Irene Richardson was killed in February 1977, also in Leeds, police warned women not to 'get into cars' and tried to get sex workers to talk to them about their clients, but simultaneously launched a draconian arresting policy, allegedly to get women off the streets and so out of danger. One hundred and fifty-two were arrested and 68 cautioned. If this crackdown succeeded in protecting sex workers, it did not protect Jayne MacDonald, who was not a sex worker and therefore not thought to be at risk. She was killed in June 1977. Afterwards, police in Leeds began extensive and sustained monitoring of soliciting areas and the places sex workers used for 'business', aiming to catch the killer by identifying the vehicles he used, and after the attack on Maureen Long in Bradford (July 1977), these covert observations were extended to Manningham.[16] This intensive surveillance of sex workers and their clientele in Leeds and Bradford, from the summer of 1977, may have affected Sutcliffe's decisions about where to target his attacks, leading him to select victims outside monitored areas when the risk of capture was too great within them. In his confession, he stated that his switch to Manchester, where he killed Jean Jordan in October 1977, was in response to police activity in Yorkshire:

> I realised things were hotting up a bit in Leeds and Bradford ...
> I decided to go to Manchester to kill a prostitute. I had read in
> a paper somewhere or a magazine of a priest chastising what

---

[16]Manningham: the main soliciting area of Bradford at the time, particularly Lumb Lane.

went on in his parish at Manchester where there obviously was prostitutes. One Saturday night in October 1977 I drove over to Manchester. (Sutcliffe's confession, January 1981)

The circumstances of Jordan's murder suggest that Sutcliffe was not as familiar with places suitable for his purposes in Manchester, and in December 1977 he again attacked in Leeds, telling his victim, sex worker Marilyn Moore, that his name was Dave. Moore survived, and a photofit based on her (accurate) description was publicised. The senior investigating officer appealed for help from sex workers, assuring them, 'I will treat any information they give me in the strictest confidence. They need have no fear that I will use this information against them.' Still the attitude among sex workers was largely distrustful, while the police exhibited a rather exasperating naivety by throwing considerable manpower into tracking down kerb-crawlers called David.

The following month, in January 1978, Sutcliffe killed twice. Both victims were sex workers – one, Yvonne Pearson, was an experienced sex worker; the other, Helen Rytka, had only been soliciting for a matter of days – but the circumstances of both illustrate the vulnerabilities imposed by criminalisation. Pearson usually took clients to the safer surroundings of her home, but was due in court on soliciting charges and afraid she would be imprisoned if she was arrested again before going to court. For some reason it seems she thought she would be less likely to be caught if she worked the streets. She was killed on 21 January and the police were notified of her disappearance a few days later. Her friends insisted she would not have deserted her children, but the police assumed she had gone 'on the run' because of her imminent court appearance. As in many recent cases, the presumption of fecklessness and unpredictability meant no one looked for her and her body was not discovered for three months. Ten days after Pearson's death, Helen Rytka was killed in Huddersfield. Her sister Rita, who had been soliciting with her that night, did not report her missing immediately because she feared being arrested. Although Helen might not have been found alive if the alarm had been raised immediately, at least Sutcliffe's car might have been spotted in the area. As it was, while all Rita's clients that night were traced, Sutcliffe was not.

West Yorkshire police responded to Rytka's death by another crackdown on sex workers, both street and off-street. However, even senior officers were beginning to question whether repression was the answer. In April 1978, only weeks after his own officers raided a house where frightened street workers had been taking their clients,[17] the Chief Constable Ronald Gregory, gave qualified backing to calls for legalised brothels. In an interview reported in *The Times* he said:

> I would not be against legalised prostitution but not in its present form. I think these girls are exploited and the prostitute industry as it is today I am against. In a different form I think it could be regularised. It could be legalised I think in some way. That would eliminate a lot of these vicious attacks ...'[18]

Gregory's temperate and realistic remarks were of course attacked on all sides, but this furore was more related to the concurrent national campaign for reform of prostitution law (see below, page 21) than the situation he was overseeing in West Yorkshire where the police were still devoting massive resources to monitoring the movements of sex workers and their clients.

The intense police activity in West Yorkshire again seems to have prompted Sutcliffe to go further afield. In May 1978, Vera Millward was killed in Manchester. Covert monitoring of all soliciting areas in West Yorkshire then began, based on the initiative started in Chapeltown the previous year. In July Manchester joined in; Sheffield and Hull followed suit. In the first month, 150,000 vehicles were logged with the Police National Computer (PNC). In Manchester, 4,000 cars were logged every night. Between mid-1978 and December 1980, when the exercise was abandoned, 5.4 million car registration numbers were checked against the PNC. The number of cars sighted astonished police and overwhelmed their resources to process all the information. Byford stated: 'The West Yorkshire Police cannot be blamed for under-estimating the extent of prostitution and the use of motor vehicles by people seeking the services of prostitutes', but having such unequivocal evidence of the reality, this exercise should have provided an enduring lesson to policy-makers in devising strategies to reduce street prostitution, by illustrating the sheer numbers of men who patronise sex workers and the impracticability of addressing the issue by targeting clients (Kinnell 2006b).

During 1978, police in Bradford attempted to promote safer working practices among sex workers, advising them not to work

---

[17]'Women "afraid of Ripper"', *Yorkshire Post*, 22 February 1978, quoted in Bilton (2003).
[18]'Police chief calls for prostitution to be legalized', *The Times*, 15 April 1978, quoted in Yallop (1981).

when drunk, to work in pairs, to note down the registration numbers of each others' clients and 'to use only certain designated areas when actually earning their fee' (Yallop 1981). Yallop's perception was that sex workers scorned this effort, after months of arrests for soliciting and raids on indoor premises where they had sought safety from the streets, but in January 1979 a completely new tactic was tried in Bradford, the first known initiative by British police to set up a 'tolerance zone'. A small area was designated where women could solicit without fear of arrest, monitored by plain-clothes police in unmarked cars. The intention was to record car registration numbers, so that if a woman was attacked, all those whose cars were spotted that night could be checked. Yallop asserts that the police were not there to prevent attacks, condemning the initiative as a cynical experiment in using the women as bait for the killer, but he also describes drawbacks for the sex workers which reflect difficulties encountered in similar initiatives today. The area was so small the women were crammed together on the pavements, which put off the clients, while the arrest amnesty also attracted sex workers from outside the area, adding to the problem of overcrowding.

Covert observations continued in other soliciting areas in the north, but no other area adopted this approach. If the intention was to attract sex workers into the Bradford zone, hoping the killer would follow, it did not work; if the intention was to offer protection to sex workers, it did. From that time onwards, Sutcliffe attacked only non-sex workers, outside red-light districts. The implications of this are chilling, not so much because, as Yallop asserted, the amnesty in Bradford was intended as a trap to lure the Ripper into another attack, or because the strategy of covert observations failed to catch the killer, but because the strategy of amnesty and intense monitoring of the movements of sex workers and clients *succeeded* in deterring the killer from these areas and these potential victims, whereupon 'innocent' women were targeted. It seems possible that unspoken lessons learned from this experiment underlie continuing reluctance to create safe areas for prostitutes to work in.

After the murders of Josephine Whitaker, a bank clerk, in Halifax (April 1979) and student Barbara Leach in Bradford (September 1979), phone-ins to a local radio station ridiculed the 'covert' monitoring of cars in red-light districts, because by then it was common knowledge. Although the police did not acknowledge publicly that Sutcliffe was no longer targeting sex workers, by the end of 1979 covert observations were halted in Hull, Manchester and Sheffield, while in West Yorkshire they were curtailed and then halted in May

1980. Sutcliffe did not immediately revert to attacking sex workers, however. As had happened before during his offending period, there was a long gap between his known attacks, and when he resumed, he again targeted non-sex workers, parking his car and approaching them on foot, suggesting that he believed the street soliciting areas were still being monitored and car registrations collected. In August 1980 he murdered civil servant Marguerite Walls; a month later, he attacked medical student Uphadya Bandara; six weeks after that, 16-year-old Teresa Sykes was attacked; two weeks later, in November 1980, Sutcliffe killed again for the last time, his victim, another student, Jacqueline Hill, in Leeds.

Jacqueline Hill's death was the only one of these four attacks which the police immediately linked to the Ripper investigation, but since the murder of Barbara Leach in September 1979, all women in West Yorkshire had felt under threat. Self-defence classes for women sprang up; some women began to carry weapons and employers made meticulous arrangements to ensure women employees got to and from work safely. Possibly this hyper-vigilance pushed Sutcliffe back to street prostitution areas, or perhaps he considered himself untouchable. He had been interviewed by police nine times in connection with the investigation; one or other of his cars was logged seven times in the first 18 days of cross-area monitoring, and 60 times before his final arrest. Nonetheless, when he was arrested on 2 January 1981, he had fitted his car with stolen number plates before driving to the soliciting area of Sheffield. He was arrested with a sex worker in his car and later confessed that he had intended to attack her. The uniformed officers who arrested him, however, were initially only interested in the stolen number plates. South Yorkshire police had ceased covert monitoring of the area for over a year.

Deluded visionary, sexual sadist or archetypal misogynist?

It was essential to Sutcliffe's defence of insanity that he thought all his victims were prostitutes, and that his attacks were not sexually motivated. However, when first arrested he made a lengthy confession, not once claiming to have received divine instructions to kill prostitutes, and in his own accounts of several attacks he acknowledged a degree of sexual arousal or admitted that he knew his victim was not a prostitute but didn't care. There was also evidence of sexual sadism: mutilations to the breasts, buttocks and genitalia of his victims; masturbation over some of his victims after attacking them; and attacking three victims while they were crouching down to urinate. Nevertheless, by the time of his trial, Sutcliffe had convinced psychiatrists that he was suffering from paranoid schizophrenia, the 'voice of God' he claimed to have heard a clear symptom of this disease. The Crown was at first willing to accept the psychiatrists' conclusions and Sutcliffe's plea of diminished responsibility, but the judge, Mr Justice Boreham, insisted that the evidence for his plea was put to a jury. Yallop, who was present at the trial, observed expressions of consternation spread around the court, including on the faces of senior police officers from West Yorkshire, with good reason. Even the limited evidence that was presented bore abundant testimony to the deficiencies of the police investigation.

The Attorney-General, Sir Michael Havers, having been instructed to actually prosecute Sutcliffe rather than acquiesce in his defence of insanity, led the prosecution for the Crown, stressing that at least half of Sutcliffe's victims were not prostitutes, 'victims whose reputation was unblemished', as he put it, but he colluded in the denigration of the other victims. For example, 'She drank too much, was noisy and sexually promiscuous – she distributed her favours widely.' Perhaps Sir Michael was having difficulty changing his focus from reasons why Sutcliffe might be forgiven for thinking some of his victims *were* prostitutes when they were not, to emphasising that many of them *weren't*, either legally or effectively, or both. Havers nevertheless argued that Sutcliffe could not have believed they were all prostitutes, and was therefore lying about the 'voice of God' defence, confronting him with the 'sexual components' of his attacks. Possibly aware that the legal and psychiatric conventions would not regard any 'sexual motive' as compatible with his plea, Sutcliffe strenuously contradicted all parts of his confession that suggested otherwise.

Psychiatrists not only argued that Sutcliffe's claim to have been acting under divine instructions to kill showed him to be suffering from paranoid schizophrenia, one doctor asserted that to have an overwhelming hatred of prostitutes was itself indicative of schizophrenic illness. It is doubtful whether such an argument could be made today, when obsessive hatred of prostitutes has become quite respectable in the context of residents' action groups opposing street prostitution, and is routinely condoned, especially if it is wrapped up in religious justifications (see page 89; Sagar 2005; Pitcher *et al.* 2006).

The ECP and WAVAW[19] protested vociferously outside the Old Bailey against the conceptual segregation of women into good and bad throughout the trial. The attention paid to the virtue or otherwise of the victims was seen as shifting the blame from the male killer onto the female victims, replicating the attitude then routinely taken towards rape victims and to women killed by their partners – if provocation or other 'bringing-it-on-herself' factor could be argued, the rapist or killer was quite likely to be acquitted (Radford 1984; Lees 1992; Bland 1984). Contemporary feminist analyses of the case also castigated the failure of the judicial process to recognise that, as Hollway insisted, 'Sutcliffe's acts were an expression – albeit an extreme one – of the construction of an aggressive masculine sexuality and of women as its objects.' She criticised the prosecution for:

> trying to prove that there was a 'sexual component' in Sutcliffe's attacks. This and the 'divine mission' were contested as if they were mutually exclusive. Yet in the face of evidence of Sutcliffe's brutal attacks, only on women, a feminist analysis sees no incompatibility between a mission to kill women and this man's sexuality. (Hollway 1981)

However, the task before the court was not to try the culpability of male sexuality in general, but to determine Sutcliffe's culpability for the crimes with which he was charged, and he was found guilty on all counts.

Paradoxically, the psychiatrists soon won their argument, having Sutcliffe transferred to Broadmoor within a few years, and Wilson (2007) seems happy to accept that Sutcliffe had a 'divine mission', allocating him to the 'visionary' category of serial killers, motivated by the belief that they have a mission to kill a certain group of people. In policing circles, the fact that Sutcliffe killed both sex workers and non-sex workers is continually overlooked; a senior officer investigating the murder of a sex worker in Norwich in 2002 said, *'there is nothing to suggest from our enquiries that there is any threat to any other members of the public.'*[20] In popular culture too, Sutcliffe is regarded as the archetypal prostitute-killer, and radical feminist assertions about how he should be understood remain largely unchallenged. While denying that his unambiguous hatred for sex

---

[19]English Collective of Prostitutes and Women Against Violence Against Women.

[20]'Tests show city vice girl was strangled', *Norwich Advertiser*, 5 April 2002.

workers was anything more specific than 'misogyny', they also claim that he was a 'typical punter'.

Sutcliffe as punter: bad or bogus?

But was Sutcliffe a punter? Crucial to his own self-image, if not to his defence, was his assertion that he was not and never had been a punter. He *posed* as a punter, a fact he admitted to explicitly in his own statements about his attacks, but the accusation of *being* a punter was one of the only comments that annoyed him during his initial police interrogation, despite the fact that he was with a sex worker when he was finally apprehended. This sex worker explained at his trial that he had agreed to pay £10 and she had spent 15 minutes trying to masturbate him to achieve an erection: many sex workers today report that failure to get an erection can provoke a violent attack. Marilyn Moore, one of the sex workers who survived, reported that Sutcliffe had refused to pay upfront and attacked her when she refused to do business with him: another common scenario in attacks on sex workers today. He himself claimed his hatred of prostitutes began when he was cheated out of £10 by a sex worker in 1969 – many sex workers today report attackers who are explicitly wreaking revenge for having been robbed by sex workers in the past. Male friends of Sutcliffe's testified that he had been obsessed with prostitutes ever since he was in his teens, but they also recalled him boasting about 'never having to pay'. In his confession he recalled that, when he first hit Helen Rytka, her reaction was to say, 'There's no need for that, you don't even have to pay.' He seems to have stolen McCann's purse after killing her; Richardson had under 50p in hers, so she hadn't been paid either, while his unsuccessful efforts to retrieve the £5 note he gave to Jordan provoked the most frenzied and disgusting post-mortem attack. It appears that his violence was indeed intimately connected with money, but that *not* paying was integral to his contempt for his victims. It also suggests that he may have been telling the truth when he repudiated the description of 'punter' – *he did not pay.* Does this make him a better man than one who does pay? Of course it doesn't.

Feminism in the Sutcliffe era

Sutcliffe's last known sex worker victim was killed 30 years ago, but his crimes have profoundly influenced public and feminist discourses on violence against sex workers and continue to do so. The radical feminist ideology of sex work which now dominates public debate also derives legitimacy from the involvement of its proponents in events of the Sutcliffe era. Bindel is one who wears this battle honour prominently; she claims: 'The Yorkshire Ripper case was my reason for becoming a campaigner against sexual violence. I was angry, like many others, that the police only really seemed to step up the investigation when the first "non-prostitute" was killed.'[21] I cannot claim any such damascene moment. I do remember Sutcliffe being arrested, and being puzzled by the sudden obliteration of the 'Geordie' connection, so I must have absorbed something about the case, but I lived outside the crucibles of women's politics, and I wasn't the only one whose frame of reference was not memorably penetrated by Sutcliffe's crimes. In an extremely limited straw poll of friends and colleagues of sufficient seniority and with an interest in the subject, one – a former Midlands sex worker – remembered that many women from 'up north' worked away from Ripper territory for the duration, but that sex-working women in the Midlands did not feel personally affected. Others, not sex workers but feminists living in West Yorkshire at the time, had vivid memories: shock at the deaths of Barbara Leach and Jacqueline Hill (both students); the intense fear of walking alone at night; the marches and self-defence classes; and the anger provoked by police advice for women to stay indoors, ignoring the fact that many had jobs which meant they had no choice but to be out after dark. One remembered that the overwhelming message from police during 1979 and 1980 was still that prostitutes were the killer's target even though, from May 1978 onwards, all of his victims had been non-sex workers. More disturbingly, one remembered a widespread belief that the police themselves were in some way implicated in the Ripper crimes – that the culprit was either a policeman himself or that the police were covering up for the killer.[22]

---

[21]This would have been when Jayne MacDonald was killed, in June 1977, when Bindel was 15; Julie Bindel, 'Prejudice in death', *The Guardian*, 21 October 2005.
[22]The currency of this belief is confirmed by Hanmer and Saunders (1984).

They also recalled that women's politics in Leeds were then strongly influenced by separatist radical feminism, and while there was disgust at the distinctions made between prostitutes and respectable women, with the implication that prostitutes 'deserved' their fate, there was no feeling of identification with women who pandered to male sexual demands by selling sex: they were letting the side down in the struggle against male dominance. These personal reminiscences tend to support Yallop's observation, questioning whether the feminist demonstrations which erupted between 1977 and 1980 were primarily inspired by outrage at the vulnerability of sex workers or whether the vulnerability of non-sex workers was more important to them. Yallop commented:

> There had been ... no public marches through the streets after the murders of Wilma McCann, Emily Jackson, and Irene Richardson, all in Leeds. There was no female outcry after Tina Atkinson had been brutally murdered in Bradford, or Maureen Long attacked in the same city, or Yvonne Pearson murdered also in the same city. No feminists took to the streets of Manchester after the murder of Jean Jordan. They were equally mute after Vera Millward had been hacked to death. There was no feminist public protest in Huddersfield after what was left of Helen Rytka had been discovered. It is abundantly clear that it took the deaths of non-prostitutes, of Jayne MacDonald in Leeds, Josephine Whitaker in Halifax and Barbara Leach in Bradford, to produce public action from women. (Yallop 1981)

Other sources which reflect contemporary feminist attitudes and concerns have little to suggest that Yallop misrepresented them. In the context of the Ipswich murders, in December 2006, Bindel reminisced about the feminist protests in Yorkshire at the time of Sutcliffe's killings, including fly-posting Leeds with mocked-up police notices requesting men to stay off the streets for the safety of women. She wrote, 'For one night only (until the police discovered our scam and the posters were taken down) the Chapeltown area, where many street prostitutes worked, was free of foot punters.'[23] How helpful to the sex workers, to take away their foot punters, when the killer was thought to use a car.

---

[23]Julie Bindel, 'Terror on our streets', *The Guardian*, 13 December 2006.

The feminist magazine *Spare Rib* carried reports of the first Reclaim the Night demonstrations, in November 1977. The Leeds group claimed inspiration from similar demonstrations in Germany, from a 'Revolutionary Feminist' conference in Edinburgh, and were 'particularly concerned because there'd been a series of women murdered in West Yorkshire', but did not mention sex work. In Manchester, where Jean Jordan had been murdered only a month before the march, 400 women demonstrated, and their report states, 'We stood in silence for two minutes in remembrance of all women who have suffered at the hands of men', but Jean Jordan is not mentioned. The only reference to prostitution is made in a report about the London Reclaim the Night demonstration, where marchers invaded Soho shouting 'sexist crap!' and slapping stickers saying 'THIS DEGRADES AND EXPLOITS WOMEN' on offensive advertising. Reporting on this demonstration, one wrote, 'an ex-prostitute told me she didn't agree with it because she thought it would be bad for the business of the prostitutes in Soho' (*Spare Rib* 1978).

Later, *Spare Rib* carried a longer description of the Leeds demonstration of November 1977, which explained the routing of the march through Chapeltown (criticised as insensitive to the large black population there): 'It was the very place where a 16-year-old girl had been found dead earlier in that year: to make a commemoration for that young girl, to say: we have not forgotten you, and we will try to make a safer space for women for the future' (Fairweather 1979). No mention is made of the vulnerability of sex workers; the 16-year- old they commemorated was the 'innocent' Jayne MacDonald, not the other, 'impure' Leeds victims: Wilma McCann, Emily Jackson and Irene Richardson. The article ended with a list of 35 Leeds organisations for or relevant to women, none of which mentioned offering any service to sex workers.

After Barbara Leach died (September 1979), 'In Yorkshire women took to the street, protesting about male violence' (Bilton 2006). When police warned women not to go out alone at night, 300 women demonstrated in Bradford, demanding that men be given a curfew instead. After Jacqueline Hill's death, hundreds demonstrated in Leeds; they challenged men in the street, asking them where they were when Jacqueline was killed, but their protests were not solely the result of her death, nor of other Ripper murders. A Women's Liberation national conference, (Sexual Violence Against Women) was held over the weekend of 22 and 23 November 1980, in Leeds, and the demonstrations took place on the Saturday night of the conference, organised by WAVAW.[24] Statements issued by the organisers of both conference and demonstrations characterise the Ripper attacks as exemplifying violence against all women, but do not mention sex work, and conference papers show that pornography was of far greater concern than prostitution (Rhodes and McNeill 1985a). The protesters targeted cinemas showing films which glorified sexual violence; there were fights between marchers and police; a sex shop in Chapeltown had its windows smashed. In London the 'Reclaim the Night' marchers 'went right through Soho and right into the foyers of the strip joints and we threw stink bombs and flour bombs.'[25] This anti-pornography stance and opposition to legal forms of commercial sex drew approval from Mary Whitehouse,[26] but there is no indication that those involved in the demonstrations made alliances with sex workers (McNeill and Rhodes 1985b; Walkowitz 1992).

An interesting perspective on wider feminist attitudes to prostitution during the Sutcliffe era is given in accounts of the PROS movement (Programme for Reform of the Law on Soliciting), a widespread and long-lived campaign for the reform of prostitution law, which began in late 1975 and culminated in the abolition of imprisonment for soliciting and loitering offences in 1982[27] (Toynbee 1977; McLeod 1982). PROS was a unique alliance between sex workers and non-sex worker supporters, such as probation officers, social workers and solicitors. Its spokespeople and National Committee members were sex workers, and its agenda was framed by sex workers' perceptions of their own problems. They campaigned for an end to imprisonment for soliciting and loitering, the reduction of fines, the removal of the term 'common prostitute' from the statute book and the eventual decriminalisation of all aspects of prostitution. McLeod's account of the PROS movement, active during exactly the same period that Sutcliffe was committing his crimes and the police were failing to catch him, mentions the 'Ripper' case once, which suggests that it was not a significant factor for feminists campaigning for the rights of sex workers, nor for many sex workers themselves. The concerns of sex workers were much more focused on their victimisation by

---

[24]WAVAW – Women Against Violence Against Women
[25]Pam Isherwood, quoted in 'Women Unite, Reclaim the Night' by Rachel Bell, the f-word website: http://www.thefword.org.uk/features/2006/01/women_unite_reclaim_the_night.
[26]Mary Whitehouse (1910–2001) – a prominent campaigner against pornography and obscenity.
[27]Criminal Justice Act 1982, s 71.

the police and the legal process than on violence in the course of their work (McLeod 1982). In March 1977, women involved with PROS were interviewed for *Spare Rib*: violence was one of the topics discussed, but the 'Ripper' was not. The only murder mentioned was one in Birmingham. One of the sex workers said 'We were terrified and we worked together for safety. I hired a room with some friends and when the law found out they raided us and that was that.' The article ended:

> They are all critical of feminists who haven't taken up the issue of the prostitution laws.... "We want women's liberation to think about the whole thing and discuss it, but not just *use* it. They have used the word 'prostitute' in a really nasty way – about housewives, to sum up their idea of the exploited situation of women. But we need allies to lobby and to publicize our programme" (Green 1977)

McLeod reflected on the ambivalent attitude of the feminist movement towards the PROS campaign:

> ... if, as feminists, women are setting their faces against men's oppression, how can they endorse prostitution or support a better deal for women whose work – on the surface – seems to reinforce men treating women in an oppressive way? In this connection, in the early days of PROS its support came more readily from feminists emphasising the economic and class origins of women's oppression ... rather than those rooting the explanation of women's oppression in patriarchy.... (McLeod 1982)

Towards the end of its campaign, PROS had participant groups in London, Glasgow, Bristol, Birmingham, Wolverhampton, Manchester and Sheffield, although not, interestingly, in West Yorkshire. I asked McLeod whether the murders had made it difficult to organise support in West Yorkshire. She replied, 'The geographical location of the Ripper attacks did not have any bearing on where the PROS groups did or didn't develop, that was related to initiatives by women working locally or by supportive probation officers who organised on the issue'.[28] It therefore appears that, despite all the organising fervour of feminists in West Yorkshire, they did not relate

---

[28]Eileen McLeod, personal communication, 9 October 2007.

to a movement where sex workers decided the agenda and spoke on their own behalf.

The writings of radical feminists in Leeds during and soon after the Sutcliffe era also suggest that they were aloof from the organisations that represented the views of sex workers, and judging from the emphasis on patriarchy suffusing the report of the Sexual Violence Against Women Conference held in Leeds in November 1980 (Rhodes and McNeill 1985a), it seems that the delegates were largely composed of those, in McLeod's phrase, 'rooting the explanation of women's oppression in patriarchy'. There were two papers addressing prostitution, one of which was by Sheila Jeffreys, then based in Leeds and describing herself as a revolutionary feminist. Jeffreys seems to have been ignorant of the PROS movement, which had then been campaigning for five years, as her paper opens with:

> There has been little discussion in the WLM about prostitution and less action. So far the issue has been aired mainly by Helen Buckingham and the ECP.[29] It has been posed as the need to protect prostitutes from police harassment and persecution by unjust laws, a need which it would be impossible to deny. Yet there has been little response from feminists, little support for imprisoned prostitutes or for prostitute groups campaigning to change the law. Why is this? One reason seems to be an uneasiness about supporting prostitutes against victimisation in a way which offers no real threat to male power and no room to criticise the institution of prostitution itself and its effects on women. (Jeffreys 1980)

She ended by saying, 'We have to work out ways in which to attack the institution of prostitution as we attack all other ways in which male supremacy is supported, whilst positively supporting women who work as prostitutes against unjust laws, the police and pimps,' without having made a single suggestion about how this might be done. The other paper on prostitution (O'Hara 1980), takes a similarly negative view of commercial sex, but hazards the view that 'workable feminist strategies around prostitution can only come out of dialogue between women who work as prostitutes and women who don't,' and concludes that feminists should support the ECP

---

[29]WLM – Women's Liberation Movement; ECP – English Collective of Prostitutes; Helen Buckingham – sex worker campaigner for prostitution law reform.

23

and PROS campaign (which O'Hara evidently *had* heard of) for decriminalisation. She argued that the 'criminalisation of prostitution forces women ... further underground and therefore makes them more vulnerable to exploitation', and even more interesting in the context of present-day discussions, she also opposed the suggestion that feminists should 'demand that soliciting of women by men be made illegal'. O'Hara observed, 'This has been done in New York, where its main effect seems to be to drive women working as prostitutes further underground and increase their vulnerability to pimps.'

O'Hara's pessimism about police-led criminal justice remedies for the abuses of prostitution was amplified by Hanmer and Saunders (1984), reporting on their 1981 survey of women's experiences of violence in Leeds. Their account is particularly revealing of the authors' own priorities and beliefs, and has especial relevance to developments in prostitution debates today, in view of Professor Hanmer's connection to the first kerb-crawler rehabilitation programme set up in Leeds in 1998.[30] They evidently regarded the Sutcliffe experience as mainly of importance in raising women's awareness of the 'male protection racket', by which male protection systems (police and judiciary) failed to restrain male violence in public places, thereby making women dependent on individual men (husbands, partners) for their safety and restricting them to private spaces (homes) where these same individual men could then attack them, also with virtual impunity from the criminal justice system. The extent of their lack of faith in the police and in police-led strategies for reducing women's vulnerability is explicit:

> The widespread rumour that the "Ripper" was a policeman, along with the police's inability to capture him, began to invalidate the belief that the collective male system, the criminal justice system, provides protection for women.... Rather than give the police more power we should be demanding less power and more accountability to women. When we demand curfew on men we mean policemen also. (Hanmer and Saunders 1984)

Hanmer and Saunders also articulated deep unease, not only with patriarchal institutions, but with heterosexuality itself. They called

---

[30]While Professor Hanmer was Director of the Research Centre on Violence Abuse and Gender Relations at Leeds Metropolitan University, the Centre set up the West Yorkshire Kerb-Crawler Rehabilitation Programme, 1998–1999, with the support of the West Yorkshire Police. (See Chapter 13, page 170.)

for a national survey of male violence against women, declaring they already knew it would reveal 'heterosexuality as a system of social relations as it is currently structured and how this system serves to normalize, even encourage, violence to women and female children'. Their interest in prostitution, or the particular vulnerabilities of sex workers, seems minimal. They mention the death of Barbara Leach, 'the first murder of a university student', as marking 'a change in reporting by newspapers and television from the stress on prostitutes to the recognition that any woman could be a victim'. This is revealing of their perspective, and the fact that their survey was done in an area with a high proportion of students: the earlier deaths of sex workers, a shop assistant and a bank clerk seem to have made no impact. They also describe the murder of student Jacqueline Hill on 17 November 1980 as raising 'the consciousness of violence to women in the Leeds–Bradford area in a way that had not occurred with the previous murders'. Their only direct statement about prostitution as a distinct issue was in the context of their call for a national study, which they claimed would also 'give us more information on the known relationship between father–daughter incest and prostitution, where women are often subject to continuing sexual and physical abuse by men who use them either as customers or pimps.' No reference is given for the 'known relationship' between incest and prostitution.

These insights into radical feminists' discourses and activities during the Ripper era illuminate their ambivalence towards prostitution and their lack of interest in engaging with sex workers in any practical way. The Ripper killings were useful for grandstanding their ideology of male sexual violence and expounding on the problematic nature of male heterosexuality, but they do not appear to have participated in an alternative form of political activism that gave sex workers a role and a voice, nor concerned themselves with the specific vulnerabilities of sex work. The only Ripper victims whom they dignify with individuality are non-sex workers. The timing of their demonstrations suggests that they, like other members of the public, became most outraged by the killings only after police activity, whether intentionally or not, had curtailed Sutcliffe's attacks on sex workers, whereupon non-sex workers became vulnerable. Perhaps the 'radicalising' factor claimed by today's radical feminists was not the vulnerability of sex workers to murderous misogyny, but the realisation that, if prostitutes were protected from it, other women ('innocent' women?) might be at risk. Joan Smith appears to acknowledge as much in her comments on the 2006 Ipswich murders:

Sutcliffe's earliest assaults, outside red light districts and on women who had nothing to do with prostitution, were disturbed by passers-by. That is when he began killing women who sold sex for a living, reverting to 'ordinary' women when the red light districts of Leeds and Bradford became too heavily policed for him.'[31]

---

[31]Joan Smith, 'Hunt vicious men, not "vice girls"', *The Independent*, 17 December 2006.

Chapter 2

What is violence against sex workers?

Is sex work 'in and of itself violence against women'?

The core of the current radical feminist position is the assertion that sex work is 'in and of itself violence against women', that no woman ever freely consents to selling sex and that all clients are motivated by the desire to dominate, humiliate and hurt. This is the contemporary orthodoxy; it is shockingly heretical to suggest any other typology for women who sell sex or men who buy; to do so leaves one open to very serious insinuations, not merely that one is terminally naive, culpably ignorant or colluding with abuse, but quite possibly part of an international conspiracy to promote prostitution and in the pay of international traffickers.[1] Despite such unnerving accusations, because my subject is violence in the sex industry, I cannot wholly ignore the 'sex-work-is-violence' line, so I will explain why I think it is a meaningless shibboleth which diverts attention from violence as sex workers themselves define it and from the structural conditions that allow it.

It is important to realise that 'violence' in the radical feminist discourse does *not* mean the beatings, rapes and murders inflicted on sex workers. Instead the commodification of women's bodies

---

[1]Madeleine Bunting, 'Sorry, Billie, but prostitution is not about champagne and silk negligees', *The Guardian*, 8 October 2007; Cath Elliot, 'What sisterhood?', *The Guardian*, 10 March 2008 (see http://commentisfree.guardian.co.uk/cath_elliott/2008/03/what_sisterhood.html and comments nos.1188566, 1188809, 1190572).

through charging for sexual acts or performances (e.g. pole dancing) is deemed the essential harm, the 'violence' which damages women. This proposition arises out of the assertion that women's (but not men's) essential being is so invested in their bodies and in their sexuality, that they are always damaged by being paid for sex (Pateman 1988). Even students who supplement their incomes with a spell of pole dancing are regarded as victims of violence, 'forced' into the commodification of their own bodies. Thus, even with clear evidence that it is possible to operate as a sex worker without suffering physical violence or economic exploitation, receiving payment for sex is considered a form of violence so severe that women can never be deemed to have made a free choice to subject themselves to it, and must be prevented from doing so.

Further, based on a selective amalgamation of sex workers' personal life stories showing a common recruitment pattern into prostitution through the deliberate manipulation of pimps and traffickers, in which each woman's capacity to consent is destroyed, it is also asserted that sex workers *never* enter prostitution voluntarily. It follows that no woman has consented to a paid sexual act, therefore, every such act is a sexual assault, so sex work *is* violence. Those who protest that they have chosen to sell sex are dismissed as deluded, damaged by a lifetime of subservience to men, the victims of 'false consciousness'; to be pitied but ignored by those formulating theories or policies.

The assertion that all those who pay for sex do so to degrade and dominate women, fiercely promulgated in support of the demand to criminalise paying for sex, is grounded in the belief that male sexuality *itself* is characterised by the desire to dominate and humiliate, and that clients, as men, naturally share these motivations. Jeffreys makes this explicit: 'Male sexuality is a perversion because its primary motivation is not pleasure, individual or mutual, or the enhancement of personal relationships, but control of and power over women.' She further asserts that men need prostitution to express their 'hatred and degrade women in ways which might endanger their other relationships' (Jeffreys 1980). The argument is not that the economic demand for commercial sex is reprehensible because it draws people into the sex industry where they are vulnerable to violence and exploitation, but that those who pay for sex are all driven by the desire to dominate and hurt the sex workers they pay.

Apart from the outrageously elitist dismissal of sex workers' opinions and choices and the totalising assertions about women's relationships to their bodies, the radical feminist ideology ignores the existence of male and trans sex workers, and the reality that women also pay for sex. By characterising clients' motivations as exclusively sadistic and controlling, it ignores a wealth of commentary showing that both sex workers and clients frequently perceive the sex worker as controlling the interaction, that many clients seek companionship and physical closeness rather than merely sexual gratification, and that many sex workers find the majority of their clients respectful, considerate and grateful (Sanders 2008; Daniels 2006).

Sex workers' experiences of violence in the form of robberies, abuse, harassment and physical and sexual attacks are also ignored in this discourse, since it leaves no incentive to distinguish between acts to which the sex worker has consented and acts which leave her physically harmed or dead. It colludes with violence, since if there is qualitatively no difference between the 'violence' of society which 'forces' a woman to become a pole dancer, and the violence expressed in beatings, rape and murder, there is no necessity to examine or reduce the latter sort of violence: merely to abhor the sex industry and demand its elimination is sufficient. It renders unnecessary efforts to restrain the violent or to protect those vulnerable to them. It side-steps the question of why some men behave as 'genuine' clients – they pay, respect the sex worker's restrictions on time, place and sexual practice, and are non-violent – but others do not.

It is not difficult to see why policy-makers have embraced the radical feminist ideology. Three decades after the young hotheads of women's activism threw stink bombs into strip clubs, smashed the windows of sex shops and bravely fly-posted the streets of Chapeltown, radical feminism has lost its cautious support for decriminalisation and any hesitation about targeting clients. It has also become muted on the subject of patriarchy, and is now entirely compatible with the views of conservative moralists loyal to patriarchal religions and ancient concepts of the role of women, while the main instrument for imposing their solutions is the police – everywhere in the world still a heavily male-dominated institution and never slow to welcome extensions of its powers. The rhetoric of saving abused women and children is a very handy smokescreen to throw around other objectives which have little to do with challenging women's subjection to male dominance under conditions of patriarchy, but have everything to do with managing property values, social values and votes.

Politically difficult proposals to improve sex workers' safety by legitimising their working situations can be rejected as legitimising violence against women, if sex work itself is deemed violence. Alternatively, such measures can be rejected lest they 'encourage' women to enter or remain in prostitution, by making it safer and, therefore, more attractive. The logical corollary of such arguments is that violence against sex workers should not be prevented, because it acts as a control on the numbers of women involved. While no one would admit that policy is driven by such thinking today, in the past the Home Office has been less squeamish. Reporting on prostitution in 1977, Polly Toynbee wrote:

> A Home Office spokesman explained to me that the official view is that prostitution is degrading to hooker and client alike, and *should be made difficult, inaccessible, unsatisfactory and even dangerous in order to discourage its spread.* (Toynbee 1977, my emphasis)

Much has been made of the durability of institutional cultures, and it seems to me that the internal culture of the Home Office – and the sub-ministries that have recently been formed out of this parent body – continues to regard violence against sex workers as a necessary deterrent.

Redefining violence in the sex industry

I believe that it is unspeakably cruel to regard physical assaults, rape and murder as useful deterrents in any context, and especially in the context of a way of life over which the most vulnerable have little choice. Refocusing on physical and sexual violence committed against sex workers, particularly that which occurs while they are directly engaged in sex work activities, illustrates starkly how the criminalisation and stigmatisation of sex work critically exposes them to danger, by undermining their safety strategies, prohibiting the development of safe sex work environments and encouraging attitudes of abhorrence, contempt and hate towards them.

The radical feminist ideology which conflates sex work with violence not only marginalises the importance of physical and sexual assault, even murder, but by stereotyping clients as uniformly abusive and sadistic, it also diverts attention from other kinds of societal violence and from other kinds of assailant. The question of *who* commits violence against sex workers is a major focus of this book, addressing the dangers posed by some but not all clients, and the dangers posed by other individuals, groups and institutions. I have scrutinised hundreds of reports of violence against sex workers, and have found that although many assailants approach sex workers *as if* they were clients or while their victims are 'at work', paying for sex is not strongly associated with violence, but *not* paying is: most violence seems to come from those who do *not* pay.

Neither is violence solely a matter of criminal acts committed by individuals. What is the 'violence' of a society which 'forces' a woman to become a lap-dancer compared to the violence of a society which drives sex workers into the most dangerous situations, which denies them protection and deliberately makes them homeless? Understanding 'violence' as including acts that cause fear, humiliation, manhandling or exposure to danger, many non-criminal acts might be classed as violence, including immigration raids and deportations, policing operations, community actions against street sex workers, evictions, politicians' statements and media exposés of sex workers. Such events are always presented as legitimate means to achieve socially desirable outcomes, uncover serious offences, 'rescue victims' or expose moral turpitude, but their intrinsically violent or abusive nature is usually ignored.

> Different types of violence were experienced from the state, family, strangers, and clients. The most harrowing entailed the occasional removal of prostitutes' children by the state, and domestic violence. (Ward and Day 2001)

Wilson (2007) comments on the social structure which allows violent criminals to operate 'by placing value on one group to the detriment of others'. He nevertheless endorses the Home Office Co-ordinated Strategy on Prostitution, which acknowledges that enforcement of anti-prostitution law may exacerbate sex workers' vulnerability, while simultaneously demanding rigorous enforcement to please those groups in society who object to it (Harrison and Wilson 2008; Home Office 2006). Hillyard and Tombs (2005) highlight the selectivity of the criminal justice system in its definitions of 'crimes', pointing out that criminal law largely ignores harmful actions perpetrated by institutions and the state. They quote Reiman's observation on 'the implicit identification of crime with the dangerous acts of the poor'.[2] In the sex work arena, the criminal justice system devotes most of its attention to the non-dangerous acts of poor women, while acts of institutional and community violence against them are not

---

[2]J. Reiman (1998) 'The rich get richer and the poor get prison', *Ideology, Class and Criminal Justice*, 5th edn. Boston: Allyn & Bacon; quoted in Hillyard and Tombs (2005).

regarded as crimes at all. They are nonetheless real and damaging, perpetuating the view of sex workers as social outcasts whom it is nobody's business to protect.

Rather than wasting police and social welfare resources trying to impose a state-sanctioned sexual ideology, I believe social policy should focus on the violence that sex workers themselves perceive as unacceptable, and on the people who commit that violence, recognising the dangers which are posed by some but not all clients, *and* the dangers posed by other individuals, groups or institutions in society. This book explores both actions which are clearly crimes and, to appropriate the language of Anti-Social Behaviour Orders[3] used so frequently against sex workers, actions which cause them fear, alarm, harassment or distress.

---

[3]ASBO (Anti-Social Behaviour Order) – an order obtained through civil law which can impose limitations on behaviour, travel, place of residence, clothing, and any other behaviour that complainers allege causes fear, alarm, harassment or distress. ASBOs have been used against street sex workers since 1998, commonly banning them from soliciting in particular areas, although the ban may apply to the whole country. The recipient of an ASBO does not have to be proved guilty of a criminal offence but breach of an ASBO is a criminal offence for which a prison term of up to five years may be imposed.

Chapter 3

Inclusions and exclusions

Which sex workers?

In this book, people are described as sex workers if they are known to have some involvement in sex work, either selling sex directly or in some other role, for example as a receptionist at indoor premises. The broader sex industry includes exotic dancing, clipping[1] establishments, pornography and telephone sex services, but although these branches of the industry may involve risks for violence, they are not explored in this book, with the exception of two homicide cases where the victims were a clip-joint hostess and a lap-dancer, which are included in Chapter 13.

Pimping and sexual exploitation of children

I use the term 'pimp' to describe men or women who use threats, violence, coercion and deception to force other people to engage in sex work and profit from their work. Although attacks and murders committed by some who deserve to be called pimps are referred to in this book, I shall not explore violence in these contexts extensively.

---

[1]Clipping – posing as a sex worker (a clipper), taking money for sex and then disappearing without giving a service. Clip-joint – a species of night club where overpriced drinks are sold and the misleading impression that sex is available is given.

Neither is the sexual exploitation of children through prostitution examined in this book.

Trafficking

The conflation of sex work and trafficking in current discourses about the sex industry ignores the enormous diversity in relationships between sex workers and others who benefit from their earnings, the wide range of factors which draw individuals into the sex industry and the differing degrees of personal autonomy exercised by sex workers (Anderson and O'Connell Davidson 2003; Agustín 2007). Because suggesting that women from overseas may be involved in the sex industry voluntarily is likely to draw down accusations of promoting prostitution, Dibb et al.'s report for the Salvation Army on trafficking in Tower Hamlets is of interest, since no one could possibly accuse the Salvation Army of underplaying the role of coercion and exploitation in prostitution. This report illustrates the wide and complex range of situations overseas sex workers may be in: of 21 case studies included, one concerned a dual-heritage British girl in danger of sexual exploitation and another was an Asian woman trying to escape from her pimp. Seven were foreign nationals who gave no indication of past or current coercion or exploitation, and three had been trafficked, but having escaped from that situation were then working in the UK sex industry voluntarily; four were brought to this country by friends or family members from their home countries and subsequently sexually exploited by these people; three had been trafficked by other people, but there was no information regarding their subsequent relationships to traffickers or other exploiters; one was trafficked as a debt-bonded domestic servant, was sexually exploited in that situation, escaped and became involved in the sex industry through coercion from a pimp, sought help and was threatened with deportation; and one claimed to have been trafficked and raped, but services trying to help her concluded she had invented her story to escape deportation (Dibb et al. 2006).

Anti-trafficking policing is deeply enmeshed in immigration agendas which are beyond my remit, so I concentrate on the changes which new immigration patterns and the corresponding changes in policing strategies have made on issues of violence mainly towards indoor sex workers (Chapters 9 and 10), rather than attempting to sift truth from hysteria on the subject of relationships between sex workers and traffickers.

Ethnicity

The ethnic dimensions of sex work are difficult to discuss for fear of contributing to stigmatising racist discourses, but I do not think either understanding or policy is well served by avoiding these areas of discomfort. I have, therefore, within the limitations of my data sources, included ethnic data if it is available. My decision to revisit the mainly Muslim community protests that drove sex workers out of Balsall Heath in the 1990s may prove more controversial. Would it not have been better to foreground the white, middle-class protests which destroyed a long-established policy of tolerating a small area of street soliciting in Edinburgh, or the white working-class actions in a mainly Protestant area of Liverpool, so avoiding possible accusations of anti-Muslim prejudice? Perhaps, but I was an eyewitness in Balsall Heath, I saw events unfold, I know the background and the context, and I know what happened afterwards. It is a complex story. I hope I have deconstructed some of the ethnic stereotypes that were attached to it, but my main intentions have been to uncover misrepresentations that were made at the time, and continue to be made, about the immediate and long-term effects of the protests in relation to sex work. Any wider repercussions are beyond my remit (see Chapter 8).

Violence by sex workers

I know of eight sex workers who were charged with homicide between 1990 and 2006: two suspects were male, both charged with killing men who had approached them as clients; two of the female suspects were charged with killing their husbands; three were charged with killing other sex workers (two victims); and one was charged with killing a client. This compares with 118 homicides in the same period where the victim was a sex worker. While I do not think it is helpful, or respectful, to stereotype sex workers as weak and helpless, the overwhelming weight of evidence I have suggests that it is they who are most frequently and severely victimised, out of all proportion to any danger they may pose to anyone else. I have not, therefore, examined violence by sex workers, although a few cases of non-fatal violence between sex workers and the two homicides of sex workers by sex workers are included.

Trans and male sex workers

In the UK little is known about violence against trans sex workers, although in Canada, the USA and Portugal, violence against this group has been highlighted by many murderous attacks over the past decade.[2] The SW5 Project in London offers a service to both male and trans sex workers, and has reported that trans women appear to be more at risk of violence than male sex workers. Elsewhere a small percentage of female sex workers are known to be transgender, but they often work alongside other females, receive services from the same agencies and are not distinguished from other women in any records or surveys of exposure to violence.

Male sex workers may encounter homophobic violence in addition to the risks of sex work, but very few media reports concerning non-fatal attacks and only two cases of homicide have been found (see Chapter 13). Available information suggests marked regional and situational variations. The SW5 Project found that male sex workers reported very little violence in the context of work, although violence was reported in the context of childhood abuse, homophobic attacks, disputes between partners or among peers, or in drug-related muggings. Very few rapes were reported, two of which had occurred while the victims were in prison, and only one while the victim was at work.[3] Gaffney stresses that since the mid-1990s in London, much male sex work has moved from the streets to indoor venues where the risks of violence are minimal, but also reported that changes in the street 'rent' scene in London have made it more dangerous. From involving mainly gay-identified men unaffected by hard drug use, he says:

> More typically today, the street-based male sex worker is covert, heterosexual, rough sleeping and addicted to crack cocaine. He blends with the general street culture, is rougher and tougher, and rarely admits to actually selling sex. Violence and illegal taxation (vigilante gangs who prey on the houseless and beggars and take their money), often associated to the crack scene, have

---

[2]'"She-male" is 34th murder', *Toronto Sun*, 27 August 2003; 'Surviving on the streets', *Washington Post*, 20 August 2003; 'Transphobia kills again', Panteras Rosa – Frente de combate à GayLesBiTransfobia, Lisbon, Portugal, 13 March 2008.
[3]Sarah Dennison-Hunt, SW5 Project, personal communication, 3 December 2007.

made the streets an unsafe venue to work, just in terms of a young man's physical safety. (Gaffney, 2006)

Connell and Hart (2003), however, describe violence against male sex workers in Glasgow and Edinburgh as extensive. Their informants had experienced violence from clients, people posing as clients, other sex workers and those organising sex work businesses, as well as in the context of homophobic attacks, street violence or personal relationships. In contrast to descriptions of indoor work in London as largely trouble-free, Connell and Hart found that brothel work was perceived as relatively dangerous. They also reported that street work was regarded as safer in Edinburgh than in Glasgow. However, the safety precautions adopted, the precipitating factors for violence (such as drug or alcohol use by attackers or victims, disputes over sexual practice and payment, etc.), the vulnerabilities imposed by hostile policing, verbal abuse and harassment from passers-by, all correspond very closely to the factors highlighted by female sex workers.

Because the vast majority of my information and experience concerns female sex workers, I refer to sex workers as female, except in particular cases where the victims have been male. However, since the available information indicates that the issues for male and trans sex workers are similar to those for female sex workers, I hope this exploration of violence in the sex industry will be relevant to male and trans sex workers and to those working with them.

Chapter 4

Prevention, Ugly Mugs and the role of outreach projects

Preventing violence

Brookman and Maguire (2003) place prevention of violence and homicide in the context of approaches to crime reduction in general, noting that strategies to reduce crime against vulnerable people or in vulnerable locations 'rely on predictions about where, when and/ or by what kinds of person offences are likely to be committed, so that interventions can be targeted at particular "hotspots" (or populations).' I also ask the where, when and by whom questions, focusing particularly on violence that takes place *when* the victims are engaged in selling sex, *where* it occurs and *by whom* the violence is committed. The question of *who* becomes a victim has largely been answered by previous explorations of sex workers' risk of violence. While the proportion who have experienced various kinds of attack may vary from survey to survey, where street and indoor situations have been compared, the most important findings are that street work is more dangerous than indoor work, and that indoor work is safer if working with other people (McKeganey and Barnard 1996; Church *et al.* 2001; Ward *et al.* 1999; Kinnell 2004). These findings are clear and unequivocal, but they have yet to have any impact on sex work policy, as Brookman and Maguire noted in the context of sex workers' risk of homicide:

> The feasibility of many preventive strategies depends largely on the legal position of prostitutes and police enforcement practices. This is clearly an area of direct relevance to homicide

reduction which would benefit from further research and more imaginative initiatives. (Brookman and Maguire 2003)[1]

The necessary 'where' and 'when' predictions for preventing violence which Brookman and Maguire outline are straightforward in relation to violence against sex workers, and the necessary strategies and technology to make significant improvements already exist. Most street soliciting areas already have extensive surveillance hardware which could be used to catch those who simply attack sex workers on the street. Attacks in vehicles or at outdoor locations where 'business' is done could also be interrupted if there were monitored areas to which sex workers could take their clients. Sex workers could be encouraged to take clients to indoor premises, where a friend or concierge was present to assist if difficulties arose. Text messaging could be used to alert police if violence occurred or was threatened. Other new technology such as mobile phones and alarms that pinpoint the holder's position also has potential. However, political support for these strategies would require the prevention of violence against sex workers to become a higher social priority than the prevention of street prostitution.

Instead, prevention of violence depends largely on the ingenuity and vigilance of sex workers themselves, in anticipating, deflecting or escaping from danger. Integral to sex workers' self-protective strategies is the identification of known or potential assailants – Ugly Mugs.

Reporting and recording violence against sex workers

Sex workers are often reluctant to report attacks to the police. They may not expect to be treated sympathetically – police may respond by telling a street worker that 'she shouldn't be out there in the first place'; if there are warrants out against her, or if she is subject to an ASBO, she may fear being locked up if she contacts the police. Those who have not had previous contact with the police may be unwilling to identify themselves as sex workers; those working indoors may fear prosecution, and those who fear deportation may not consider

---

[1]This statement is omitted from Brookman and Maguire's summary of their findings on reducing homicide (Brookman, F. and Maguire, M., 2003, *Reducing Homicide: Summary of a Review of the Possibilities*, RDS Occasional Paper No. 84. London: Home Office).

it an option. If they do report an attack, they may be detained for long periods and may be questioned about matters that are nothing to do with the incident, while a woman who is under pressure from a pimp to earn a set sum every day, or one who is supporting a drug habit by her earnings, may be deterred from reporting simply by the amount of time it will take.

Even if attacks are reported to the police, there does not appear to be much consistency in how such crimes are recorded, and no data on violence against sex workers are available through the criminal justice system. Consequently, much of the information I present about violence towards sex workers comes from 'Ugly Mugs' collected by outreach workers in different projects around the country, from project reports and personal communications from outreach workers, and from media coverage of attacks, particularly those referring to cases which have resulted in a prosecution.

The Ugly Mug system

Sex workers' strategies for resisting violence have always included warning each other about attackers. Miller's accounts of street workers in the USA show that, even when there were conflicts between women, they expressed a group culture of solidarity regarding the obligation to share such information (Miller 1993). Some escort agencies and brothels in Britain have had warning systems for many years, but with the emergence of organisations for sex workers' rights and health promotion, other systems were developed, using both old and new communications technology. Agencies working with sex workers now frequently operate an 'Ugly Mug' scheme, by which violent incidents are logged and warnings circulated to sex workers of potential assailants.[2] This element of dissemination is unique to the Ugly Mug system, since even if attacks are reported to the police, they have no mechanism to ensure that other sex workers are warned about dangerous individuals.

Sex workers are often happier to report attacks to outreach workers for dissemination through the Ugly Mug system than they are to report such attacks to the police, but this depends on outreach workers

_____

[2] The term 'Ugly Mug' was coined by the Prostitutes' Collective of Victoria, Australia, in the 1980s, and adopted in the UK from 1989 onwards. Some prefer the term 'Dodgy Punter', but since many of the assailants described are not 'punters', I use the term 'Ugly Mug'.

encouraging women to do so, and having the right conditions to facilitate this exchange of information. Most projects are not funded to address violence, and levels of contact with sex workers may be inconsistent or limited. Severe interruptions in reporting occur when projects are closed due to insecure funding, but maintaining the necessary levels of contact is never easy. Outreach sessions may take place regularly, but it is completely unpredictable which sex workers will be contacted during them. Stringent anti-prostitution operations also reduce the numbers of women making contact during outreach; sex workers may temporarily relocate to other 'beats', and those who remain are under pressure to keep conversations with outreach workers brief, so that they can make their money and leave the area as fast as possible. These conditions are not conducive to the careful recall of details of attacks, and the destabilisation of sex workers' soliciting patterns means that a woman who has been attacked may not meet an outreach worker for weeks afterwards. Drop-in centres are often better environments for reporting attacks, although again police operations can limit sex workers' access to such premises and some ASBOs ban sex workers from the areas where drop-ins are situated.

Contact with indoor sex workers also depends on project resources and orientation. Some projects are aimed at street workers only, so do not contact indoor workers at all, and even where outreach to indoor workers is routine, sex workers may be reluctant to report attacks for fear of attracting police attention to their premises. These fears have grown since the Home Office strategy on tackling prostitution was implemented (Home Office 2006), its demand for aggressive policing of indoor sex work undermining relationships of trust built up over many years between sex workers and outreach projects as well as, in some areas, trusting relationships between sex workers and police.[3]

What Ugly Mugs can tell us

Ugly Mugs describe the experiences that sex workers themselves define as violence, and shed some light on the identity and behaviour of attackers. However, there is no national Ugly Mug database at present, nor, even if one existed, would it reflect the total incidence of violence in the sex industry, because many areas do not have an

---

[3]See page 115.

outreach project, not all projects run Ugly Mug schemes[4] and even
ones that do would not claim to be in contact with every sex worker
in its catchment area or hear about every attack on those with whom
they are in contact. Also, there is no reliable method of establishing
the baseline population of sex workers against which numbers of
attacks can be compared, so it is not possible to estimate overall
prevalence.

Further, since their purpose is to warn other sex workers about
individual attackers, Ugly Mugs concentrate on descriptions of
assailants and their modes of making contact, rather than on details
of the actual attacks. Consequently, the information available for
categorising different kinds of violence, or for exploring 'reasons'
for the attack (however unreasonable these might be) tends to be
patchy. For example, an assailant may say he has been robbed by
a sex worker and is getting his revenge by attacking another: this
may be the motivation behind more attacks, but unless the assailant
voices this rationalisation, the sex worker will not know. Sometimes a
woman will add to her account her own interpretation of the attacker's
behaviour – such insights are very valuable, but a sex worker who
is being assaulted has other things on her mind than interrogating
her assailant about his motivations, so often these cannot be known.
Ugly Mug reports cannot, therefore, provide a firm measure of
incidence or prevalence of violence, nor answer all questions about
why an attack has occurred, but are nevertheless extremely valuable
for understanding the types of violence experienced by sex workers
and how risk of different kinds of violence varies depending on the
style of work.

Apart from unequivocal descriptions of physical and sexual
assault, Ugly Mug reports cover a very wide range of incidents, such
as

- unsuccessful attempts to gain access to sex working premises;
- suspicious behaviour while in sex work premises;
- 'weird' behaviour that has caused anxiety but not physical harm;
- peeping toms, covert photography;
- blackmail attempts, threatening letters and telephone calls;
- people posing as police officers or other officials;
- verbal abuse, threats, intimidation, pestering, stalking;
- stealing, mugging, robbery, bad cheques;

[4]Of projects affiliated to the UK Network of Sex Work Projects, 77 per cent
operated an Ugly Mug Scheme in 2007.

- throwing missiles: fireworks, stones, bottles, urine, dirty nappies, eggs, etc.;
- harassment by gangs of youths, residents, vigilantes;
- street workers being driven at or thrown out of moving cars;
- threats with weapons;
- refusal to pay, forcing or attempting to force return of money after sex;
- objections to condoms, tampering with or removing condoms;
- requests for unacceptable services;
- forcing or attempting to force acts which have not been agreed or paid for;
- kidnap, being held against one's will.

Ugly Mug reports from many different areas and agencies will be used to illustrate the variety and nature of attacks, identify components of danger and suggest strategies for prevention. I am able to refer to datasets comprising all reports made over differing periods in London, Huddersfield, Bristol, Merseyside, Edinburgh and Bournemouth. I have also collected dozens of individual Ugly Mugs from many other areas. Altogether I have examined well over a thousand Ugly Mug reports, and while local differences in presentation of the information they contain makes it difficult to compare one area with another, the same themes and types of attack emerge time and time again. These themes and categories are used to analyse the nature of violence and those responsible for it in subsequent chapters.

The role of outreach projects

Responding to violence against sex workers has been a major concern of outreach projects for many years. The Ugly Mug system was introduced in Birmingham in 1989 (Kinnell 1995), and by 1990 had been adopted by projects in London; the Working Women's Project in Streatham was producing a monthly Ugly Mugs List by 1992 and the Praed Street Project in Paddington offered self-defence classes to sex workers from the early 1990s. Their experience helped to inform the Southampton *Resistance!* project, a sex worker-led self-defence training programme based on women's experiences of violence, set up in 1994 and lasting several years (Blackwood and Williams 1999). In 1995 the Doncaster Streetreach project, with support from the Suzy Lamplugh Trust, investigated safety issues for street workers, adapted the Trust's safety training methods to their needs and produced a leaflet, *Working Girls, Working Safe*, drawing on sex workers' own knowledge and experience (Watson 1995).[5] O'Neill and Barbaret (2000) refer to the Ugly Mug system operated by the outreach project in Stoke-on-Trent in the 1990s. The London Ugly Mugs List, which collates reports from several agencies, also dates back to the mid-1990s. In 1998 the One25 Project in Bristol reported:

> We have seen an increase in violence on the streets, and a number of the women have been attacked or raped ... (named officers) have been willing to meet women away from the Police Station in order to take statements in connection with attacks ... 120 Personal Attack Alarms have been ... given freely through the outreach programme. In addition, as part of our Training Programme for volunteers, a session on Self Defence for women will ... be open to all workers connected with One25, including the female sex workers. (One25 Project, Annual Report 1997/8)

In 1998 the Harbour Centre, Plymouth, reported on their consultations with outreach projects prior to setting up a service for sex workers, stating 'we were advised to initiate an "Ugly Mugs" List.... Several projects offer practical safety advice such as self-defence classes and leaflets. We purchased an excellent "How to work safely" leaflet written by sex workers from the Praed Street Project in London' (Curren and Sinclair 1998). In 2001, the Leeds Genesis Project outlined the importance attached to the issue of violence, and the crucial role outreach workers play in liaising between sex workers and the police to encourage reporting of attacks:

> Street workers particularly are regularly confronted by punters who are verbally, sexually, and physically violent towards them, yet 77% of women who reported an incident to us this year chose not to report it to the police. Women do not feel comfortable about reporting such incidents for many reasons and we continue to facilitate this process through our incident report forms. These allow us to take a detailed description of the attacker and type of violence experienced. From this details

---

[5]In 2006, the Home Office commissioned the Suzy Lamplugh Trust to develop personal safety training for those involved in sex work and to produce a safety leaflet, similar to the *Working Girls, Working Safe* document that was produced with support from the Suzy Lamplugh Trust in Doncaster in 1995.

are used to put together a 'dodgy' punter description.... We also note whether the incident has been reported to the police and if not, the reason why.... In many incidences, with support, a woman will feel able to work with police. (Genesis Project 10th Anniversary Annual Report 2001)

In 2000, with Home Office funding under the Crime Reduction Programme, the Liverpool Linx Project and Merseyside police developed improved instruments for the collection of data about attacks, and new communications technology was employed to disseminate warnings about attackers more quickly. Rapid progress was made, doubling the frequency with which attacks were reported; there were important court cases where Ugly Mugs were used in evidence, and the Ugly Mugs system, including the essential role of the outreach project in operating the system and giving women support during the judicial process, were praised by investigating officers (Penfold *et al.* 2004; Sanders and Campbell 2007). Similar successes in securing convictions with the help of Ugly Mug reports have occurred elsewhere, including Bournemouth, Coventry and Plymouth. The credibility and integrity of the Ugly Mug system has thus been subjected to legal scrutiny on several occasions.

Despite all these initiatives, outreach projects have been criticised for failing to address sex workers' vulnerability to violence. Barnard *et al.* (2001) alleged: 'There has been a tendency to overlook those features of sex work that affect directly the health of prostitutes, but do not have any obvious health consequences for others. Client violence to prostitutes is one such topic.' The Home Office document *Paying the Price* (2004) re-echoed this theme: 'Outreach and drop-in projects have tended to focus on sexual health issues but increasingly it has become clear that harm minimisation should also take account of other risks, including the danger of physical assault.' It also described Ugly Mugs as being set up in Liverpool in 2000, in reference to the Merseyside scheme, which was to *enhance*, not start, the Ugly Mug system, suggesting a wilful denial of the long-standing efforts of outreach projects to address violence.

Paying the Price (Home Office 2004) cited the Merseyside scheme as an example of good practice, but by the time *Paying the Price* was published, the Linx Project had closed, illustrating how little sustained interest there has been in preventing violence against sex workers. In 2006, a new Merseyside initiative was launched: an Independent Sexual Violence Advisor (ISVA) was appointed to the Armistead Project, one of 30 ISVA posts funded as part of the National Sexual

Violence Action Plan, but the only one to be based with a sex work project.[6] In the first full year of this appointment, the number of Ugly Mug reports given via the outreach project doubled over the previous year's total, and the proportion of service users reporting attacks rose from 9 per cent to 21 per cent (Stoops and Campbell 2008). As before, prioritising the issue of violence combined with good police liaison has resulted in several offenders being prosecuted.

Outreach workers have also found that sex workers value the recognition Ugly Mugs give to the violence they suffer. Many have encountered dismissive attitudes from the police and from others when they have tried to describe a frightening or violent occurrence, whereas having that experience recorded as an Ugly Mug is a tangible statement that someone, somewhere, thinks the event they have suffered is important. Ugly Mugs are thus not only a tool to address sex workers' safety but demonstrate active concern for their well-being.

Nevertheless, Bindel has attacked Ugly Mugs on the grounds that 'such schemes can only reduce, rather than eliminate harm, and can be seen as a way to maintain women in the sex industry, as opposed to assisting their exit from it' (Bindel 2006), vindicating the point made in Chapter 2, that the radical feminist approach is essentially dismissive of sex workers' vulnerability to violence: compared to the aim of stopping commercial sex altogether, preventing beatings, rape and murder is viewed as a distraction from the core task. Bindel and Atkins (2007) reiterate these criticisms, also stating that the 'police should not be leaving voluntary organisations to compile Ugly Mug databases, but should take on the responsibility and share intelligence with those supporting women in prostitution', again illustrating the peculiar reliance of radical feminists on the police to prioritise the safety of sex workers.

Crimestoppers[7]

The government's *Co-ordinated Strategy on Prostitution* (Home Office 2006), while demanding universal adoption of rigorous enforcement

---

[6]Again with short-term funding from the Home Office.

[7]Crimestoppers – a national telephone service whereby crimes can be reported anonymously. The organisation is an independent charity, but works closely with the police, to whom the information given by callers to the phone line is passed on.

methods that make street sex work dangerous and discourage the reporting of violence, nevertheless proclaimed its determination to 'ensure justice', for sex workers who experience violence and heralded an initiative to encourage sex workers to report attacks via Crimestoppers, adding:

> A crucial element of the new arrangement is to ensure that, where appropriate, warning information reported to Crimestoppers is routed back without delay to local Ugly Mugs schemes and made available to those on the streets.

In August 2006, the 'Campaign to Stop Violence Against Prostitutes' was launched. This consisted of posters and stickers advertising the Crimestoppers phone number. Dr Tim Brain, ACPO[8] lead on Prostitution and Chief Constable of Gloucestershire, welcomed the scheme but stressed that it was a response to individual victimization:

> As *individuals* they are entitled to the full protection of the law. The Crimestoppers 'STOP' campaign will assist *individual* prostitutes in identifying those so-called clients who have a history of abusing prostitutes by way of physical violence. (Emphasis added)

Dr Brain's choice of language suggests he felt it important to indicate that the campaign was not an attempt to improve the safety of sex workers in general. The Home Office Minister, Vernon Coaker, was less grudging, announcing:

> We must ensure that victims' interests and needs are put at the heart of the criminal justice system, and although we want people to have the confidence to report all crimes to the police, this joint initiative means that those involved in prostitution can anonymously pass on vital information to help bring offenders to justice and to reduce the risks to others on the street.[9]

The princely sum of £20,000, or 25 pence for every sex worker believed to be operating in the country, was allocated to meet these

---

[8]ACPO – Association of Chief Police Officers.
[9]*Campaign to Protect Women Involved in Prostitution*, Press Release, Home Office, 21 August 2006.

laudable aims. In comparison, it was predicted that the full cost of investigating and prosecuting the five Ipswich murders would be £19 million.[10] With the current toll of homicide of sex workers running at an average of nine per year (2004 – 2007), the costs per year to the Exchequer must, therefore, be in the region of £34 million. It might be thought that it was worth the government's while to invest rather more heavily in prevention, if only to save money.

By April 2008, no evaluation of the uptake or effectiveness of the Crimestoppers initiative appears to be available or even planned, and despite the Home Office's recognition of its crucial importance, no system of passing on intelligence about attackers to those working with sex workers seems to be in place.

---

[10]'Anger at red-light killings bill', *Evening Star*, 27 January 2007.

Chapter 5

Who attacks sex workers?

> To ensure the safety of our staff we are unable to include
> information about attackers who are known to be ponces, police
> or other prostitutes on the Ugly Mugs List.

This disclaimer, formerly included by one project for sex workers
on its Ugly Mug forms, is a salutary reminder that violence in the
sex industry is not the exclusive province of those who approach as
clients, and this chapter sketches some other identities of assailant:
pimps, partners, family members, acquaintances, police, robbers
and members of the general public, as well as clients and other
predators.

Ugly Mug reports are usually about violence in the working
environment, but sex workers also encounter violence in other
situations. The relative frequency of violence from different sources
is hard to judge, but one project which records all 'Violent Incidents'
reported by their service users, listed by different categories of
assailant, is the SWEET project in Huddersfield.[1] Of 61 violent
incidents over a nine-month period in 2007, 34 per cent of reports
related to violence from a pimp, partner, ex-partner or other family
member; 31 per cent related to violence from other people, such as
muggers, vigilantes, acquaintances, other sex workers, drug dealers
and men committing sexual violence who did not approach as clients;
and 34 per cent related to men approaching as clients (see Table 5.1).
A similar figure was reported by Ward and Day (2001), who found

---

[1]SWEET – Sex Worker Empowerment, Education and Training.

Table 5.1 Violent Incident Reports, SWEET
Project, January to October 2007

Assailant	Reports	%
'Client'	21	34
Partner/pimp/ex-partner	19	31
Family member	2	3
Other	19	31
Total	61	99

that 40 per cent of recent assaults on women surveyed between 1989 and 1991 were committed by clients.

Thirty-four women reported one or more violent incidents to the SWEET project, under a quarter of service users seen during the period: 13 reported violence from 'clients'; 14 violence from a pimp, partner, ex-partner or family member; and 15 reported violence from other people, showing that several of the women had experienced violence from multiple sources, and that violence from 'clients' was no more frequent than violence from other people.

Pimps, partners, families and acquaintances

That's my husband of 12 years. Don't call him a pimp![2]

Understanding sex workers' private relationships is hampered by demonisation of those who profit from the prostitution of others, but the common 'pimp' stereotype of a man who has no emotional relationship to the sex worker, regarding her merely as a source of income, may be misleading. These relationships may be of many years' standing; they may have children together, and the relationship may have pre-dated the woman's involvement in selling sex. While a partner's violence may be primarily calculated to coerce her into commencing or continuing in sex work, there are other scenarios where violence appears more similar to that which occurs in numerous relationships where neither partner has any involvement in the sex industry. It should also be remembered that not all partners are male, and that other family members can be violent and coercive. Violence

---

[2] 'Asbos for Paddington prostitutes who made residents' life misery', *Mail on Sunday*, 22 November 2006.

in private relationships may also be more hidden than violence at work, and be more difficult for the sufferer to report, either to the police or to welfare agencies, since sex workers are often inhibited by the same issues that prevent other victims of domestic violence from acknowledging or seeking to escape abusive relationships: love, fear, self-blame, inadequate support structures and feeble judicial responses (May *et al.* 2000; O'Neill 1996; Phoenix 1999).

> He tried to help ... feed her heroin habit by robbing in Debenhams and Marks & Spencer in Sheffield's Meadowhall Centre. But Alan was a bad shoplifter and Lynne was a bad addict. He kept getting caught ... they have been together since they were 16.... In their world of prison, heroin addiction, violence and pimps, Lynne and Alan offered each other a gentle, strung-out shoulder. (O'Kane 2002)

With the spread of drug dependence among street sex workers and their partners over the past decade, there has been wider acknowledgement that coercion by a partner is not the driving force behind all women's involvement in sex work. Where partners are themselves heavily drug dependent, they may be incapable of exerting any purposive control, although cocaine use may increase aggression. If both partners are drug users, their drug consumption may initially be financed by the male partner's thieving until he is arrested and imprisoned. The woman may then turn to sex work while her partner is incarcerated. When released, the partner may acquiesce in or encourage her involvement, or may object and become violent as a result. Sanders (2005) and McLeod (1982) also report that sex workers often sell sex without their partners' knowledge, illustrating how seriously sex workers regard the necessity of separating their working lives from private relationships, and how great is the fear of losing those relationships should these boundaries fail. Where she has been selling sex without her partner's knowledge, violence may arise if he finds out.[3]

Even relationships that are clearly exploitative and abusive can take different forms. Ashley Wright exemplified the violent, abusive, sadistic, career pimp. He was convicted of 16 offences, including three rapes in 2002. It was alleged he had raped, beaten and tortured 12 sex workers in Birmingham over a 20-year period.[4] Steven Wilson, also of

---

[3]See pages 198–200.
[4]'Face of evil', *Sunday Mercury*, 9 June 2002.

Birmingham, forced his wife into sex work as a teenager, subjected her to nine years of violence, then murdered their two young sons when she left him.[5] Barrington Taylor, of Sheffield, who was convicted of robbery and assault in 2007, was described as a:

> well known character to the sex working/drug using community. He dabbles as a crack dealer and could loosely be referred to as a pimp, who uses extreme violence (both sexual and physical) to control and intimidate women. Most of the women are aware of Barrington and his reputation; many have been his victims over the years.[6]

A third of the 'Violent Incident' reports taken by the Huddersfield SWEET project related to violence from a pimp, partner, ex-partner or other family member. Fourteen women reported violence from these sources, under 10 per cent of service users seen by the project during the period. The reports show that women are encouraged to report this kind of violence, and to seek help to escape from abusive situations, which suggests that the extent of violence in the personal lives of sex workers may not be as great as it is often assumed to be.

> [In a street attack on] another prostitute who had failed to pay back money she was alleged to have owed ... [She] was frisked by her before being punched to the ground and kicked. Two men who were passing intervened and saved her from further injury, but she still needed hospital treatment for a broken nose, black eyes and cuts.[7]

Ten (16 per cent) of the 'Violent Incident' reports made to the SWEET project involved violence from acquaintances, and in half of these the assailant was a woman. Plumridge (2001) reported on violence between sex workers in New Zealand, and Daniels' account of her experiences as a sex worker in Britain illustrates the sometimes volatile relationships between sex workers, with competition for business, conflicts over private partners and through female-on-female pimping (Daniels 2006). Extreme incidents are rare, but seven of the suspects

---

[5]'Boys killed in revenge by "evil" father', *The Guardian*, 26 March 2003.
[6]See http://www.swwop.org/success_stories.html; 'Prostitute claims pal raped and robbed her', *The Star*, 21 December 2005.
[7]'Prostitute attacked rival', *Doncaster Star*, 27 July 2007.

charged with homicide of sex workers in the UK between 1990 and 2006 were women, five of whom were known to be acquaintances of the victims and three were sex workers themselves (see Chapter 14).

Police

Sex workers in other countries frequently report abuse by law enforcement personnel (Miller 1993; Phal 2002). In New York 27 per cent of sex workers reported assault by police (Thukral and Ditmore 2003). In Britain violence by the police is now rarely mentioned, but 30 years ago it was not such a taboo subject. During the Sutcliffe enquiry, it was alleged that two vice officers in Manchester raped a sex worker, threatening to kill her and make it look like a 'Ripper' murder (Yallop 1981). When investigating prostitution in 1977, Toynbee wrote, 'Everyone I met in the prostitution world believed that all vice squads are corrupt from top to bottom ...' (Toynbee 1977). This section is not intended to vilify the police service – there are many reports of good relationships between sex workers and police, but these examples indicate how much our expectations of police behaviour have risen in recent years. However, there is still abuse of sex workers by law enforcement personnel, and attention needs to be drawn to the difficulties that sex workers face in getting redress if abused by people in positions of power over them.

Among sex workers interviewed in Liverpool (2000–2001), more than half said they would not report *any* attacks to the police and 24 per cent reported violence from police officers themselves, a similar proportion to the 27 per cent reported in New York (Campbell 2002). The Liverpool report did not explore the circumstances of this violence: some may have been incidents of rough handling when arrested rather than attacks in other circumstances. That 'rough handling' during arrest can be extremely violent was illustrated in March 2007, when footage of a young woman being punched repeatedly by a male officer was made public.[8] Other alleged incidents of police abuse suggest that those involved were indulging in forms of bullying: one concerned an officer who forced sex workers to sing Christmas carols for his entertainment; another that officers turned a fire hose on some

---

[8] She was not a sex worker: Emine Saner, 'Taking a beating', *The Guardian*, 9 March 2007 (see http://www.guardian.co.uk/crime/article/0,,2029923,00.html).

women in the back of a police vehicle.[9] These incidents might be dismissed as 'having a laugh', but they betray enjoyment in exerting power, in humiliating sex workers, and the fire hose episode suggests a subtext of contempt for them as 'dirty' women, an attitude also revealed by an officer who was convicted of soliciting an Ipswich sex worker in 2007. He repudiated the charge saying he was a 'hygiene freak' and that the sex worker had smelt 'quite unclean'.[10] Although the sex worker may have resented this gratuitous insult, she is not reported to have made any complaint of violence or non-payment against him, but in 2003 a Bolton policeman was accused of approaching sex workers for business while in uniform and then not paying them. The women complained to other officers and he was convicted of soliciting a woman for prostitution. He was fined and ordered to pay costs, but the court did not order him to make any financial reparations to the women he had bilked of payment, so his victims may not have felt entirely satisfied with the verdict.[11]

Sexual abuse has also been alleged. In 2001 an officer was accused of indecently assaulting four sex workers in his police van, on the pretext of searching them for weapons, during a police crackdown after the murder of a local sex worker. When one woman threatened to report him, he allegedly replied: 'Who do you think they will believe – a daft prostitute smackhead or me?' They did not believe her: he was acquitted on all counts.[12] However, sometimes sex workers, whether daft smackheads or not, are believed. In April 2008, a police community support officer who had used his position to extort sex from sex workers in Birmingham was found out because other sex workers had not been intimidated into compliance and had reported him to other officers. He admitted to two charges of misconduct in a public office, one of false imprisonment and one of rape. The judge sentenced him to nine years imprisonment, 'to deter him and others from misusing their positions'.[13]

---

[9]Private communications to the author.
[10]'Detective guilty of kerb crawling', *BBC News*, 12 September 2007 (see http://news.bbc.co.uk/go/pr/fr/-/1/hi/england/suffolk/6990975.stm).
[11]'Policeman on duty picked up prostitutes', *The Guardian*, 23 March 2004.
[12]Smackhead – heroin user; 'Policeman "assaulted prostitutes"', *BBC News*, 15 October 2002 (see http://news.bbc.co.uk/1/hi/england/2330747.stm); 'Policeman cleared of vice assaults', *BBC News*, 23 October 2002 (see http://news.bbc.co.uk/1/hi/england/2353659.stm).
[13]'Support officer admits misconduct', *BBC News*, 8 April 2008 (see http://news.bbc.co.uk/go/pr/fr/-/1/hi/england/west_midlands/7337476.stm).

Robbers and muggers

In the early hours of last Saturday morning Dawn was pulled from a client's car by a knife-wielding maniac and horrifyingly attacked. She was rushed to hospital after a taxi driver found her slumped in the street ... [she] had been repeatedly stabbed in the stomach. Surgeons were forced to remove one of her kidneys.... Her friends and colleagues were horrified when they learned robbery may have been the motive for the attack.... She was savagely knifed as she tried to flee, and her 'bum bag' containing up to £100 was cut from her waist.[14]

Extreme violence associated with robbery can be directed at both street and indoor sex workers. Robbery is the main form of violence at indoor sex work premises: 63 per cent of attacks reported by indoor workers to the London Ugly Mugs List included robbery or theft, but while such robberies were frequently accompanied by physical violence, only 16 per cent involved sexual violence. In contrast, 51 per cent of attacks reported by street workers involved robbery or theft, but two-thirds of these events also involved sexual assault.[15] At indoor premises, therefore, robbery seems to be primarily an acquisitive crime, although the gratuitous violence frequently meted out by such assailants may also indicate hatred and contempt for those who make their money in this way. Robbery from street workers, however, appears more often to be an additional form of humiliation in the context of sexual violence than a method of income-generation, although this picture may be changing, as those working with street sex workers now report frequent muggings unconnected with sexual violence by drug users and others.

Community violence

The threat of violence is ever-present. Women are subjected to threats, abuse ('tourists' and 'vigilantes' driving past, throwing stones, paint, eggs and dirty nappies, for instance), rape and assault. Women often have black eyes and bruised mouths. One woman was kidnapped by a group of men and beaten with jump leads, supposedly in revenge for 'taxing' (theft of wallet, etc.) of

[14]'Maniac could kill next time', *Metro News*, 11 October 1990.
[15]See pages 84 and 121.

one of their friends. They later discovered they had attacked the wrong woman, but did not see this as an issue. There has been very occasional violence between sex workers. (Hobbs 2004)

Harassment, victimisation and abuse by a wide range of perpetrators is commonplace and widespread in street soliciting areas, and as the above description indicates, while individual women suffer, they are not targeted as individuals, but as members of a group regarded as legitimate objects of aggression. Adults, gangs of youths and even children – of both sexes – participate in these public displays of hatred and contempt for sex workers, but very little action is taken or disapproval expressed, especially when the aggressors can be seen as justifiably aggrieved by the presence of sex workers in their neighbourhood. The potential for violence of organised community actions against sex workers is examined in Chapters 7 and 8, but hatred for sex workers as community pollutants may also be expressed by individuals and gangs committing sexual assaults and robberies.[16]

Clients: the good, the bad and the bogus

The sex industry in Britain has traditionally operated with many conventions which may surprise outsiders who imagine it to be a chaotic maelstrom of sexual aggression and vulnerability. In reality both street and indoor workers have clear expectations of how clients should behave, and how 'the business' – i.e. the complete transaction between sex worker and client – should proceed. A 'genuine' client respects these conventions and fulfils the conditions of the 'client contract': the expectation that he will pay for the service requested; will use condoms as required; will not force acts which have not been agreed to or paid for; will not to rob the sex worker nor the premises on which she works; and will be non-violent (Sanders 2005). These expectations and conventions are rooted in the understanding that the sexual interaction is *business*, and provided that clients understand and abide by these rules, they protect the sex worker financially, physically and emotionally.[17]

---

[16]See pages 90 and 152–3.
[17]These conventions, in which the sexual encounter is clearly defined as 'business', may be less common among male sex workers (Connell and Hart, 2003; Bloor *et al*. 1992).

The first stage of negotiation between sex worker and client is to agree a price for a specific act. Selling sex is not organised like an 'eat-all-you-can' restaurant, where for a fixed price the customer can help himself to whatever he fancies and go back for seconds as often as he likes; it is strictly à la carte. Sexual interactions are divided into parcels, each of which is separately chargeable, and, despite all the hand-wringing over 'commodification' of bodies, the more the interaction is commodified, the more control the sex worker retains. If a certain price has been agreed for hand relief, the client cannot expect oral sex as well for the same price; if he wants something different, he must pay extra; if he wants more time, he must pay again, etc. Clients are expected to understand that they get only what they pay for, and attempts to force an act which has not been agreed to or paid for will be regarded as at least a violation of the rules, if not a sexual assault. The universal expectation among female sex workers is that payment should be made in advance of any sexual contact. This establishes the subsequent interaction as 'business' and is the basis on which consent is given. Refusal to pay upfront or haggling over the price are signals that the 'client' does not recognise the sex worker's right to set her own price on the services she offers, does not intend to abide by the conventions and may turn violent.

> [On first visit punter tried to negotiate reduced price for service.] On second visit woman agreed to slightly reduced price, but punter then began asking lots of personal questions, then complaining about service, and became very aggressive and threatening, demanding his money back. Eventually left after woman had called a friend to come and help. (London 2003)

Agreement must also be reached about where the sexual interaction will take place and how much time the client is buying. If working from fixed premises, the 'where' is not an issue, but both escorts and street workers must negotiate the venue with each client, and the sex worker's aim is to arrange a place where she feels safe, however marginal this perceived safety may be. A 'genuine' client accepts the sex worker's choice of venue without dispute and any quibbling may indicate trouble ahead.

> The driver refused to take her to a specified location and took her to a car park between two industrial units.... The woman

tried to leave and after a scuffle the man took her to a secluded part of the car park where he raped her repeatedly.[18]

Agreement over time is most straightforward for escorts whose rates are explicitly based on the time spent with each client, and while street workers may not specify a time limit, it is generally understood that their 'going rate' is too low to allow much time with each client. For sex workers in other working environments, the time spent with each client may be flexible, but where there is an agreed time limit and the client wants to exceed it, he must be prepared to pay extra.

> ... after 3hrs woman wanted to finish – client up till then very nice; immediately began kicking her and threatened to rob place. (London 2003)

> ... paid upfront, went to flat woman knew about, took too long, when she said time up, became very threatening, aggressive, smashed up furniture in flat. (London 2003)

There are further conventions which clients are expected to abide by: they must understand that maids (receptionists) at indoor premises do not provide sexual services and any attempt to touch someone in this role will be met with great disapprobation. Nor is overt sexual behaviour at inappropriate times or in inappropriate places acceptable: one Ugly Mug report described a client who caused great offence by exposing himself in the waiting area of a brothel. Clients are also expected to be polite: Sanders (2005) describes one street worker's technique of initially refusing all would-be clients; those who shout insults will not get another chance, but those who come back a second time and ask nicely are accepted. There are also limitations on emotional obligation: while romances and friendships may develop between sex workers and their clients, this is neither expected nor necessarily welcome. Clients who cannot accept that their relationship to the sex worker is confined to the interactions for which they have paid cause problems. They may fantasise that the sex worker is a girlfriend and become a nuisance with numerous visits and phone calls, or develop stalking behaviours which are rightly perceived as potentially dangerous. One report describes a client who evidently did not understand these more subtle conventions: 'pushy ... wants to

---

[18]'Prostitute suffers "brutal" rape', *BBC News*, 24 February 2006 (see http://news.bbc.co.uk/1/hi/england/manchester/4749232.stm).

start touching women as soon as inside flat. Acting strange; kneeling on floor whilst talking … haggles over money … refuses to leave.' He was denied entry on subsequent visits, then started harassing and threatening the women with repeated phone calls, vindicating their assessment that his bizarre behaviour was ominous.

Resisting the client role

Reactions of rage when the sex worker tries to enforce her expectations of the transaction, most obviously in refusal to pay but also through refusal to accept other conditions, such as using condoms or respecting time restrictions or prohibitions on certain forms of sexual practice, demonstrate resistance to the client role, and is frequently associated with violence. Violation of the accepted conventions may be flagrant and obvious acts of aggression, or may appear relatively insignificant to outsiders, though regarded very seriously by sex workers themselves, both because disregard of the conventions may breach the emotional and practical boundaries which separate sex work from other kinds of relationships and because it can indicate potential for committing serious harm. Even forcing a kiss is breaking an important taboo for many sex workers: if refusing to kiss clients helps to maintain clear boundaries between sex-as-business and sex in personal relationships, such an act can feel very intrusive and threatening. Refusal to respect the sex worker's personal boundaries is also a signal for further trouble:

> He asked for kissing but it was explained that the woman didn't do this. He became rough during the service grabbing the woman's face really tight and making her kiss him. After the service he started screaming and shouting and saying that he wanted his money back. (London 2001)

Refusal to use a condom, or deliberately removing or tearing condoms, are clear violations of the sex worker's rules and safety precautions and are much more invasive than unwanted grabbing or kissing, because protection from contact with clients' semen both serves an essential disease prevention purpose and forms an important differentiation between paid-for sexual acts and those in personal relationships, where not using condoms emphasises the intimacy of private sex. Condom use is standard practice in commercial sex, and while sex workers have always reported client resistance to condom use, any man approaching a sex worker for 'business' ought to anticipate the expectation that condoms will be required. Despite this, there are many reports of men reacting violently as soon as they are asked to use a condom, indicating that it is the role of client which is being resisted:

> Smith had paid the prostitutes for a massage and other sexual services at flats in Aberdeen but when they insisted he should wear a condom he attacked them.[19]

> ... tried to take the condom off during business, then grabbed the woman and pulled her hair out. He then robbed her of a considerable amount of cash. (Midlands 2003)

Similarly, attempts to force acts which the sex worker has not agreed to demonstrate refusal to recognise that consent has been given only on the basis of payment for separate units of sex/time, and refusal to acknowledge the ownership the sex worker has in her own body and her right to hire it out on her own terms.

> He tried to do several things during the service, which the woman said she did not do. He then asked for his money back. When the woman refused he got aggressive and put his hand round her throat and tried to strangle her.... She kicked him in the groin and left. (London 2001)

Sometimes the client becomes violent because he is 'not satisfied' with the service given. This usually means that he has failed to get an erection or ejaculate, problems which are often related to alcohol or drug use, which in themselves may precipitate violence. Disputes over time limits are also frequently related to these factors.

> Woman agreed to business ... however he could not maintain his erection. He asked for his money back & when refused went on to drag the woman over a wall & onto floor then pulled her coat off, running away with it & contents. (Midlands 2007)

---

[19]Ally McGilvray, 'Freed early, double rapist is banned from city's red light area', *The Scotsman*, 6 July 2007.

... seems to have difficulty doing business and becomes aggressive ... pays reduced amount or not at all. (North West 2003)

Was impotent, put a knife to her throat. Another woman reported that when she did business with him he took Viagra, coke and alcohol and cut her face with a knife. (South West 2003)

Miller and Schwartz (1995) quote Weisberg's observation that the 'most common factors precipitating [violence] ... are mutual misunderstandings regarding sexual acts to be performed, failure to satisfy a customer, and refusal to perform requested sexual acts.' Here 'mutual misunderstandings', 'failure to satisfy' and 'refusal to perform' are lumped together with – perhaps – an undertone of weariness with sex workers' lack of communication skills and intransigence, and without any apparent appreciation of the normal conventions involved in negotiating paid-for sex or acknowledgement that sex workers have every right to 'refuse to perform requested sexual acts'.[20] It is evident that some clients, and perhaps some commentators, believe that the sex worker is obliged to render 'satisfaction' under any circumstances, but sex workers cannot be blamed for the erectile problems of drunk or drugged clients; they also have the right to be paid for their time and to consider their own comfort and their opportunity costs. Neither does the evidence from the London Ugly Mugs List support the assertion that these problems are the most common factors precipitating violence. Dissatisfaction with the sexual encounter as a cause for violence or intimidation was mentioned relatively infrequently. Among indoor workers, only 6 per cent of incidents involved 'dissatisfaction' and another 9 per cent concerned clients forcing or trying to force acts that had not been agreed or paid for (Chapter 10). Nor is 'failure to satisfy' an excuse for violence or robbery. Often the attacker in these circumstances will not only take the money he has paid himself, but rob the woman of all the money she has, so cannot be likened to a dissatisfied customer demanding a refund for faulty goods: he is a thief and a rapist, but not a client.

---

[20]D.K. Weisberg (1985) *Children of the Night: A Study of Adolescent Prostitution.* Lexington, MA: Lexington Books.

The 'client disguise'

Sanders (2005) describes sex workers' screening methods to identify men who mimic client behaviour but do not intend to fulfil the client contract. This concept of the mimic, or 'client disguise', deserves wider recognition, since sex workers' accounts of violence show that most 'client' attacks are committed by men who only pretend to be clients until they have manoeuvred the sex worker into a position of vulnerability. Many robberies also involve men who mimic client behaviour when approaching sex workers, and there are instances of vigilantism where perpetrators pretend to be clients, luring women into situations where they can be attacked.[21]

> He agreed to pay her for a sex act and took her to the alleyway where he turned violent and demanded her takings. When she said she had no money, she was knocked to the ground and raped by Lewis, who threatened to beat her up unless she did as he said.[22]

There are also many instances where the imitation of client behaviour extends to paying for and having sex before forcing refunds, where paying upfront and so getting sex without any struggle seems to be an elaboration of the 'client disguise'.

> The 26-year-old woman was attacked as she got out of the man's car.... The attacker had paid the woman for sex, then punched and kicked her about the face and body. He lunged at her with a knife and grabbed the money back.[23]

> ... had completed business when he demanded the money back. She refused, jumped out of car and ran off. He reversed the car in pursuit, hitting a parked vehicle whilst doing so. Punter caught up with victim and hit her around the head, knocking her to the floor. She dropped her bag which he then picked up and ran off ... (Midlands 2008)

McKeganey and Barnard (1996) point out that only a minority of interactions between sex workers and clients involve violence, and the

---

[21]See pages 84 and 122–5.
[22]'Rapist jailed for "wicked" vice girl attack', *Bolton News*, 3 August 2007.
[23]'Knife attacker may strike again', *Bolton Evening News*, 3 December 2003.

accounts which sex workers themselves give via Ugly Mug reports, describing situations which they regard as abnormal and unacceptable, indicate that violation of the 'client contract' is the exception, not the rule. Attackers are, nevertheless, commonly described as 'clients', but examination of numerous reports of such attacks demonstrates that a high proportion of this violence comes from those who do not pay, and since the defining characteristic of a client is payment for sexual services, these attackers are, therefore, *not* clients, even though they may have approached the sex worker *as if* they were clients.

The 'non-client excuse'

Attackers may also claim that they were *not clients*, that they did not know their victim was a sex worker until she asked to be paid and that this request provoked rage. Joseph Harrison, who killed a sex worker in Aberdeen in 2005, claimed he had 'lost control' when she propositioned him; Matthew Rounce, convicted of murdering a Hull sex worker in 2001, claimed that he had not realised that she was a sex worker and that he had 'lost his self-control' in the subsequent dispute over payment.[24] Likewise, Stuart Burns, convicted of the murder of a Leeds sex worker in 2004, claimed 'it was only when she began quoting prices to him that he realised she was a prostitute and ... went "ballistic" because he felt degraded.'[25]

Many men might find it insulting to see themselves as insufficiently attractive or persuasive to obtain sexual partners without offering monetary inducement: when a well-known and attractive man is exposed as a client, there is public amazement that such a man would 'need' to pay, the implication being that only the physically repellent resort to such expedients. Outbursts of rage and sexual violence in response to demand for payment cannot, however, be explained merely as the expression of wounded self-esteem. Although unfamiliarity with the common norms in the UK sex industry may sometimes lead to misunderstandings, such stories have to be regarded with scepticism, since it is almost universal practice among female sex workers to make the commercial nature of the transaction

---

[24]Trial Judge Report 2004/320/MTS; Matthew Leslie Rounce; in High Court judgment rejecting Rounce's appeal for reduction of sentence, 4 November 2005 (see http://www.hmcourts-service.gov.uk/cms/144_7503.htm).
[25]'Life jail for body-in-bath killer', *Yorkshire Post*, 29 October 2005.

explicit at the outset, and in most accounts of such attacks the victim was approached in circumstances which suggest that the assailant did know she was a sex worker, so must have anticipated the request for payment. For example, Joseph Harrison, who claimed he had 'lost control' when asked for payment, was caught on CCTV, chatting happily to his victim while withdrawing money from a cash machine.[26] It seems possible that the 'non-client excuse' is proffered in the belief that violence will be regarded as an understandable reaction to being asked to pay for sex.

Examination of the language and behaviour of men who use the 'client disguise' or the 'non-client excuse' reveals common attitudes of contempt towards sex workers and numerous instances where rape and other types of assault have been used to demonstrate their power, to deny that they are clients and to deny the woman's right to receive payment. It appears that these aggressors do perceive the woman's status as a sex worker as a sanction to rape and abuse, but that through their violence and refusal to pay they are asserting that they are *not* clients.

Other predators

There is no word in common usage that conveys the equivalent of 'homophobic' or 'racist' for attacks which seem to arise merely from hate of sex workers, but there is a category of aggressor, which the evidence collated here suggests is at least as numerous as any other category, for which some such convenient label is needed. These are men who attack sex workers without any pretence of being clients, without any known personal grievance, sometimes even without any obvious sexual motive. Shane Haynes of Huddersfield is an example. Angry with his partner over access to their child and intoxicated with alcohol and cannabis, in October 2007 he went out 'to clear his head', taking with him a 20 cm kitchen knife. He walked over a mile to the street soliciting area where, with almost no apparent preamble, he stabbed sex worker Geraldine Brocklehurst several times, severing her jugular vein. She bled to death within minutes. He admitted he intended to harm her but did not say why. His barrister claimed the attack was not premeditated, citing the fact that Haynes had made no attempt to avoid CCTV cameras, nor to drag Geraldine 'to

---

[26]'Asking for it?', Tanya Thompson, *The Scotsman*, March 3 2007.

a remote and secret place'.[27] He had, nevertheless, armed himself before leaving home, directed his steps towards the street soliciting area and directed his knife into the neck of the first sex worker who spoke to him. Haynes would appear to have felt an overwhelming compulsion to vent his rage, not on anyone, not on any woman, but on a sex worker – any sex worker. This kind of attack may be related to the concept of 'collective liability', whereby sex workers are held to be collectively liable for perceived wrongs committed by 'all women in changing times' (Miller and Schwartz 1995).[28]

There are also many people who have attacked and killed sex workers who have also committed violence against non-sex workers. Some are infamous, such Michael Sams who is better known for kidnapping estate agent Stephanie Slater in 1992 and holding her to ransom. Sams was also convicted of murdering sex worker Julie Dart a few months previously, allegedly as part of his kidnapping plans, to convince police that he should be taken seriously (Britton 2001). Also, Ron Castree, eventually convicted of murdering 11-year-old Lesley Molseed in 1975, who was only identified as her murderer when his DNA was taken after attacking a sex worker in 2005.[29] Neither of these offenders, nor many others whose names are only likely to be remembered by their victims or their victims' relatives, are readily classifiable by sex work-related terms. They are serial predators who seem to target sex workers only because they are easy to attack.

---

[27]Andrew Hirst, 'Why Shane Haynes killed Geraldine Brocklehurst remains mystery', *Huddersfield Daily Examiner*, 1 March 2008. This case is not included in the analysis of sex worker murders as it occurred after December 2006.
[28]See Chapter 12.
[29]Castree was not prosecuted for this attack so is not included in any dataset in this book. Paul Byrne and Patrick Mulchrone, 'Child sex fiend gets life in jail', *The Mirror*, 13 November 2007.

Chapter 6

Street sex work: the context of violence

Legal framework

In England and Wales the Sexual Offences Act 1956 increased the criminalisation of indoor sex work, pushing sex workers onto the streets; the 1959 Street Offences Act made soliciting and loitering imprisonable offences, pushing women back off the streets, although this effect was only temporary (Self 2003). The Criminal Justice Act 1982 removed imprisonment for soliciting and loitering, but the Sexual Offences Act 1985 criminalised kerb-crawling. Fines were increased under the Criminal Justice Act 1991 and Anti-Social Behaviour Orders (ASBOs) were introduced in the Crime and Disorder Act of 1998. Although not originally intended to control soliciting, ASBOs were quickly adopted for this purpose, introducing a far heavier threat of imprisonment than had been removed in 1982: while the 1959 Act allowed a maximum of three months imprisonment, breach of an ASBO can result in up to five years imprisonment (Sagar 2007). Meanwhile, kerb-crawling law has become more stringent. Scotland has similar provisions, although kerb-crawling was not criminalised there until October 2007, and it is expected that kerb-crawling will be criminalised in Northern Ireland during 2008. New instruments for forcing sex workers to engage with 'exiting' programmes, with the reintroduction of imprisonment for failure to comply, were included in the Criminal Justice and Immigration Bill 2008. However, encountering vigorous opposition in the Lords, these clauses were dropped to expedite the passage of the Bill through Parliament.[1] It is nevertheless likely that further attempts will be made to introduce similar reactionary measures in future.

Enforcement policies, however, vary from place to place, contributing to differing local patterns of sex work. In many areas enforcement against street work has been pursued energetically for decades, but in a few places, if the location of street work has not offended senior police officers or local residents, sex workers have avoided arrest by working in informally designated areas and at certain times of day. The government's *Co-ordinated Strategy on Prostitution* (Home Office 2006) sought to remove any local tendency towards toleration, but chief constables have considerable autonomy is deciding their own priorities which may allow for a continuing variety of policing approaches in the future.

Playing the numbers game

Although there can be no firm statistics about an activity that is criminalised, stigmatised and covert, a mapping exercise carried out in 2005/6 estimated there were between 50,000 and 80,000 female sex workers in the UK, of whom 28 per cent (14,000 to 22,400) were street workers (UKNSWP 2008).

In some areas the number of street sex workers seems to have fallen, possibly due to police enforcement, interventions assisting women to 'exit' prostitution, or the increased use of mobile phones, enabling street workers to arrange meetings with clients without public soliciting, thus becoming less visible. Elsewhere there has been little obvious change in overall numbers, although soliciting locations frequently change in response to policing operations, which sometimes even displace sex workers to neighbouring towns.[2] However, claims of dramatic falls in the number of street workers should be treated with caution, because it is always in the interests of those supporting repressive policies to pronounce imminent success. A classic ruse is to compare the total number of sex workers known to police or to an

---

[1]Clauses preventing prison officers from going on strike were a higher priority for the government: 'Laws dropped to ease strike bill', *BBC News*, 28 February 2008 (see http://news.bbc.co.uk/go/pr/fr/-/1/hi/uk/7268971.stm).

[2]Sex workers were displaced from Southampton to Bournemouth in the 1990s and from Doncaster to Scunthorpe in the 2000s.

outreach project at some point in the past, which typically includes every individual seen over the course of a year, to the number seen soliciting on any particular night, which will be a small fraction of the annual total. In Stoke-on-Trent in January 2008, police claimed there were only 45 street workers compared to 187 four years earlier, while an agency supporting sex workers simultaneously stated they had seen 130 women in the previous nine months.[3] In 2007, police in Leeds claimed their tough policy was a great success, contrasting the 31 women found by the outreach project over a two-week period, with the 300 known to have been working two years earlier, while in Ipswich in 2008, it was claimed that 100 street workers had been reduced to 'one or two'.[4] There is no street soliciting area in this country where it is possible to count 100 women at one time, never mind 300. Even in Glasgow in 1991, when the total sex working population was estimated at 1,150, the average number seen on any one night was 22 (McKeganey *et al.* 1992).

Drug use

Heroin and crack are major problems among street sex workers today, but this situation has arisen relatively recently. Heroin dependency was common among street workers in some areas, such as Glasgow and Liverpool, by 1990, but relatively insignificant elsewhere (Cusick 1998). However, from 1990 onwards, crack cocaine began to have a severe impact on street workers. Women who had never previously been drug dependent began using crack, and over time this increased levels of heroin use, as sex workers self-medicated against crack's side effects (May *et al.* 1999; Green *et al.* 2000). The steadily falling cost of heroin may have hastened this trend. Not every woman doing street work became drug dependent within a few years, however, and different areas were affected at different times – some places are still more affected by opiates than other drugs – but street work became an increasingly drug-dominated milieu, which itself led

---

[3]Catherine Bruce, 'Police shut six brothels in sex trade crackdown', *The Sentinel*, 3 January 2008.

[4]Charles Heslett, 'Plight of the vice girls driven to danger', *Yorkshire Post*, 24 February 2007; 'Pride over town's response to killings', *Evening Star*, 24 February 2008.

non-drug users to move to other forms of sex work.[5] In some areas, the police facilitated this transformation, targeting their arrests at non-drug using sex workers; who were seen as having chosen to sell sex, rather than the drug-users who were seen as having no choice.

The Home Office strategy to eliminate street work foregrounds the importance of addressing sex workers' drug problems, but street prostitution existed long before either heroin or crack use became associated with it and, therefore, may not vanish once these addictions have been eliminated. Leaving aside questions of how long it takes the average addict to become completely drug-free and gainfully employed in other ways, or whether our social structure is incubating new generations of potential drug-using sex workers, and if so whether the current drug treatment programmes will keep up with them, history suggests that women with the lowest status in society, those in the most desperate financial need, will find their way into street prostitution, whether they are drug users or not.

Safety, policing and violence on the street

For much of the twentieth century street prostitution took place in localities with little or no resident population, such as docklands and industrial or commercial areas, or was pushed into poor and run-down neighbourhoods where those who objected to it had no political influence to move it, and where, perhaps, there was more sympathy with an activity which siphoned off profit from the upper and middle classes to the benefit of the underclass. However, urban renewal programmes, gentrification and new immigration patterns changed perceptions of street prostitution in areas where it was once tolerated, and by the 1990s, with large-scale redevelopment of old industrial sites, city centres and ports, the desire of the developer for a cityscape of monolithic respectability and affluence has frequently become paramount in shaping urban environments (Hubbard and Sanders 2003). The Home Office signalled its support for these priorities in *Paying the Price* (2004), which places 'the nuisance caused to neighbourhoods through noise, litter and harassment' and 'the impact on the neighbourhood in terms of undermining economic regeneration and neighbourhood renewal' first in a list of problems caused by the sex industry, above both violence against sex workers

---

[5]'Drugs lead to prostitution boom', *BBC News*, 9 April 2003 (see http://news.bbc.co.uk/go/pr/fr/-/1/hi/england/bristol/2931983.stm).

and abuse of children. The subsequent *Co-ordinated Strategy on Prostitution* (Home Office 2006) reaffirmed these priorities, even while acknowledging that enforcement to discourage street prostitution could undermine sex workers' safety. The impact of these forces on the policing of street prostitution and on the well-being of sex workers has been seen from King's Cross to Edinburgh and from Ipswich to Manchester. Examples are given below, which also illustrate other influences on policing, including the varying attitudes of senior officers and the effect (or not) of sex worker murders on the policies pursued.

In 1983, Sheila Anderson, a street sex worker in Edinburgh, was murdered. She had either jumped from or been pushed out of a moving car and was then run over repeatedly. In trying to solve this case, Edinburgh police realised that the lack of trust between them and sex workers impeded their investigation and prevented women from reporting other attacks.[6] Anderson's death motivated Edinburgh police to designate Britain's first semi-official tolerance or 'non-harassment' zone, which lasted until December 2001. The Edinburgh zone was lost because the character of the traditional area for street soliciting, Leith, was transformed by new developments on the old waterfront, the new Scottish Executive buildings and the gentrification of the area. New residents regarded street sex work as offensive, and a sustained campaign of harassment was launched against the women. In the last full year that the Edinburgh zone operated, there were eleven violent incidents reported to the outreach project; in the second full year after losing the zone, 111 violent incidents were reported.[7] Half of these incidents were described as 'harassment', and the report detailing this deterioration commented:

> Many of the incidents reported as harassment by sex workers other citizens would have categorized as a more serious crime against them. The women's tolerance of violence and what they accept as 'normal' treatment by clients and other members of the general public has shifted dramatically over the last two years. (SCOT-PEP 2004)

---

[6]'Hunt for brute after car crash mutilation of hooker Sheila', *Daily Record*, 5 December 2007.

[7]'Attacks rise after tolerance scrapped', *BBC News*, 5 July 2002 (see http://news.bbc.co.uk/1/hi/scotland/2095675.stm).

In the 19 years the Leith zone operated, there was one murder of a street sex worker in Edinburgh: the culprit was arrested within three days and convicted of murder. In the same period in Glasgow, there were seven murders, four suspects were tried, and one convicted of murder. After the seventh Glasgow murder in 1998, Strathclyde police issued safety leaflets and rape alarms to street workers. They also established a safety zone, not arresting sex workers who stayed in an area that was covered by CCTV (O'Kane 2002). No more street workers were murdered while 'at work' in Glasgow until 2005, by which time the policy had been abandoned.[8]

In September 2007, police in Dundee reported similar transformations in the urban landscape, and in public attitudes. Chief Inspector Tonks spoke of residents' increasing intolerance for sex work activity:

In Dundee, prostitutes have favoured the Blackscroft area to operate which is an area currently undergoing massive regeneration both commercial and residential. With the increase in new business and housing developments in these areas, there is a commensurate increase in the number of complaints about the activities of prostitutes and those who use the services of prostitutes.[9]

Tayside police planned to respond by targetting kerb-crawlers as soon as Scottish law came into line with English kerb-crawling legislation. The following month, the Edinburgh project, SCOT-PEP, again reported on the impact of hostile policing: widespread dispersal of sex workers to isolated areas at the edges of the city and a doubling in the rate of attacks reported over the previous year. The senior police officer in Leith expressed concern that the newly introduced kerb-crawling law would 'mean prostitutes working further away from the gaze of CCTV cameras and police officers, putting themselves in more dangerous situations.'[10]

---

[8]'Rape alarms for Scottish prostitutes', BBC News, 4 March 1998 (see http://news.bbc.co.uk/1/hi/uk/61974.stm); Cara Page, 'Vice in Scotland: cops in war on vice', The Daily Record, 14 February 2004.

[9]'Plans for kerb-crawler crackdown', BBC News, 19 September 2007 (see http://news.bbc.co.uk/go/pr/fr/-/1/hi/scotland/tayside_and_central/7002379.stm).

[10]Nicholas Jury, 'Red alert as attacks on city's vice girls double', The Scotsman, 17 October 2007; Michael Howie, 'Kerb-crawling law 'could put prostitutes at greater risk'', The Scotsman, 23 October 2007.

Bolton's approach to street prostitution has also fluctuated. In 2000, naming and shaming of kerb-crawlers was deemed the magic bullet, and on 30 September 2001, legislation giving police the power to arrest kerb-crawlers came into force. Twelve days later, on 11 November 2001, 17-year-old Carly Bateman was murdered, and six months after that, on 1 June 2002, Danielle Moorcroft was murdered. Local MP Brian Iddon called for brothels to be legalised and police admitted that they 'were fighting a losing battle against prostitution in the town.' An immediate renewed purge on kerb-crawlers was announced, but within a month residents of another district were complaining that the women had simply moved into their neighbourhood. In February 2003, another crackdown was reported, with 'hundreds of people targeted', but also that the police had, in their view, soft pedalled on enforcement during the Carly Bateman murder enquiry so as not to alienate potential witnesses. Carly's killer was arrested in January 2002, but Moorcroft's killer was still at large and was not arrested until February 2005, two and a half years after she died.

Whether or not the failure to identify Moorcroft's killer affected police attitudes to sex workers in October 2005, it was reported that those who stayed within Bolton's traditional soliciting area were less likely to be arrested, an area well-covered with CCTV. A senior police officer described the benefits of this policy: 'A partnership with outreach and health workers had forged better links with women who work on the streets, meaning they were more likely to stay within the zone. Chief Supt Lea said he was now confident that more attacks were being reported.' CS Lea attributed their recent successes in convicting a sadistic pimp and violent attacker to better liaison with sex workers via the local outreach project. He was nevertheless concerned that the police could not monitor women's safety once they had left the designated area with their clients.

Despite these benefits of cooperation and a de facto tolerance zone, by November 2007 it was back to business as usual in Bolton. Inspector Phil Spurgeon insisted, 'We have never tolerated it and there has never been a tolerance zone.' By March 2008, 107 people had been arrested, 49 of them sex workers. The justification for this reversion to aggressive enforcement was explicit: 'Police say the "aggressive" new approach is driven by a 2,000-name petition handed to Bolton Council, the redevelopment of the Shiffnall Street area and the opening of the Merchant's Place flats and office complex in River Street.'[11]

---

[11]'Twelve accused of kerb crawling', *Bolton Evening News*, 22 August 2000; 'Brothels could help save vice girls' lives says MP', *Manchester Evening News*,

In Sheffield, before 2001, street workers could avoid arrest if they worked away from pubs and residential areas.[12] They congregated near the university, attracted by the very lighting and security cameras that had been installed to deter them. Superintendent Steve Hicks said: 'The extra security made them feel safer and, surprisingly, it didn't seem to deter the punters.' But the arrival of a new senior police officer and new blocks of luxury flats signalled a change to 'zero tolerance', forcing the women to an old industrial estate with few lights and no CCTV. To coincide with the new powers of arrest for kerb-crawling which came into force on 30 September 2001, police announced an intensified crackdown on kerb-crawlers: 'We want kerb-crawlers to know that if circumstances permit, they will be arrested, handcuffed and taken to the police station and charged.'[13] Within a week, sex worker Michaela Hague, who had been soliciting in the new area, was murdered. A month later, police appealed for an important witness, the client of another sex worker, to come forward, offering him 'amnesty from prosecution in return for his evidence'.[14] This potential witness did not come forward, and Michaela's murderer has not yet been identified, seven years after her death.

A sex worker described the conditions in which she was working:

> There are no bright lights or high-quality CCTV cameras.... There's no lighting, no security, nothing well lit. The only people round here are weirdos and punters. It's just basically scary and horrible.... They should put us in an area where we'll all be safe, which is well lit and with cameras, things like that. The police go round arresting us, making it hard for us to work. We've had to go so underground, it's unbelievable. (O'Kane 2002)

---

5 June 2002; 'Murder police in kerb-crawl purge', *Manchester Evening News*, 24 June 2002; 'Fury as red light girls move in', *Bolton Evening News*, 17 July 2002; 'Anger as pimps and dealers swamped streets', *Bolton Evening News*, 6 February 2003; 'Prostitute's fears after friend is murdered', *Chorley Citizen*, 24 October 2005; Edward Chadwick, 'Police in vice trade crackdown', *The Bolton News*, 20 December 2007; Paul Keaveny, 'Kerb crawlers are shamed', *The Bolton News*, 6 March 2008.

[12]Kath Grant, 'Street wiser', *The Guardian*, 7 March 2001.

[13]'City cracks down on kerb crawlers', *Yorkshire Post*, 30 September 2001.

[14]'Amnesty offer in vice girl murder', *Yorkshire Post*, 4 December 2001.

In June 2003, Chief Superintendent John Brennan, whose previous robust approach to prostitution in Doncaster had driven many women to work in Sheffield, described the two main soliciting areas around Kelham Island and Sheffield University, admitting that a crackdown in one area merely shifted the women to the other.[15] Nevertheless, in February 2004, it was reported that complaints about street prostitution had fallen 'following the relocation of the city's main "red light" area [to] the back streets of the Kelham Island, which is largely an area of small industrial businesses.'[16] Sadly, by September, complaints had risen in the Kelham Island area too. Inspector Morley, who does not seem to have been in the area very long, said: 'The area has *traditionally* been a focus for that sort of activity ...' (emphasis added). ASBOs were threatened against the women who only six months before had been deemed to be causing less of a nuisance than in their previous locations. The women moved again, into a neighbouring district. In December 2004, police brought their mobile CCTV unit to this area, claiming an instant reduction in the numbers of sex workers and kerb-crawlers,[17] but by March 2005 were threatening kerbcrawlers with court proceedings to take away their driving licences, and ASBOs were in use against women who 'refused help'. Nine months later, the police warned that a 'zero tolerance campaign against kerb-crawlers and prostitutes' would be launched in January 2006. One wonders what their previous campaign had been, but the new one was again pronounced a great success in June 2007, although problems were reported in nearby Doncaster, possibly seeing a return of CS Brennan's displaced persons from 2002. Two gunpoint attacks on sex workers in the Kelham Island area in December 2007 and February 2008 suggest that CS Brennan's comments during 2003, of enforcement pushing sex workers from place to place, remain more accurate that the repeated claims of victory over vice. They also illustrate the dangers that Sheffield street workers still face, a point made by one of the readers commenting on the report of yet another crackdown on kerb-crawlers in March 2008, which appeared on the website of the Sheffield *Star*:

---

[15]Personal communications, September 2002; 'Help city's 500 vice girls – plea', *The Star*, 13 June 2003.
[16]'Street prostitution complaints fall after red light area switch', *The Star*, 2 February 2004.
[17]'VICE GIRLS BAN', *The Star*, 17 September 2004; 'Mobile CCTV targets vice girls', *Yorkshire Post*, 16 December 2004.

What are the police doing about Michaela. SIX YEARS!!! What are they doing about the girl that got raped in January? If they had released details of the December attack earlier, this rape could have been avoided. No, pick on the weak. Bully the vulnerable. Drive them all to unsafe, dark areas where more will get killed and raped.

Nine out of ten of the Sheffield readers' comments on this news item expressed similar attitudes.[18]

Reducing the public nuisance of street prostitution has also been prioritised over murder investigations elsewhere. Bradford sex worker Rebecca Hall was missing for two weeks before her battered body was found in April 2001 by a member of the public, in an alleyway on the heavily policed beat.[19] Over the next few days, Detective Chief Superintendent Max McLean made several appeals for information from members of the public, but while sex workers gave all the help they could, nine days after Rebecca's body was found, he said: 'The response to our appeals has been rather disappointing. What will find Rebecca's killer is information from the public.' Three days later, the front page article in the local paper announced a fresh 'PROSTITUTE CLAMPDOWN', in response to complaints from businesses and residents. Rebecca's murder is mentioned as if the dead bodies of murdered sex workers was just one aspect of the nuisance of street prostitution:

> The move comes in the wake of the murder of Rebecca Hall, whose battered body was found lying naked in the notorious red light area of Lister Hills. Detectives are still trying to catch the killer.... Businesses based along Thornton Road and City Road have also written in to Bradford council leader Margaret Eaton complaining about the effect prostitution has had on the area. Detective Superintendent Geoff Dodd, the squad's overall

---

[18]'Persistent kerb crawlers in city to face driving ban', *Yorkshire Post*, 1 March 2005; 'New crackdown on prostitution', *The Star*, 29 December 2005; Paul Whitehouse, 'Kerb-crawl crackdown success', *Yorkshire Post*, 5 June 2007; 'Woman suffers gunpoint sex ordeal', *BBC News*, 20 February 2008 (see http://news.bbc.co.uk/go/pr/fr/-/1/hi/england/south_yorkshire/7254575. stm); Claire Lewis, 'Street vice crackdown', *The Star*, 27 March 2008 (see http://www.thestar.co.uk/news/Street-vice-crackdown.3918888.jp).
[19]Beat – street soliciting area.

commander, said the priority would be to target kerb-crawlers and to starve the 'demand' for prostitutes.

DS Dodd announced: 'I issue this warning to anybody who does undertake kerb-crawling or pimping – the police will always press for prosecution at court.' His threats against those who might have been able to help the murder investigation may or may not have deterred their involvement in kerb-crawling or pimping, but they do appear to have been discouraged from any contact with the police. Six days later DCS McLean was again begging for cooperation with the murder investigation:

> We've had a disappointing response to our appeal ... I would stress the confidential nature of our enquiries and that the hotline is free and confidential. Our detectives do not care under what circumstances you knew Becky, but if you did, please come forward.[20]

Months passed, and although no progress was made with the murder investigation, aggressive policing of street prostitution continued. Local residents were said to support the police, but five out of seven of those quoted in the local paper either expressed scepticism about the long-term effect, called for more to be done to help the women or asked why prostitution could not be legalised.[21] These cautious and tolerant voices were not heeded and the Bradford crackdown continued:

> Nearly 200 kerb-crawlers have been shamed in a new crackdown on the sex trade on Bradford's streets. Vice squad officers have handed out 195 warning orders to men caught cruising the red light areas in cars as part of a scheme to stop the damaging effect on the quality of life for residents.[22]

---

[20]'Streets of fear', *Telegraph & Argus*, 2 May 2001; "Cracker' called in', *Telegraph & Argus*, 5 May 2001; 'Prostitute clampdown', *Telegraph & Argus*, 8 May 2001; 'Help us trap killer of tragic Rebecca', *Telegraph & Argus*, 14 May 2001.

[21]'Firm backs vice drive', *Telegraph & Argus*, 31 July 2001; 'Public backs vice squad crackdown', *Telegraph & Argus*, 1 September 2001.

[22]'200 kerb-crawlers shamed in crackdown', *Telegraph & Argus*, 30 August 2006.

But the murder of Rebecca Hall is still unsolved and street prostitution in Bradford continues.[23]

In complete contrast to the above approaches to female street sex work, in April 2007 the Birmingham Community Safety Partnership announced a 'yellow card scheme' to address the dangers faced by male street sex workers. It was aimed at kerb-crawlers, following 'concerns that rent boys and gay men … have been subjected to attacks by "non-clients".' A senior police officer explained, 'We have to be careful with how these cards are issued as there's a high suicide rate among men who engage with male prostitutes or are prosecuted for homosexual acts. Many who do this are married, family men who are not "out", so there is a risk of exposing a life people don't know about.'[24] The description of attackers as 'non-clients', the distinction made between 'gay men out "cruising" legitimately' and 'kerb-crawlers', and the concerns voiced by the police for the effect of the initiative on clients are extremely interesting. The contrast with the approach taken to female sex workers and their clients or 'non-clients' is quite startling. Attacks on female sex workers are not usually regarded as hate crimes, the victims' participation in selling sex is commonly viewed as wilful self-exposure to the risk of violence, and the effect of exposing their clients to public censure is considered just punishment rather than something to be avoided. However, rather than demanding that male sex workers and their clients are treated as harshly as those involved in female sex work, the attitude of the police and other agencies involved in the Birmingham initiative could inspire a more sensitive approach to all sex workers and their clients.

Effects of zero tolerance on sex workers' safety strategies

… the working girls are scattered thinly over the now vastly dispersed soliciting areas. We visited the sites of all the Liverpool murders since 1990, or at least the places where the bodies were found, including the tree not three yards from the pavement where Anne-Marie Foy was found. It was decorated with the Liverpool United shield and motto 'You'll Never Walk Alone'

---

[23]'Kerb-crawl ruling sparks outcry', *Telegraph and Argus*, 14 July 2007.
[24]'Yellow card scheme targets gay kerb-crawlers', *Birmingham Post*, 13 April 2007.

– but they do. These days, all the girls walk alone, no possibility of them looking out for each other.[25]

There are precautions that street workers can take against violence: working in pairs, one recording the car registration number of the other's client and raising the alarm if she does not return to her usual pitch within the expected time; using visual clues and intuition to decide whether a client seems 'safe'; agreeing the service, price and place to do business before getting in the car; telling a friend where she is going with the client; and doing business where it is possible to call for assistance if necessary. Zero tolerance undermines all these meagre safety strategies: traditional, close-knit and geographically limited soliciting areas have been broken up, with sex workers dispersed over much wider areas and rarely working within sight of each other, nevermind noting down the car numbers of each other's clients. Having time and light enough to assess a client or negotiate a deal are infrequent luxuries and anti-kerbcrawling measures reduce the numbers of clients, further limiting any residual level of choice over whether to accept a client or not.

Doing business is the time of greatest danger, because the sex worker and client leave the beat where there may be other people who might help in a crisis, usually finding privacy only where it is isolated and dark. Some street workers used to take their clients to their own or to friends' homes, where there would be someone to help if there was trouble, but now many are homeless, few have access to indoor premises and those who do risk eviction if they use their homes for business. This has been a deliberate policy on the part of social housing providers, and some local authorities have put pressure on private landlords to evict sex workers if they take clients to their homes or solicit in the neighbourhood. In 2000, in Middlesbrough, it was reported that the local authority were 'to urge private landlords to take action against vice girls living in their rented flats and houses. The move follows suspicions that prostitutes in Middlesbrough are avoiding traditional police target areas in order to ply their trade in the neighbourhoods where they live.'[26]

Instead business is often done outdoors, in vehicles, alleyways, industrial units, parks, derelict buildings and country areas outside town. However, this is a constantly changing situation. In the early

---

[25]Author's diary: Liverpool, August 2007.
[26]'Landlords recruited in drive to stop vice', *Northern Echo*, 25 November 2000.

2000s, Sanders (2005) found that street workers who had previously 'done business' in cars or outdoors were being driven by intense policing and community protests to take their clients indoors, often to crack houses, the only places where some sex workers could find a roof over their heads. But from 2002, police began using new powers to close down crack houses, making sex workers roofless once more, and by 2004 a survey by the homelessness charity Shelter, found unprecedented levels of homelessness among street workers (Davis 2004).

An alternative is to go to the client's home, which may be private and free from police surveillance but not always safe. The proportion of sex workers who were murdered at a suspect's home more than doubled in the 17 years to 2006 (see Chapter 13), while the London Ugly Mugs List shows that the proportion of attacks on street workers taking place indoors doubled between 2000 and 2005. Given the high rates of homelessness among street workers, it must be assumed that these indoor locations were often the clients' homes.[27] Miller (1993) noted that choosing the place for 'business' was a key element of street workers' safety strategies, with indoor venues preferred only if they were *not* the client's premises, a viewpoint shared by a Glasgow sex worker commenting in 2007 on the effects of the different policing approaches she had experienced:

> When I first started going out it was a lot safer – there were tolerance zones and it felt like the police were there to protect you – but now they've taken all that away. I used to feel I could go to the police if I had a problem but that's changed, even though I've had a few bad experiences. People have started changing how they work [in response to the new kerb-crawling legislation]. They are going out of areas that they usually work in because clients don't want to risk coming into ... [Glasgow's red light district] where the cameras are. Last night a friend of mine went all the way back to a flat in Cumbernauld ... I don't go back to flats, even in an area I know. As soon as that door's locked, that's you stuck. What I have started doing is going out later – two or three in the morning – to avoid the police ... I didn't used to go with anyone too drunk or under the influence of drugs, but now I do because I just want to get out of there quick, before the police come. It has got more dangerous. You just need to look [at the Ugly Mug reports]. There used

---

[27]See pages 82–3.

to be about eight reports a month, now it's around three a night.[28]

To follow this sex worker's advice, the next section explores what Ugly Mugs can tell us about violence against street workers.

---

[28]'Girls will now take more risks', *BBC News*, 15 October 2007 (see http://news.bbc.co.uk/go/pr/fr/-/1/hi/scotland/7045355.stm).

Chapter 7

Street violence: individual and community aggression

The following exploration of individual and community violence directed at street workers utilises sex workers' descriptions of attacks given via Ugly Mug reports. All such reports appearing in the London Ugly Mugs List (LUML) between September 2000 and April 2005 have been analysed, with supplementary information from media accounts and Ugly Mug reports from elsewhere.

The London Ugly Mugs List

Between September 2000 and April 2005, the LUML carried 142 reports of attacks on street workers,[1] less than 2.5 reports per month – surprisingly few, considering the large numbers of sex workers believed to be active in London and the high levels of violence they are believed to experience. There may be fewer street workers in relation to indoor sex workers in London than in the past: Ward *et al.* (2004) reported that the proportion of street workers among those attending one London service between 1985 and 2002 fell from 18 per cent to 3 per cent, reflecting a marked fall in the relative importance of street work in the catchment area of that service, although it is not known whether similar changes affected other parts of London. In the period 2000 to 2005, no street soliciting area in London avoided wave after wave of police action against street prostitution, which may partly account for the small numbers of street Ugly Mug reports. It

---

[1]Indoor attacks reported to the LUML are analysed in Chapter 10.

may also have discouraged women with insecure immigration status from street work, which, despite increasing numbers of women from overseas at indoor venues, remained dominated by British women.

An outreach worker in south London describes the conditions which have affected levels of contact between sex working women and outreach projects, and the reporting of attacks:

> There are about 60 individual women street working in Streatham/Brixton at any one time and an outreach session will usually see about 10–20 women over 2–3 hours. However a lot of the women now work off mobile phones and it is quieter than it has been in the past. There is a lot of violence on the streets and attacks are underreported to the Ugly Mug list. Women will often warn other women about attackers in our drop-in but won't sit down and complete an Ugly Mug sheet for various reasons. ... The amount of women working on the streets has remained constant in the time I have been in Lambeth (7 years) but the women are less visible due to mobile phones and the way in which they continually go in and out of the crack houses as opposed to just standing in one spot all night. (June 2007)[2]

Location of street attacks

> Woman got in car, joking with client. Took her to indoor premises where he kicked in the door. Once inside said he wouldn't pay and would rape her; pulled out knife. Woman smashed a window ... and escaped. (LUML 2003)

There was a decline in the proportion of attacks which took place inside a vehicle between 2000 and 2005, from 40 per cent to 16 per cent of street attacks, while outdoor attacks rose and those which took place indoors nearly doubled (see Table 7.1). This could reflect sex workers choosing to be outside rather than trapped by central locking devices, or indicate increased trade from clients on foot, perhaps abandoning cars in response to anti-kerb-crawling strategies, or more poverty, therefore, fewer car owners in the client population. Increased violence from 'people on the street', rather than those specifically identified as clients, might also have been a factor, or

---

[2]Nicki Pruss, outreach worker, south London, personal communication, 19 June 2007.

Table 7.1 LUML: location of street attacks, 2000–2005

	2000–2002	%	2003–2005	%	2000–2005 n	%
Car	30	40	11	16	41	29
Outside	33	44	37	55	70	49
Car/outside	4	5	6	9	10	7
Indoors	6	8	10	15	16	11
Missing	2	3	3	4	5	3
All	75	100	67	99	142	99

even increased forensic awareness by attackers. The rise in attacks at indoor premises – usually a place chosen by the client – may indicate rising levels of homelessness among street workers and more avoidance of police surveillance.

> Took her to his nearby flat … arranged price outside and also said he would be alone. Once in flat man only had half the money so girl declined business. Man called out and 2 men appeared who held her down whilst the original man raped her. (Midlands 2002)

Reporting of violence to the police

> … went for business and everything was ok. After the service the man demanded his money back. The working woman argued with him and said no. He followed her … grabbed her scarf and wrapped it round her neck and squeezed until she collapsed … This man may have thought she was dead when he left her. It is likely this man will attack again so please be careful. This has NOT been reported to the police. (London 2007)

Only 16 per cent of Ugly Mugs reported by street workers to the LUML stated that the police had been informed. This may underestimate the level of reporting, since it is believed that many reports of violence against sex workers have been made via Sexual Assault Referral Centres. Unfortunately it has not been possible to obtain any data to confirm this from the Metropolitan Police.

Types of street attack

Types of street attack are given in Table 7.2. Eighty-one reports (57 per cent) described some form of sexual assault, from removing condoms to rape; in 73 per cent of these, physical violence was also used, and in 48 (59 per cent) the assailant refused to pay, took his money back and/or robbed her of all her money. A third of all 'money crime' reported by street workers to the LUML – 18 per cent of all incidents, did not involve sexual assault. This kind of incident is also reported elsewhere:

> [Attack by man and woman] The victim was approached ... by the male who asked for business. She refused, as she felt wary. He grabbed her by the throat and demanded money. He was then joined by the woman who also began to violently attack the woman who gave them her money so as to get away. (Liverpool 2003)

> Pestered girl and followed her ... Punched her several times in the face, causing injuries and then stole her handbag. (Bournemouth 2006)

Twelve reports (8 per cent) stated that problems arose because of dissatisfaction with the service, such as not achieving an erection or ejaculation.

Table 7.2 LUML: types of street attack
(n = 142 – NB categories overlap)

Type of attack reported	n	%
Sexual assault*	33	23
Sexual assault & robbery/theft	48	34
All sexual assaults	81	57
Robbery/theft	25	18
All robbery/theft	73	51
Other incidents	36	25
All reports	142	100

*Sexual assault: in these cases no robbery or theft was mentioned in the report, but this does not mean that robbery or theft did not take place.

A quarter of all incidents did not involve either 'business' or sexual assault. They included:

- muggings and robberies;
- stalking or pestering;
- assaults or aggression from men with whom the women refused to do business;
- physical assaults by men taking revenge for having been robbed by someone else;
- physical assaults by vigilantes;
- physical assaults for unknown reasons.

Not paying for sex

> ... he handed over the agreed money to the girl. Then he started to get angry and saying why should he pay for it, became violent, took his money back, and tried to rape her. She got away. (London 2003)

> This man was on foot and had done 'business' earlier in the evening with the same woman. When he came back at 3am he asked for 'business' again and as they were walking ... he grabbed her bag and ran off. (Midlands 2008)

The LUML reports show that many perpetrators do not qualify as 'clients', since they *did not pay for sex*. Half the reports (73, 51 per cent) specified that the assailant refused to pay, took or demanded his money back after sex or simply robbed the victim without any pretence of being a client. This probably underestimates the extent to which attackers refused to pay, since the victim might not consider it necessary to say that her assailant did not pay when describing a violent rape or other assault. Fourteen (10 per cent) did not indicate whether the assailant had paid or not, and only 24 (17 per cent) mentioned that the assailant did pay and did not mention that he took his money back (although he may have done). Eleven of these incidents involved clients not wanting to use condoms or becoming difficult for other reasons such as being told their time was up, and 13 involved violence.

Three-quarters of the attacks were committed by those who did not pay, and only 13 (9 per cent) involved violence from an assailant who seems to have paid. These reports sometimes include the victim's observation that the attacker appeared to get aroused by violence: one describes a client who started to strangle the woman, saying 'he wasn't going to kill her but he got off on strangling. She kicked him as she had been shown by Personal Safety team': he apologised, and gave her an extra £20. Other assailants were less easily deterred, seeming to believe that having paid gave them the right to inflict any kind of assault they chose. This is the kind of scenario which fits most closely with the stereotype of men who pay for sex because they want to degrade, humiliate and hurt, but the evidence of the LUML indicates that this type of client is rare, and that violence is far more frequently associated with refusal to pay.

> ... approached woman and pulled a knife out threatening her and saying he wanted a service but was not going to pay. She managed to get away unhurt. (Bournemouth 2006)

The finding that much of what is called 'client violence' comes from people who either make no pretence of being clients or refuse to conform to the defining characteristic of a client – paying for sex – confirms a 2002 survey of violence against street workers, which found that 55 per cent of attacks involved robbery, refusing to pay or forcing refunds.[3] It is also reflected in Ugly Mug reports from other regions. Of 18 reports to the One25 Project in Bristol between January and October 2007, half describe robbery, theft or refusal to pay; of 43 reports to the Merseyside Linx Project, over three months in 2003, 19 (44 per cent) were attacks by those who approached as clients but then refused to pay and/or robbed the woman of all her money, and of 29 street attacks reported by sex workers in Huddersfield over a nine-month period in 2007, only two specified that the client did pay but was violent during or after the sexual encounter, while nine (31 per cent) described 'clients' refusing to pay or forcing refunds.[4]

People in the vicinity

The advantage of monitoring soliciting areas and the places to which sex workers go with clients to do business is shown in reports where sex workers have been able to flag down police patrol cars, or other

[3]Multi-centre survey conducted for Channel 4 television; Vikram Dodd, 'Law increases danger, prostitutes say', The Guardian, 16 September 2002.
[4]Data from SWEET Project, Huddersfield, 2007 (see pages 49–50).

security personnel have intervened in attacks, and sometimes outreach workers are also 'in the vicinity' and able to assist:

> We met a woman on the streets who was very distressed. She had previously received an "Ugly Mugs" leaflet that we produced (information given to us by other women about recent attacks and rapes) and recognised one of the men. When she tried to leave, he began to get very aggressive with her. We were on outreach when she flagged us down, and we were able to get her into the safety of our vehicle, call the police and then take her to the police station.[5]

> ... the woman ran to a nearby police van and told officers: "That car, go and get it, he's just raped me."[6]

> She was raped twice on university grounds and told she would be burnt alive. She was saved by two security guards.[7]

The advantage of working in areas that are not deserted or far from houses is also reflected in reports:

> Afterwards tried to keep her in car – woman kicked out windscreen, but he didn't let her go until he saw people walking towards the car. (London 2005)

> The 23-year-old woman was allegedly beaten up on wasteland in Scunthorpe, north Lincolnshire. She managed to escape and knocked on the door of a nearby property.... The resident of the house called an ambulance.[8]

The environment which affects sex workers' vulnerability to violence includes the behaviour of other people in the vicinity. I was recently given an anecdote from someone who had visited a vicarage in an area of street soliciting and witnessed a sex worker being forced into a car by several men. She called out to those on the steps of the

---

[5]*Annual Report, 2004*, Trust, 94 Brixton Rd, London SW9 6BE.
[6]'Brutal rapist faces life in jail', *Evening Gazette*, 19 October 2007.
[7]'Rapist's "voices" plea rejected', *BBC News*, 15 August 2005 (see http://news.bbc.co.uk/go/pr/fr/-/1/hi/england/nottinghamshire/4153272.stm).
[8]'Arrest over prostitute attack', *BBC News*, 30 July 2003 (see http://news.bbc.co.uk/1/hi/england/humber/3109601.stm).

vicarage, begging them to phone the police, but they ignored her. The vicar's wife took the view that if they had done so, the vicarage might become a target for attacks.

> The woman screamed to people in the vicinity but nobody came to help her. (LUML 2001)

Some sex workers encounter more helpful reactions from 'people in the vicinity', and interventions by others have certainly saved lives.[9] In April 2008, Coventry police thanked members of the public who had not only helped a woman escape from two rapists, but went to court as witnesses.[10] Ugly Mug reports also often describe helpful interventions from passers-by:

> The car pulled up by the woman on Canning St; he got out and began shouting abuse at her then punched her to the ground. A passer-by came to her assistance ... (Liverpool 2003)

> A man wanted his money back, the woman refused and got out of the car, he ran after her, held a knife to her throat and demanded his money again. A passer-by stopped and the woman got into their car and was driven to a nearby pub. (Midlands 2003)

Public responses of a very different kind are, nevertheless, not only common but frequently tolerated, if not commended, as the next section illustrates.

Community violence

> At the moment our clients report frequent abuse (mainly verbal) from residents and gangs of teenagers. This is something they find difficult to cope with and it also hinders them working in certain streets. This has escalated to teenagers throwing bricks and lighted fireworks at the women and similar. (London 2007)[11]

---

[9]See page 157.
[10]'Man guilty of raping prostitute in Hillfields park', *Coventry Evening Telegraph*, 3 April 2008.
[11]Nicki Pruss, outreach worker, south London, personal communication, 19 June 2007.

Harassment, minor assaults and muggings of street workers by 'people in the vicinity' are so common in many areas that such incidents are often not even recorded as Ugly Mugs, even though this atmosphere of hostility and abuse provides the context and arguably the cause for many more serious attacks. Where reports are taken of abuse by people not identified as 'clients', they can form a high proportion of all violent incidents. Half of all incidents reported to SCOT-PEP (Edinburgh) in 2003 concerned harassment by members of the public, compared to 10 per cent which involved a sexual assault (SCOT-PEP 2004), while 42 per cent (18/43) of attacks reported on Merseyside during 2003 were by people who exhibited no 'client behaviour' beyond, in some cases, posing as a client in order to lure the victim to a place where she could be attacked. The perpetrators ranged from gangs of local boys and girls aged between 8 and 16 to older youths and adults. Some attacks were combined with robbery or attempted robbery; some involved men saying they wanted 'business' and thereby luring the women into side streets where others were waiting to attack them. In one case a man who asked for sex drove the woman to a place where she was violently assaulted by a gang, including being stabbed in the head.[12]

Four males walking through red light area. One male pretended to be a punter, he was violent towards her and hit her hard in the face ... (Huddersfield 2007)

[Five males in a car] The car mounted the pavement and drove towards the woman who jumped out of the way, they were shouting obscenities and that they would kill her. (Midlands 2008)

It might be thought those claiming a moral agenda of 'ridding the streets' of prostitutes would abstain from robbery and sexual violence, but both have been committed by people expressing superiority to and disgust for sex workers. For example, Mohammed Irfan, jailed for nine years for rape, assault and indecent assault on sex workers in Bradford, had 'told one of his victims that he "couldn't stand prostitutes" and threatened there would be vigilante-style "lynches" to rid the streets of them.' His accomplices were also convicted of robbing their victims.[13] Violence of this kind can also be fatal, as was

---

[12]Liverpool Ugly Mugs, July, October and December 2003.
[13]'Students jailed for prostitute attacks', *Telegraph & Argus*, 8 March 2005.

demonstrated by Darren Brown, who killed a sex worker in Ipswich in December 2003, because he objected to her working near his house.[14]

Cleaning the streets

Miller and Schwartz (1995) drew attention to the constant 'verbal abuse [which] labels and stigmatizes the women, creating contexts in which violence against them becomes legitimized', while Lowman (2000) described the 'rhetoric of disposal' used by Canadian media and anti-street prostitution action groups, drawing associations between the intensity of such rhetoric and the incidence of sex worker homicides. Lowman argued that the social acceptability of language which equates sex workers with rubbish legitimises the actions of those who attack and kill them. The rhetoric of 'cleaning the streets' and 'waging war' on sex workers and clients is also invoked in numerous anti-street prostitution announcements in the UK, in which sex workers and their clients are portrayed as hate figures, social outcasts who deserve public humiliation and punishment for the social and environmental pollution they are deemed to cause.

In Wolverhampton in 2005, the local press proclaimed, 'The battle against street sex in Wolverhampton's traditional "red light" area continues, as community development workers work ... to clean up the district.' Two months later, a somewhat misleading poster campaign against kerb-crawlers was launched, featuring 'a dramatic image of a kerb-crawler trapped in the gutter with the headline: Kerb-crawlers end up behind bars' – misleading, because kerb-crawling is not an imprisonable offence, but also explicitly endorsing hate, with the added message 'Wolverhampton hates kerb-crawling. So get out & stay out!'[15]

In May 2007, Home Office Minister Vernon Coaker declared:

---

[14]'Guard kicked prostitute to death', BBC News, 11 October 2004 (see http://news.bbc.co.uk/1/hi/england/suffolk/3733984.stm).
[15]'Blitz on city's red light zone', icwolverhampton, 19 December 2005; 'We'll rid city of vice trade', icwolverhampton, 21 February 2006 (see http://icwolverhampton.icnetwork.co.uk).

Local communities are fed up with street prostitution – sexual activity taking place in their parks and playgrounds, condoms and discarded needles littering the streets and innocent women mistakenly targeted and abused by men on the prowl. For the residents it is intimidating, unpleasant and unsafe.[16]

Equating sex workers with rubbish is often reflected in the way the bodies of murder victims are treated (see Chapter 14) and in non-fatal violence. Carol Ives, a 63-year-old sex worker from Hull, was thrown in a skip after being beaten so badly that the man who found her could not tell if she was a man or a woman. The police treated the case as attempted murder, saying: 'this person felt they were dealing with a piece of rubbish.' Her injuries were consistent with having been punched to the ground, her head stamped on, and then dragged face down over concrete before being thrown into the skip.[17]

The police also make public statements which reinforce prejudices and fears about sex workers. In 2003, police in Reading 'issued a warning that a prostitute working in the town has AIDS. This follows the naming and shaming of prostitutes, the cautioning or charging of 30 sex workers and the sending of letters to kerb-crawlers.'[18] This kind of vilification has been less blatant in recent years, but has not disappeared. In February 2008, Northampton police announced that a

---

[16]*New crackdown targets kerb-crawlers*, Press Association, 12 May 2007 (see http://www.ananova.com/news/story/sm_2328683.html?menu=).

[17]A local fireman, Barrie Jackson, was tried for attempted murder after Carol's blood was found on his shoes but was acquitted. He was, however, sentenced to two years imprisonment for an attack on another woman three weeks before the attack on Carol Ives. Jackson was murdered in April 2005, allegedly in revenge for an assault he was believed to have made on yet another woman. The two men convicted of his murder were sentenced to a minimum of 17 years each. 'Warning after skip attack on woman', *Evening Press*, 12 November 2002; 'Woman in skip left to die', *BBC News*, 13 October 2003 (see http://news.bbc.co.uk/1/hi/england/humber/3188060.stm); 'Hammer killers given life terms', *BBC News*, 9 November 2005 (see http://news.bbc.co.uk/1/hi/england/humber/4422200.stm).

[18]Brian Thornton, 'Police AIDS 'witch-hunt' criticised', *BBC News Online*, 2 July 2003 (see http://news.bbc.co.uk/1/hi/england/berkshire/3038666.stm) http://news.bbc.co.uk/1/hi/england/berkshire/3038666.stm

rehabilitation course for kerb-crawlers, 'deals with the realities of using prostitutes including the risk of sexually transmitted infections.'[19]

Miller and Schwartz (1995) highlight the concept of 'collective liability', whereby all persons in a class or group are held responsible for all the others in the same category, and can be punished for the perceived offences of any other group member or of the group as a whole. Miller and Schwartz relate this behaviour to sexual attacks by men identified as clients, but 'collective liability' is also explicit in the blanket imposition of ASBOs, whereby it is not necessary to demonstrate that a particular sex worker has caused alarm or distress to anyone, only that sex workers in general are alleged to have done so.

'Collective liability' also appears to underlie expressions of community abuse of sex workers, some of which have acquired an image of respectability, if not heroism, for taking on these public enemies and cleansing their own neighbourhoods.

---

[19]'Police blitz traps 105 kerb crawlers', *Northants Evening Telegraph*, 12 February 2008 (see http://www.northantset.co.uk/news/Police-blitz-traps-105-kerb.3766008.jp).

Chapter 8

The cleansing of Balsall Heath

The geography of visible prostitution has been the focus of moral concern and political remedies for generations, but until relatively recently it was regarded as the business of the police to combat street sex work in areas where it was deemed unacceptable. During the 1990s, however, this changed. Day *et al.* (1996) noted increasing intolerance of street prostitution by local residents from the start of the 1990s, when street workers in Tower Hamlets had to wear sunglasses to protect themselves from aerosol attacks by vigilantes and gangs patrolled the streets of Birkenhead with Rotteweiler dogs. Several areas saw community actions against street prostitution, in which local residents directly prevented sex workers from soliciting and discouraged kerb-crawlers from driving along the streets. Some police spokesmen initially expressed disquiet about the potential for vigilantism in these community activities, but when they were successful in driving street work out of neighbourhoods where formerly the police had to invest heavily in enforcement in response to community demands, objections about 'potential for vigilantism' became muted. Local politicians also enthusiastically aligned them-selves with these protests, and over the past few years they have slotted easily into New Labour concepts of community responsibility for tackling anti-social behaviour.

No residents' action against street prostitution is better known or has gained greater commendation than that which drove sex workers out of Balsall Heath in Birmingham between 1994 and 1996. This achievement was greeted with uncritical approval at the time and has acquired almost legendary status since. The 'Balsall Heath model' is commended to neighbourhoods similarly affected in a Demos publication of 1999,[1] mentioned favourably in *Paying the Price* (Home Office 2004) and again by the Office of the Deputy Prime Minister in 2005.[2] Successive Home Secretaries have made pilgrimages to the site of this triumph, the Conservative Party leader David Cameron has paid homage[3] and those that claimed the glory have busily advised residents groups elsewhere, while the better politically connected have advised the government on community issues (Cohen 2000). Various important – and false – claims contribute to the legendary status of the Balsall Heath action: that it was supported by all sections of the community, did not lead to displacement of the problem elsewhere and was non-violent. Because the 'history according to the victors' has been written into many accounts where the authors have inadvertently been misled by the highly sanitised version that has been so widely propagated since, as an eyewitness I feel an obligation to other commentators, as well as to the 'vanquished', to offer a minority report.

Balsall Heath: the background

In the mid-1980s the main soliciting area in Birmingham covered an area of both relatively prosperous housing, Moseley, and its poorer neighbour, Balsall Heath. A far less active soliciting area also existed in north Edgbaston, another fairly prosperous neighbourhood, a couple of miles north-west of Balsall Heath. Between 1984 and 1986, a local residents group in Moseley used direct methods to prevent street workers operating there.[4] Their actions were viewed with suspicion by the police as tantamount to vigilantism, as illustrated by the title of a report which documented this community action: *The Police versus the North Moseley Residents' Association Action Group* (Cooke 1986). Cooke quotes a senior police officer as saying:

---

[1]C. Leadbeater and I. Christie (1999) *To Our Mutual Advantage*, Demos (see http://www.demos.co.uk/files/Toourmutualadvantage.pdf).
[2]*Neighbourhood Management – Working Together to Create Cleaner Safer Greener Communities*, Office of the Deputy Prime Minister, March 2005.
[3]Gaby Hinsliff, 'The muesli offensive', *The Observer*, 2 July 2006.
[4]Hubbard (1998) and Hubbard and Sanders (2003) describe subsequent events in Balsall Heath, but not the earlier manifestation of geographical 'cleansing' in Moseley.

The Action Group are not really concerned with the eradication
of prostitutes ... but it has become more of an obsession with the
group, combined with a deep hatred of prostitutes themselves.

Up to 40 activists at a time would stand around the women, preventing
them from soliciting, following them if they moved elsewhere,
generally harassing both sex workers and clients, and despite the lack
of police support, the action group eventually succeeded in pushing
almost all soliciting activity north into Balsall Heath. In view of the
events which took place a few years later in Balsall Heath, it should
be noted that in Moseley the protesters were mainly white British.[5]

By September 1987, when the outreach project for sex workers
began, very little soliciting took place in the areas targeted by the
Moseley action group, but the overall numbers of street workers
remained constant. Before the Moseley 'purge' in 1982, McLeod
estimated approximately 200 street sex workers in Birmingham
(McLeod 1982). Two years after the Moseley area was cleared, in
1988, the outreach project interviewed 213 street workers,[6] nearly all
working in Balsall Heath, demonstrating that the women had merely
been displaced a few streets away. The same number of sex workers
were then concentrated in a much smaller area, which was also
more ethnically diverse.[7] At the 1991 census, 45 per cent of the local
population originated in the Mirpur region of Pakistan-administered
Kashmir (Hubbard 1998).

Balsall Heath also contained two small streets of terraced
houses, Court Road and Cheddar Road, many of them occupied
by sex workers using the 'window' method of soliciting.[8] Unlike

---

[5]Cooke's paper states that only 50 per cent of the demonstrators were local
residents.
[6]Hubbard (1998) suggests a substantial increase in the numbers of sex
workers in the area over McLeod's estimate of 1982, based on police figures
of 890 individuals arrested for street prostitution offences in 1989. I also
used this figure for my estimates of numbers of sex workers in Birmingham
(Kinnell 1989). However, I eventually discovered that the figure of 890 did
not relate to individual women but to individual court appearances, and as
most street sex workers were before the court repeatedly the figure of 890
seriously exaggerated the number of individual women involved in street
prostitution.
[7]Sagar (2005) describes the Balsall Heath action as 'more ethnically homogenous'
than the neighbourhood she studied in Cardiff, but homogeneity seems to
have followed rather than preceded the anti-prostitution demonstrations.
[8]Window soliciting was also reported in Southampton during the 1980s.

the windows in Amsterdam, those in Balsall Heath were the front rooms of small houses whose front doors opened directly onto the pavement. The connection between window work and street work was strong: customers could access both street workers and window workers in the same area; soliciting charges were used against the window workers as well as street workers, as they were visible from 'a public place', and women moved between the windows and the streets according to personal circumstances.[9]

It has been suggested that prior to 1994, the police were 'tolerant' of sex work in Balsall Heath, contributing to an explosion in the numbers of sex workers in the area (Hubbard and Sanders 2003). However, of the 213 street workers interviewed in 1988, 90 per cent had been cautioned or prosecuted for soliciting or loitering within the previous 12 months, 46 per cent had been prosecuted over 20 times and 45 per cent had served prison sentences for non-payment of fines. Numerous reports in the local press also show that the police devoted considerable resources to addressing the problem, for example:

> A special squad of 17 officers is assigned to patrolling the streets.... Latest figures reveal that 1367[10] prostitutes were arrested in 1987, 713 down on the year before.... One girl at work on Mary St last night was arrested twice within an hour. Another, among the 12 taken in for questioning yesterday, had been brought in 17 times since October.[11] (January 1988)

Police efforts to combat prostitution in 1988 were reported with uniform optimism. A senior officer is quoted saying that £500,000 was spent annually on policing prostitution; letters to kerb-crawlers are claimed as '100%' effective. A year later, the police are still 'waging war' on kerb-crawlers and had made 800 arrests of sex workers. Another year on, the city council starts to use planning law to stop women working from the windows, while the police announce another 'Blitz

---

[9]Hubbard and Sanders (2003) have been misinformed about the legal status of the 'window' workers. The legal status of window workers being liable to soliciting charges was established in *Behrent v. Burridge*, Royal Courts of Justice, 26 May 1976, before judges Widgery, Donaldson and Boreham.

[10]This figure refers to the number of arrests, not the number of individual sex workers (see note 6 above).

[11]'Paying for sex – by credit card', *Evening Mail*, 15 January 1988.

on kerb-crawlers' and 'declare war in Vice Alley'.[12] Between 1990 and 1993, press reports reflect a less enforcement-orientated approach. Concern for sex workers' safety begins to creep into the picture, and various city council initiatives to address the problem holistically are announced. Some councillors call for 'tolerance zones'[13] or the legalisation of brothels: the police express scepticism, they continue to target kerb-crawlers, use WPCs as decoys[14] and continue to arrest sex workers. However, by 1993 the vice squad comprises nine officers compared to 17 five years earlier, and annual cautions and arrests are down to 600 compared to nearly 1,400 in 1987.[15] This reduction might indicate that the numbers of sex workers had declined but could also reflect reduced police input. Even so, it cannot be said that the police ignored the situation. From 1987 to 1994, repeated drives were made against kerb-crawlers; hundreds of street workers were arrested every year and the number of houses used for window work declined.

During this period the outreach project made contact with thousands of sex workers, but usually no more than 25 to 30 were contacted on the street or in the windows during a single outreach session. Violence from clients and those posing as clients was reported frequently, but apart from residents throwing occasional buckets of water or children throwing stones, there was little community aggression directed at the women. There were isolated incidents of vigilantism when groups of residents harassed sex workers, but none of these occurrences was sustained or apparently well organised. Although residents' protests had prevented the siting of a clinical service for sex workers in the neighbourhood, there was no overt hostility to the outreach project either.

---

[12]*Evening Mail*, 4 February 1988, 10 February 1988, 4 April 1988, 23 April 1988, 22 September 1988, 30 June 1989, 29 August 1989, 17 September 1990; *Birmingham Post*, 30 June 1989, *Daily News*, 6 June 1990, 25 September 1990.
[13]Birmingham city councillors had debated establishing an official 'red-light' zone as early as 1981 (*The Times*, 31 July 1981, in Self 2003: 272 and 284 note 69). However, without central government or police support, no action was taken and the political will fizzled out.
[14]That is, female police officers posing as sex workers.
[15]*Evening Mail*, 17 September 1990 and 7 November 1991; *Metronews*, 11 October 1991; *Birmingham Voice*, 3 September 1992; *Sunday Mirror*, 14 March 1993; *The Independent*, 19 April 1993.

Events between 1994 and 1996

In June 1994 there was a dramatic change. Responding to announcements that, owing to reorganisation of the city's police, Balsall Heath would no longer have a dedicated vice squad, the local Muslim community, with the advice and foreknowledge of the police, mounted a campaign against both street and window sex workers. This campaign, originally the 'Balsall Heath Citizens' Patrol', was led by local resident Raja Amin, with the support of a prominent community activist Dr Dick Atkinson (Cohen 2000), at least one councillor[16] and one Church of England vicar (Lean 1996). It was strongly asserted that the whole community supported the campaign, but the overwhelming majority of its 'foot soldiers' were Muslim men, mobilised through the mosques. Local councillors, doubtless impressed by the numbers of potential electors among the protesters, voted unanimously to support the residents. They also had massive sympathy in the press, which proclaimed the campaign a total and instant success. Melanie Phillips in *The Observer* wrote:

> Elders of the Muslim community staunchly positioned themselves outside their houses to take on the prostitution racket. Within a week, most of the prostitutes had gone. The pickets' main weapon was embarrassment. Punters cruising into Balsall Heath in their cars took one look at the throng standing implacably near the girls and turned away.... Under Raja Amin's rules, the pickets were instructed to offer no violence except in self-defence. Apart from one or two scuffles, there has been none.[17]

In the *Daily Mail*, Jessica Davies began, 'The old men are devout Moslems.... Wearing flowing kurtas, the national robes of their native Pakistan, they play cards on a Birmingham street corner.' This peaceful behaviour, combined only with a few placards and noting down of car registration numbers, had, claimed Davies, not only rid the area of kerb-crawlers but virtually eliminated petty crime.[18] In *The Guardian*, Maggie O'Kane devoted more space to the

---

[16]Ken Hardeman, Conservative, Moseley, 'Red light district pickets vow to carry on working', *Birmingham Post*, 30 July 1994.
[17]Melanie Phillips, 'When a community stands up for itself', *The Observer*, 17 July 1994.
[18]Jessica Davies, 'Decent people are venturing out again. For the first time in years they feel safe', *Daily Mail*, 23 July 1994.

perspective of the sex workers and others with reservations about the demonstrations, but she too wrote: 'The patrol initiative, which came from the well-organised Asian community, is for the most part peaceful. Elderly men sit at the corners in armchairs beside six foot-high posters warning 'Kerb Crawlers: The Wife Will Find Out'.[19]

The reality was very different. In the daytime, the protesters were indeed mainly older Muslim men sitting quietly by their placards and noting down car registration numbers. But after dark, crowds of up to 500 young men, many apparently bused in from other areas, patrolled the streets, armed with baseball bats, hockey sticks and dogs. They harassed, intimidated and at times physically attacked sex workers, clients and any others they identified as connected with sex work. The local press reported one sex worker's experience:

> Birmingham vice girl Lorraine, aged 26, has been working the streets of Balsall Heath for six years and has been attacked several times by customers. But she says the recent weeks of anti-vice campaigning by local residents have made her life hell. "We can't go out and work because of all the groups of men on the street," she says. 'The other night I was dragged into a car by a gang of men and called a slag and a slut. I have never been so scared. The people who live here moved into the area because it's cheap housing – and they knew damn well that it was a red light area, so why are they up in arms?'[20]

Much was made of the contrast between the 'dignified Muslim elders' with their admirable traditional morality and the déclassé white prostitutes with their black pimps, for example: 'Prostitutes spat at them and shrieked abuse that they were dirty Pakis ruining their business. Pimps threatened them.'[21] That most of the sex workers were indeed white facilitated their condemnation; the tone of the coverage implied they were ignorant, racist, poor whites who needed a sharp lesson in cultural awareness.

Again, the reality was rather different. In the year before the Balsall Heath campaign began, 70 per cent of street and window sex

---

[19]Maggie O'Kane, 'Cruising, abusing or on the game', *The Guardian*, 23 July 1994.
[20]'It's made our life real hell', *Birmingham Evening Mail*, 20 July 1994.
[21]Melanie Phillips, 'When a community stands up for itself', *The Observer*, 17 July 1994.

workers contacted by the outreach project were white, 25 per cent were black or of mixed heritage and the remaining 5 per cent were Asian: Hindu, Sikh and Muslim,[22] a markedly higher percentage of non-white sex workers than Hester and Westmarland (2004) found ten years later in other provincial cities.[23] Many white sex workers had black partners and tended to live their private lives within the black community; some had Asian partners, and were not necessarily excluded from those communities either. Not only did many of the women working in Balsall Heath in the early 1990s have extensive personal links outside the white community, they also had daily contact with clients from every ethnic and cultural background – hardly a respectable expression of integration, but a reality which few at the time, or since, have acknowledged.

The monolithic ethnic stereotypes so cheerfully trumpeted by some bore heavily on others. Black men walking or driving through the area were accused of being pimps. An Asian sex worker had to endure particularly virulent insults, all the more hurtful because the 'boyfriend' who benefited most from her earnings diplomatically joined the 'pickets'. A British sex worker, whose partner was a Muslim, was hit by a protester. When the police arrived to investigate the disturbance, their first instinct was to arrest her: she challenged one of the onlookers to swear on the Holy Qur'an that he had not seen the attack, which he declined to do. No one was charged. A sex worker driving through the area had her windscreen smashed by a gang armed with hockey sticks: the police refused to take action unless she could name her assailants. As this culture of intimidation became normalised, verbal abuse and violence by white and African-Caribbean youths was also reported. Such attacks continued for months. O'Kane quotes a 'window worker': 'There's a whole heap of psychopaths out there. Vigilantes pretending to be clients beating up on you.'[24]

Harassment and intimidation were also directed at other women, including those helping women out of prostitution. A woman curate had stones thrown at her car, was interrogated when she walked her

---

[22]H. Kinnell (1993) *Safe Project Report 1992/3*. Department of Public Health Medicine, South Birmingham Health Authority.
[23]In Stoke-on-Trent, Hull, Manchester and Kirklees (Hester and Westmarland 2004).
[24]Maggie O'Kane, 'Cheap tricks leave city girls no time for legal niceties', *The Guardian*, 6 May 1995.

dog and vilified for wearing a short-sleeved clerical blouse.[25] Women students from a nearby college who drove through the area in a minibus were surrounded by vigilantes who attacked the vehicle with baseball bats. One woman expressed her views in a local paper:

An angry Birmingham mother ... claims vigilante groups patrolling Balsall Heath are making the streets a virtual no-go zone for women. The patrols, set up last month to combat prostitution and kerb crawling, are targeting any female who dares venture outside.... Women simply attempting to cross the road are being accused of being prostitutes, she claims ... her five months pregnant daughter feels unable to go outside to make important telephone calls. 'For her to go to the phone she's got to pass two gangs,' she said, 'and she's too scared to go to the shops' .... A spokesman for West Midlands Police said: 'We are reacting on complaints but we haven't received that many. If this girl is being intimidated she should make an official complaint.'[26]

Hostility towards both sex workers and those who expressed any support for them was evident at a public meeting held in the first month of the campaign. A Muslim woman who described herself as a socialist and spoke up for the sex workers was shouted down, and one woman who said she was a sex worker was forcibly removed from the meeting. Interestingly though, the meeting also approved the idea of a toleration zone on the Dutch model pioneered in Utrecht. Local councillor, Bhagrat Singh, said: 'I think we have to have a tolerance zone.... There will be practical problems implementing it, but it is the lesser of two evils.'[27] In Parliament, local MP Dr Lynne Jones called on the government to review prostitution legislation to allow such zones. She was dismissed by the Home Office Minister, David Maclean, who simply intoned all the current provisions of the law which Dr Jones had already argued were ineffective.[28]

The police have often been portrayed as initially wary of the 'potential for vigilantism' in the demonstrations but were soon won over by their peaceful, law-abiding nature (Lean 1996). They were shy to admit that they had foreknowledge of the planned campaign

---

[25]'From vice town to vigilante hell', *The Observer*, 6 December 1998.
[26]'Mother hits out at vigilante groups', *Metro News*, 4 August 1994.
[27]'Red-light area may get official approval', *The Independent*, 20 July 1994.
[28]'Prostitution', *House of Commons Hansard Debates*, 19 July 1994, cols 289–95.

and direct experience of its less attractive features. At the local Police Consultative Committee on 6 July 1994, the police presence at planning meetings held in one of the local mosques was made explicit, while the Divisional Commander, Colin Macdonald, reported that he had driven through the area to see what was going on and had his car rocked by a gang of youths.[29] Even so, the police exhibited a stolid indifference to complaints by others:

> The mother-of-five said the noisy gangs had met until 2.30 a.m. most nights over the past three weeks.... When her husband asked them to be quieter he was verbally and physically abused, (she claimed). She said other neighbours had been spat at, windows had been smashed, and children had been slapped by the members of the vigilantes. *'I felt more comfortable when the prostitutes were working in the area as I knew that the girls weren't going to do me any harm....* But now I feel as if I can't go out at night. ... We are all fed up with it now, *but the police say their hands are tied and cannot do anything about it.*[30]

There may be several explanations for the inactivity of the police. Low morale following the disbandment of the Regional Crime Squad in 1989 and subsequent embarrassing investigations may have played a part,[31] as may the memories of the 1991 Handsworth riots[32] after which the police were openly accused of racism in their dealings with the predominantly black community in that part of Birmingham. They may also have been mindful of the applause ringing from the council chamber to the pages of the national press for the 'brave' stand taken by the residents. The 'bravery' of standing up to the wicked pimps was made much of – a police officer reminisced: 'We thought any day one might wind down his car window and blast away at the pickets with a gun' (Lean 1996), but if any threats were made, none were carried out. From the perspective of the outreach project, far from squaring up to the threat to their livelihood, the real pimps, the career exploiters and abusers (as opposed to men who were merely

---

[29]I attended this meeting: Outreach Project Team Meeting Minutes, 12 July 1994.

[30]'Mum in fear of vice vigilantes', *Evening Mail*, 28 July 1994 (emphasis added).

[31]J. Lewis and N. Morris, 'Outcry over great escape for Midland crime squad', *The Birmingham Post*, 20 May 1992.

[32]'Mobs run wild in Handsworth, *Evening Mail*, 3 September 1991.

partners of sex workers), decamped with their girls as soon as the campaign kicked off and set them to work elsewhere. They were the most vulnerable sex workers of all, and the project lost touch with nearly all of them immediately.

The vigilante action did affect levels of contact between sex workers and the outreach project but not as much as has been suggested (Hubbard and Sanders 2003). Numbers of women working in the area initially dropped, and by the second week of the protests the Drop-in was closed permanently, after seven years of operation, because it was sited in the middle of the area targeted by the vigilantes and women trying to reach it were chased and stoned. However, the sex workers quickly adapted to the changed situation. Contrary to claims that the protesters' actions had successfully cleared the area of sex workers, the women simply moved to its perimeters which were not picketed. When the protests began, they covered most of Balsall Heath, but a small section which did not have many Muslim residents and was notorious for crack dealing and violence was left alone. Shortly before the campaign started, a sex worker was thrown off a third-floor balcony in this neighbourhood by a crack dealer to whom she owed £30. Crack use was not then as ubiquitous among street workers as it has become, so many sex workers had previously avoided these streets, but when they were prevented from working their usual beats, the numbers soliciting there rose considerably. Soon the outreach team were contacting as many sex workers as before. In fact, street outreach contacts between April and July 1994 dropped by only 9 per cent in comparison to the same period in 1993, and over the following four months street contacts *rose* by 33 per cent compared to the previous year, largely because many women who previously worked from the windows, where the picketing was most intense, switched to working the streets.[33] Sex workers had not been 'cleansed' from Balsall Heath, they had been displaced less than a mile away.[34]

It was not until early in 1995 that pickets appeared in this last corner of Balsall Heath, but by then their targets had extended to include systematic harassment of those seen as 'supporters' of sex workers. Outreach staff were harassed both when they were working and, those that lived in the area, when they were not. In one incident the outreach van was surrounded by dozens of demonstrators, some

---

[33]H. Kinnell and A. Stackhouse (1995) *Safe Project Activity Report*, 1994/1995.
[34]*The Independent* referred to sex workers being 'cleansed' from Balsall Heath (26 July 1994).

of whom were masked; their leaders forced their way onto the vehicle, harangued the outreach workers and personally threatened them.[35] The outreach project was blamed for every discarded condom found, but it was not only those supplying condoms who were targeted. A group of nuns whose mission has been for many years to befriend sex workers (though never to distribute condoms) were verbally abused and physically impeded as they walked around the area to talk to the women.

By the end of March 1995, another change was evident from the project's activity data: contacts made with women working in north Edgbaston rose from 19 in 1993/4 to 96 in 1994/5, a rise of 500 per cent.[36] Thereafter the numbers of women moving across town to solicit increased relentlessly. Like Balsall Heath, it was a traditional area of street soliciting but had previously attracted very few street workers who were dispersed over a much larger area. Consequently, the impact of street sex work had been negligible, but less than a fortnight after picketing was extended to cover the last refuge of the sex workers in Balsall Heath, the Conservative MP for Edgbaston, Dame Jill Knight, who had been fulsome in her praise of the Balsall Heath protests the previous summer,[37] expressed outrage that sex workers had moved to the more affluent streets of her constituency.[38]

Despite the exodus of women from Balsall Heath, press reports make it clear that some remained. *The Evening Mail* referred to the pimps and prostitutes as 'human scavengers' who had previously swamped the area day and night, now taking a 'last futile stand' in the north-west corner of Balsall Heath; O'Kane spoke to one sex worker who had 'hung on in Cheddar Road, where she claims the vigilante groups are now buying properties the prostitutes have been forced to leave and renting them to homeless families.'[39] A year after the pickets began, the *Evening Mail* reported continuing disquiet among residents of Balsall Heath:

> These vigilantes are making our lives a complete misery. I don't condone prostitutes plying their trade in residential areas such as this, but the situation is worse now than before they

---

[35]'Condom minibus stays on the road', *Birmingham Post*, 22 April 1995.
[36]H. Kinnell and A. Stackhouse (1995) *Safe Project Activity Report*, 1994/1995.
[37]'Street fighters', *Birmingham Evening Mail*, 24 August 1994.
[38]'MP's fury at condom hand-out', *Birmingham Post*, 22 February 1995.
[39]Maggie O'Kane, 'Cheap tricks leave city girls no time for legal niceties', *The Guardian*, 6 May 1995.

started their patrols. There have been numerous incidents where totally innocent residents have been intimidated. For example, a female neighbour of mine was followed home at 4 o'clock in the afternoon recently. She was wrongly accused of being a prostitute in front of her two young children she'd just collected from school. She felt humiliated. Motorists have had their vehicles attacked as they drive through the area because the pickets think they are kerb-crawlers.[40]

The marginalisation of such 'dissenting voices' (Campbell and Hancock 1998; Scoular et al. 2007), illustrates how intense the pressure was for all residents and other interested parties to either assent to the dominant discourse – that the protest was peaceful, supported by the whole community and successful – or to remain silent and, in terms of behaviour, to either conform to the vigilantes' demands or to stay at home. Instead, all parties except a few outspoken residents colluded with the fast-developing myth that the problem of street prostitution in Balsall Heath had been solved to everyone's satisfaction.

Unimpeachable evidence that the 'pickets' had not driven out prostitution, nor eliminated other crimes, comes from the minutes of a police and community liaison meeting held in November 1995, attended by Assistant Chief Constable Tim Brain.[41] The minutes report operations to combat drug dealing in Balsall Heath, but also that robbery 'continues to be a problem' and burglary was 'on the increase'. Plans were announced 'to mount a two-week operation to target drug pushers and prostitutes in Benmore Avenue and adjoining roads.' A resident reported that 'as a result of the activities of Street Watch[42] ... prostitutes were now active on the main Bristol Road' causing traffic problems when kerb-crawlers stopped to negotiate business, and that the prostitutes were active from 5 a.m., three operating from houses in Cheddar Road which they owned.[43]

---

[40]Anti-vice gangs are 'scaring residents', *Birmingham Evening Mail*, 8 June 1995.

[41]Tim Brain, now Chief Constable of Gloucestershire and Association of Chief Police Officers' spokesman on prostitution.

[42]The 'Citizens' Patrol' had become a formally recognised 'Street Watch' group by mid-1995.

[43]Minutes of the E3 Consultative Committee Meeting held on Wednesday, 8 November 1995 at the Sparkhill Social and Cultural Centre, Stratford Road, Birmingham.

The Balsall Heath effect

The apparent success of the protests rapidly encouraged similar residents' actions elsewhere. Day *et al.* (1996) mention attacks by young Asian men on sex workers in Leicester, one of whom was shot in the leg, gangs of young men committing serious assaults on sex workers in Bradford and other residents' actions in Derby and Streatham. Nevertheless, the police attitude was frequently indulgent. Sagar (2005) documents how Cardiff police encouraged residents in Grangetown to form their own Street Watch group in 1996, drawing attention to the legally dubious methods employed by the activists, and to their divisive influence within the local community. However, the power of the official version of events in Balsall Heath is evident in Sagar's account, which contrasts the problematic aspects of the Grangetown experience to the unalloyed success in Birmingham. Similarly, Moore, reporting on vigilante activity in Bradford in 1995, commented: 'While the action has ostensibly been modelled on a similar campaign in Birmingham's Balsall Heath, where prostitution was beaten by peaceful picketing, the scenes here are more menacing. Punters have been stoned and prostitutes have been picked up and physically carried from the area.'[44] The incidents and atmosphere Moore described were in reality extremely similar to those in Balsall Heath, but in Bradford it seems that commentators had no difficulty in recognising what was happening as vigilantism. As in Balsall Heath, sex workers were merely driven into new areas, and as Sagar comments:

> When the mission is a popular one, then, regardless of the tactics employed, the criminal actions of the community are often exonerated. Arguably, Street Watch members are not, nor are they likely to be, held accountable for vigilante acts against street prostitutes. (Sagar 2005)

The aftermath: 1998–2007

Some sex workers were still in Balsall Heath and still suffering abuse and harassment over three years after the vigilantism started. In December 1998, *The Observer* reported on the plight of a woman who had received anonymous letters threatening to burn her out, had

---

[44]Anna Moore, 'Bradford's moral guardians', *The Independent*, 29 May 1995.

her windows smashed, an airgun fired into her house and lighted fireworks pushed through her letterbox. The secretary of Street Watch denied that its members were responsible, but added: 'These are the actions of people who feel threatened by the activities of this woman. If there is a downside to this, it is very, very small – to say otherwise is to present a very skewed picture.'[45]

The extreme disparity between the violence against this woman and the degree of 'threat' she could possibly pose to her neighbours illustrates the point made by Miller and Schwartz (1995), that attacks on sex workers are routinely dismissed because 'prostitutes' lives are not valuable enough for violence against them to be taken seriously.' Miller and Schwartz were talking about sexual attacks by men assumed to be clients, but the minimal value placed on this woman's life by the Street Watch secretary vividly conveys how 'placing value on one group to the detriment of others' creates 'victims of a social and economic system that does not see value in their lives and routinely excludes them from the protection of the state' (Wilson 2007).

The Pyrrhic nature of the vigilantes' victory in Balsall Heath is evident in contemporary press reports throughout the years that followed. In July 2000 it was reported that Birmingham City Council was considering using paid informants to help drive sex workers from residential areas. Residents in Ladywood said their streets were 'overrun by prostitutes'.[46] Residents of Edgbaston claimed to have seen 'sleeping bags lined up by the vice girls at night'. A city councillor announced: 'Kerb crawlers who are caught in the area will be prosecuted, named and shamed in court and fingerprints and DNA samples will be taken.'[47] In October 2000, the city council again contemplated a toleration zone to 'minimise the social nuisance being inflicted on Edgbaston, Ladywood and Harborne', which of course drew forth horrified responses from church spokesmen but, most interestingly, was supported by the former leader of the Balsall Heath pickets, Raja Amin, who was quoted as saying: 'As long as the red-light area is located well away from residential areas, I welcome

---

[45]'From vice town to vigilante hell', *The Observer*, 6 December 1998.
[46]Ladywood: Clare Short MP's constituency, adjoining Edgbaston; 'Sex and the city council', *BBC News*, 21 July, 2000 (see http://news.bbc.co.uk/1/hi/uk/844587.stm).
[47]'Anger as vice girls use alley', *Birmingham Evening Mail*, 15 September 2000.

it.'[48] Amin's statement calls into question the assumed monolithic attitudes of 'the Muslim community', behind which the city council hid its cowardice six years earlier.

Edgbaston residents copied tactics used in Balsall Heath, harassing both sex workers and outreach workers.[49] The outreach van was targeted, staff were threatened and vandalism attempted on the vehicle. No action was taken against those responsible and, in July 2000, the outreach team were banned from the soliciting area. Instead, their van was parked over a mile away at sites suggested by the police. One site was outside a block of flats which was renowned for drug dealing and firearms, and where, at the time, no mail was being delivered because postal workers had been attacked so frequently. Mail deliveries were restored to these flats only when the police agreed to escort a postman once a week. No police escort was offered to the outreach project. The nuns were also intimidated by protesters and their car was reported for kerb-crawling.

In February 2001 residents from the neighbouring borough of Walsall, who were also confronting the difficulties of street prostitution, commented: 'We have seen from Birmingham's example what happens when the vice scene is merely shifted.'[50] By February 2003, Birmingham City Council and the police had issued 21 ASBOs and 25 civil injunctions against sex workers; at least six ASBOs had already been breached and the women given prison sentences of up to four months. The ineffectiveness of this approach was already evident by May 2003, when police admitted, 'Soliciting is a problem that blights the Edgbaston area and we will do everything we can to eradicate it.[51] Despite ten years of evidence that the Balsall Heath action had merely displaced street sex work, in April 2004 Melanie Phillips repeated her 1994 eulogy in the *Daily Mail*. After a highly selective and uncritical sketch of events in 1994/5, she wrote: 'Street prostitution largely vanished from Balsall Heath – and it was not displaced to other areas.'[52]

The final irony is that, after more than a decade of ferocious efforts by community groups, the police and city council, street sex work in Birmingham has now established itself in other areas with

[48]'Brum in vice district call', *Evening Mail*, 21 October 2000; 'Church fury at red-light zone plan', *Evening Mail*, 23 October 2000.
[49]'The Edgbaston protesters were mainly white British.'
[50]'Driven apart!', *Evening Mail*, 26 February 2001.
[51]'Prostitute barred from streets', *BBC News*, 20 May 2003 (see http://news.bbc.co.uk/1/hi/england/west_midlands/3043475.stm).
[52]Melanie Phillips, 'The State turns pimp', *Daily Mail*, 9April 2004.

a substantial Muslim population. By January 2007, 'Birmingham's largest red light area'[53] was Small Heath:

> At night Small Heath in Birmingham is alive, not with the traders that populate the area in the day but prostitutes walking the length of Coventry Road ... West Midlands police say that 93% of all those stopped for kerb crawling in Small Heath were from the local area. That's why they're about to head out and distribute leaflets in English and Urdu[54]

What will happen next, I wonder? It seems unlikely that the authorities would adopt quite such an indulgent view of busloads of young Muslim men gathering in the streets to impose higher moral standards as they did in 1994. Indeed the approval expressed in *Paying the Price* (Home Office 2004: section 7.8) for local communities 'reclaiming their streets', where Balsall Heath is cited as a good example, has been replaced in the *Co-ordinated Strategy on Prostitution* with 'action must be sensible and sensitive – there is no place for vigilantes to "reclaim the streets"' (Home Office 2006: 15). But who knows? Perhaps intimidating prostitutes would be seen as a relatively harmless and wholesome activity, expressing 'shared values'? Society needs its scapegoats, after all.

---

[53]'Leaflets aimed at kerb-crawlers Small Heath', *BBC News*, 17 January 2007 (see http://news.bbc.co.uk/2/hi/uk_news/england/west_midlands/6270001.stm).

[54]Anna Cunningham, 'Operation Reassurance', *BBC News*, 18 January 2007 (see http://www.bbc.co.uk/birmingham/content/articles/2007/01/17/operation_reassurance_feature.shtml).

Chapter 9

Indoor sex work: policy and policing

I have had an incident reported to me today of a brothel that was held up at gunpoint last night .... The house reported the incident immediately to the Police who came and I believe closed them down. (Project worker, South 2003)

Indoor sex work has traditionally been regarded as much safer than street work, and its relative safety is illustrated in the figures for sex worker homicides. While it is estimated that over 70 per cent of female sex workers in the UK are indoor workers (UKNSWP 2008), only 22 per cent of sex work-related homicides between 1990 and 2006 were of indoor workers.[1] However, as with street work, legislation and law enforcement jeopardise indoor workers' safety by penalising the safest indoor method – working with other people. The laws surrounding indoor sex work[2] criminalise those who profit from or organise the prostitution of others and those responsible for premises classed as brothels, which are defined as places used by more than one sex worker for the purposes of prostitution. Hence it is not sex workers themselves who are liable to prosecution, but the owner, manager or landlord of the establishment. However, a maid[3] may also be regarded as assisting in the management of a

---

[1]See Chapter 13.
[2]Mainly the Sexual Offences Acts 1956 and 2003.
[3]A maid does not offer sexual services but acts as a receptionist, helping to screen out unwanted clients and giving company and assistance to the sex worker when required.

brothel, and premises used by different sex workers, working alone but at different times, may also be classed as brothels. Consequently, indoor sex workers may operate completely alone, making them more vulnerable to attack. Criminalisation also discourages contact with the police so attacks are not reported, allowing violence to continue and escalate. Nevertheless, in the past many police forces have been relatively tolerant towards indoor sex work, unless there were concerns about under-age girls, drug dealing or trafficking.

Whittaker and Hart (1996) explored strategies for avoiding violence among indoor workers at sex flats in London in the mid-1990s. They identified several factors which contributed to safety, some of which depended on the experience and skill of both sex workers and maids in managing client behaviour, including intuition about a client's potential for violence, adopting an assertive stance towards clients and building up a clientele of 'regulars'. These interpersonal defence mechanisms are also reported by street sex workers (Sanders 2001), but other protective devices were specific to working indoors: screening clients through 'spyholes', a lighted environment which was the sex worker's 'territory' and the almost universal presence of a maid, able to intervene if there was any trouble. There was also widespread willingness to call for police assistance in emergencies. This confidence was clearly based on the assumption that the police would overlook the fact that sex work was taking place on the premises when investigating violence. While such trusting relationships between sex workers and the police were not universal, there was, nevertheless, a widespread view that discreet indoor sex work was relatively harmless, and certainly provoked far fewer demands on police time than street work.

However, things were about to change. The same authors (Whittaker et al. 1996) reported that during the year 1994/5, women from former Soviet Union countries began working in sex flats in central London. A study comparing women who first attended a sex work clinic in central London between 1985 and 1992 with those first attending from 1996 and 2002 found that 25 per cent of sex workers who first attended in the earlier period were not born in the UK, compared to 63 per cent in the later period (Ward et al. 2004). By 1999 as many as half the indoor sex workers known to outreach projects in central London were from overseas, mainly from the Balkans and eastern Europe; in outer London the proportion was about a third, but outside the London area numbers of overseas sex workers were negligible (Brussa 2000). Nevertheless, from 2000 onwards, the indoor sex industry became the focus of increasing anxiety about immigration and trafficking, a focus which has progressively intensified and extended beyond the London area to all parts of the country.[4] The Home Office's current strategy on prostitution (Home Office 2006) seeks to remove any local tendency towards toleration, some effects of which are explored below.

While it is undoubtedly the case that abusive trafficking situations have been uncovered, there has also been an increase in hostile policing and prosecutions relating to indoor sex work where no evidence of trafficking or coercion is adduced. In 2002, acting on claims that local brothels were full of trafficked women, 150 police officers and 20 immigration officers raided eight sex work premises in Glasgow. Despite this massive expenditure of law enforcement resources, only nine women were described as having entered the country illegally, and Glasgow police stated that they had 'uncovered no evidence that women are being trafficked or held against their will in saunas'.[5] In 2004, over 300 police and immigration officers raided various addresses in Yorkshire. Forty-seven women were arrested at two saunas for 'immigration offences'.[6] This operation was reported at the ACPO[7] National Vice Conference later that year and hailed as a great victory over the evils of trafficking. However, three years after the original raids all charges relating to one of the saunas were dismissed. It transpired that local police were aware that the business was operating as a brothel and made regular visits to check that there were no underage girls, illegal workers or drugs on the premises. Provided these 'ground rules' were followed, the sauna operators had, in the judge's words, 'a reasonable and legitimate expectation that their activities were at best tolerated and they would not be prosecuted'. It was also reported that:

> The final bill for the police operation and following legal proceedings is believed to total more than £1 million. The move was sparked by intelligence that illegal immigrants were working

---

[4]Association of Chief Police Officers, *Operation Pentameter*, Press Release, 21 February 2006.
[5]Iain Wilson, 'Immigrant prostitutes claim asylum: police raid city saunas to combat human trafficking', *The Herald*, 6 December 2002.
[6]'Man released after parlour raids', *BBC News*, 18 April, 2004 (see http://news.bbc.co.uk/go/pr/fr/-/1/hi/england/west_yorkshire/3634309.stm).
[7]ACPO – Association of Chief Police Officers.

there – but despite the operation attracting nationwide attention no evidence was ever found to back up the allegations.[8]

Even where sex workers from overseas are involved, abuse and coercion are not universal (Dibb *et al.* 2006), but cases of 'trafficking' where no evidence of coercion or violence can be found receive little attention in the debates about anti-trafficking policy.

On 29 January 2008, the front-page headline in the *Birmingham Mail* was 'Nine girls seized in vice raid'. The story began: 'Police have swooped on a suspected brothel in Birmingham, taking nine young women into care.'[9] Underage girls rescued and taken to the nearest children's home? Well, no. The women were aged 19 to 28 and were taken into police custody. In what other context would being taken into custody be called 'being taken into care'? Trafficked sex slaves then? Not that either. The following day, the *Birmingham Mail* carried another, much less prominent article, admitting 'Brothel workers "voluntary"'. Although the raid was part of Pentameter Two,[10] a police spokesman admitted, 'The nine women found there had not been subject to human trafficking and had come to work in the United Kingdom of their own volition'. They were, however, still being interviewed by police and immigration officials.[11]

In the same issue of the *Birmingham Mail*, there was another report describing police operations against different indoor premises in Birmingham. In December 2006, an undercover officer visited a suburban house and found an 'oriental lady' wearing only a dressing gown. He believed the house was being used as a brothel. A week later another undercover officer visited, found a man and an 'oriental lady' in her underwear, a £50 note and a pornographic magazine. In January 2007, police checked out a newspaper advertisement – quite possibly in the *Birmingham Mail* which carried between 50 and 60 adverts for 'escorts' and 'massage' everyday – for 'Oriental Beauties Massage' and traced the advert to the property in question. The police, obviously feeling they did not have enough evidence, then mounted a surveillance operation for *four months*, finally raiding the

---

[8]'Legal victory for brothel owner', *The Star*, 30 March 2007 (see http://www.sheffieldtoday.net/viewarticle.aspx?articleid=2193921&sectionid=58).
[9]Will Oliphant, 'Nine girls seized in vice raid', *Birmingham Mail*, 29 January 2008.
[10]Pentameter One and Two – the designations given to nationwide policing operations to combat trafficking 2006–2008.
[11]'Brothel workers "voluntary"', *Birmingham Mail*, 30 January 2008.

premises in June 2007. What else might the officers committed to this four-month surveillance operation have been doing with their time? Catching people who had attacked sex workers perhaps? Another point of interest, in the context of the alarming claims made about 'sex slaves' being forced to have sex with 40 clients every day, during the four-month surveillance period at these premises, the average number of males visiting per day was 12.[12]

In 2004, a brothel owner in Cardiff was fined £5,000 and given a four-month suspended prison sentence, despite the fact that foreign nationals were found working at the premises. The judge said, 'You ran efficiently and discreetly a fully functioning and successful brothel …. You had regard for the safety, health and hygiene of your staff and premises. There was nothing naive, second-rate or particularly sordid about your business … (and you were not) party to coercion or corruption.'[13] Another case at Cardiff Crown Court, in January 2008, is a spectacular illustration of the perverse outcomes of current enforcement policies towards indoor sex work. In this case, the judge commented that while such prosecutions were intended to address situations where sex workers are coerced, threatened and trafficked, no one had 'suffered any physical or psychological damage' and that, like the Yorkshire case referred to above, the police had been fully aware of the premises concerned, making regular visits to check there were no under-age girls or drugs. It also transpired that the police had only decided to prosecute the brothel owner after she had taken two trafficked women to the police herself, fearing for their safety. She told the BBC, 'I think Pentameter had all the right reasons for starting the operations off but in terms of success, and capturing traffickers, no, they got far more success from people in the sex industry, in the know, passing information on.'[14]

Outreach projects also have reported that law enforcement responses to new immigration patterns have had a considerable impact on indoor sex workers, both those from overseas, and UK citizens (Campbell 2007). Reports have been received of British women, working together for safety reasons, being charged with

---

[12]Madeleine Bunting, 'Sorry, Billie, but prostitution is not about champagne and silk negligees', The Guardian, 8 October 2007; Gary Marks, 'Brothel's 12 customers a day – claim', Birmingham Mail, 30 January 2008.
[13]'Cardiff brothel owner ran exemplary business', BBC News, 18 November 2004 (see http://news.bbc.co.uk/1/hi/wales/south_east/4022747.stm).
[14]'Sex trafficked victims "missing"', BBC News, 4 February 2008 (see http://news.bbc.co.uk/go/pr/fr/-/1/hi/wales/7225281.stm).

brothel-keeping; of raids involving the use of police dogs, of police filming women in their underwear and such footage being subsequently broadcast on television; of police visiting British sex workers, saying they were checking the premises for migrant or trafficked women, finding none, giving reassurances that no action would be taken, but then returning shortly afterwards to arrest and charge them. Sex workers from several parlours in one area of the country reported being more frightened by the police raids than they had ever been by clients, every one of whom said they felt violated by their treatment at the hands of the police. All had previously had good relationships with the police and all had previously passed on information to them about any suspicions they had regarding trafficked women or under-age girls. Sex workers at some indoor premises – some where there are migrant women, in this country legally and working voluntarily, others where only British women are working – have severed long-standing contact with outreach projects due to a climate of fear engendered by repeated raids and deportations.[15]

> They raided two 24 hour well run parlours where they had no evidence of trafficking, they claimed some evidence of migrant workers, but all women present at raids were British. So they put 30 women out of work two weeks before Christmas.... The two owners are charged with brothel keeping, both are people I have known for 8 years and were reasonable owners whose places have good working conditions. (Project worker's report, North, January 2008)

These cases demonstrate that prostitution law and current enforcement practices are not designed to promote safe and non-coercive environments, since those managing indoor sex work in a responsible way no longer benefit from police discretion as they might have done in the past. Also, if violence is defined as including activities which cause fear, humiliation, manhandling or exposure to danger, such 'official actions' can be regarded as a form of legalised, institutional violence.

---

[15]Personal communications to the author, January 2008.

Chapter 10

Violence and indoor sex work

This exploration of violence against indoor sex workers focuses on the situation in London since there is ample information regarding the indoor sex industry in this area, but examples from other areas will also be given. The primary source of information is the LUML, which collates reports of attacks on sex workers from different parts of London. The LUML is uniquely useful as it constitutes by far the largest volume of such reports from indoor sex workers (often sparsely represented in other areas), and the information is presented in a reasonably consistent format, allowing for a number of variables to be explored. Ugly Mugs do not give any details about those who have been attacked, except the kind of work they were engaged in at the time, so they cannot give a demographic profile of those reporting violence nor of how this profile has changed in recent years. Neither can the LUML reflect the extent or distribution of either sex work or violence in London, since not all sex workers are in touch with a project that contributes to the list, but it does reflect the range of incidents which sex workers themselves regard as sufficiently dangerous or disturbing to warrant alerting other sex workers to the perpetrators. The picture that emerges of work-related violence against indoor sex workers should also help dispel some misconceptions about their vulnerability and the extent to which clients threaten their safety.

The London Ugly Mugs List, September 2000 to April 2005

The period covered by the LUML reports was a time of change in the London sex industry, with increasing numbers of overseas sex workers entering the off-street sector, and intensifying anxieties about illegal immigration and trafficking undermining relationships of trust between sex workers and the police, and possibly lessening contact with outreach projects as well. Changing immigration patterns may also have affected the organisation of sex work businesses, their clientele and the characteristics of attackers. To explore whether these changes influenced the kinds of attacks reported through the LUML, several variables have been compared by the time period in which the attack took place. The first time period is from mid-2000 to December 2002, the second from January 2003 to April 2005.

Although the earliest bulletin analysed was issued in September 2000, the earliest incident reported occurred in May 2000, demonstrating that sex workers' contacts with projects contributing to the list may be infrequent, and attacks therefore may not be reported until weeks or months after they occurred. The last incident occurred in April 2005.

In the 57 bulletins of the LUML issued from September 2000 and April 2005, there were 454 reports of attacks on indoor sex workers, an average of 97 per year.[1] Comparison of the four full calendar years 2001 to 2004 shows an absolute decline in the number of reports from 2002 onwards: 137 reports were made in 2001, 101 in 2002, 84 in 2003 and 63 in 2004. The increasing proportions of non-UK sex workers in London could have resulted in reduced contact with outreach projects or more reluctance to report attacks due to language barriers, or more anxiety on the part of foreign sex workers about contact with 'officials' for fear of coming to police or immigration officers' attention. Other factors could also be relevant: there are now various Internet sites where sex workers themselves post descriptions of bad clients and internal evidence from the LUML suggests that indoor workers became less likely to report certain types of event which will be explored below. However, the decline in reporting also reflects lack of contact between indoor sex workers and outreach projects in south London from 2003 onwards. Some projects in south London that were previously regular contributors to the LUML closed down or ceased to work with indoor sex workers. Overall, reports from projects in south London declined from 49 per cent of the total in

---

[1] The LUML changed to digital format in May 2005.

2000 to 2002, to 11 per cent in 2003 to 2005, illustrating the crucial role of outreach workers in collating reports of violence against sex workers.

Style of indoor work in London

In 2004, a mapping exercise[2] estimated that about two-thirds of indoor sex workers in London operated from sex flats, saunas and massage parlours, and a third via escort agencies, while Ward *et al.* (2004) reported that among sex workers attending a central London clinic between 1996 and 2002, 34 per cent were working from sex flats, 14 per cent from saunas or clubs and 38 per cent via escort agencies or madams. The great majority of Ugly Mug reports to the LUML (88 per cent) were made by women working from 'sex flats', while only 7 per cent were made by those working in saunas and 5 per cent by escorts (see Table 10.1).[3] The small numbers of reports from escorts and those working in saunas, compared to those working from sex flats, raises the question as to whether the difference is due to lack of contact between outreach projects and sauna workers or escorts, or whether sex flats are particularly unsafe.

Working indoors in a fixed environment which the sex worker controls (unlike doing outcalls or escort jobs to hotels and clients' homes) allows for the installation of security hardware: CCTV, reinforced doors, complex entry systems and panic alarms, all of which have become increasingly common since Whittaker and Hart reported in 1996. The presence of other people at indoor premises

Table 10.1 LUML reports: style of indoor work (n = 454)

Workstyle	n	%
Flat	402	88
Sauna	30	7
Escort	22	5
Total	454	100.0

[2]S Dickson (2004) *Sex in the City: Mapping Commercial Sex across London.* London: POPPY Project.
[3]Because more than one assailant was involved in many incidents reported to the LUML, values given in all the tables relate to the number of incidents, not to the number of assailants, unless specifically stated otherwise.

is also a major deterrent to violence: other sex workers – a friend, partner or sometimes a regular client – often act as the sex worker's guardian, even if a maid, receptionist or formal security personnel are not present. These protective elements are usually present at sex flats, so the high proportion of Ugly Mugs from such premises may reflect better contact levels between them and outreach projects, and repeated targeting for robbery, which is evident in the type of attacks reported.

> This man came out of the waiting area holding a gun.... He then saw the dog in the flat and the man stayed away from the dog. The dog was close to the safe where the money was kept. The woman stayed close to the dog and the man picked up a bag of condoms and ran out. (LUML 2005)

Some flat workers do entertain clients alone to avoid brothel-keeping charges, but although they do not have protection from other people, they often employ security technology and/or keep a large dog to monitor visitors and deter attacks. Only 7 per cent of attacks (33 out of 454) were reported by lone workers, although this information was not given or was unclear in 16 per cent of reports so the proportion may have been considerably higher. Under 3 per cent of attacks at flats and saunas clearly state that the woman was alone when the attack occurred and reports from escorts constituted under 5 per cent of the total (22 out of 454). Given that working with other people is a key deterrent to violence, the nature of attacks on lone workers compared to those in groups will be explored further below.

Excluding suspect persons: singles and groups

> The first impression that he gave made the women anxious. He was sweating a lot and had a threatening attitude. When asked if he had been there before he became defensive. Luckily he was between 2 locked doors and because the woman was questioning him he left. (LUML 2001)

At indoor premises, attacks can be prevented by refusing admission to those regarded as suspect, recognised as having committed a previous attack or who fit Ugly Mug descriptions. Received wisdom is against admitting people who arrive in groups, since they present a higher risk for robbery – though not necessarily other forms of attack. In 70 incidents (15 per cent of reports), an individual or group was not admitted to sex work premises. The judgement that men arriving alone are less likely to cause trouble is reflected in the Ugly Mug reports. Over 90 per cent of 'singles' were admitted throughout the period, with no significant change over time, but the proportion of groups who were admitted rose from 64 per cent to 83 per cent between the first and second periods.

> One man came to the flat, agreed the service, and once alone with the woman punched her straight in the face. And let in 2 other men. One head locked the maid and put a big steak knife to her throat and robbed the flat. (LUML 2000)

Sex flats rely heavily on maids to monitor those seeking admission, and where there is a rapid turnover in those fulfilling this role, there is inevitably less experience of vetting potential trouble-makers. There may also be greater pressure on both maids and sex workers to maximise earnings, militating against a cautious admissions policy, but it should be stressed that sex workers do not have a rogues' gallery of e-fits to refer to in assessing whether putative clients should be trusted: at best there may be a previous description in an Ugly Mug bulletin, which may be less helpful to those whose first language is not English. Neither can 'gatekeepers' be criticised for lack of caution in whom they admit when assailants come to the door armed with weapons and force entry through sheer intimidation and violence.

> ... four men broke through the kitchen window armed with knives and some sort of spray. The men threatened the girls and wanted money. (LUML 2006)

Some groups are more subtle in their methods, gaining entry separately then joining forces inside the premises, having one member of the group receive a service as a client on an earlier occasion, or having a person with the external appearance of a reliable customer gain entry first, who then lets in his accomplices.

> A group of men carrying out violent robberies, 2 black guys and a white man whom they get to ring the bell first. Once the door is open to him they all rush in. They rob the women of their money and mobile phones. They have been known to take handbags, car keys, punters' belongings and cars. Violent if resisted. (Midlands 2004)

Exclusion of potential attackers may not terminate the incident: those excluded may hang around outside, making repeated attempts to gain admission, hammering on doors and windows, disturbing the neighbours, making threatening phone calls and sometimes attacking sex workers after they have left the building. One group even assaulted passers-by outside the flat, possibly with the intention of intimidating the women into admitting them. However, nearly all cases of violence, robbery or sexual assault involved people who were given admission to sex work premises or were encountered on outcalls, so the following analysis excludes the incidents where suspect persons were refused admission.

Types of attack or other incident

Excluding the 15 per cent of reports where potential trouble-makers were excluded from working premises, there were 385 reports concerning those who were admitted to working premises or encountered on 'outcalls'. Many incidents involved robbery or theft combined with either sexual or physical violence, sometimes both, making it difficult to divide the reports into exclusive categories of attack. Table 10.2 shows five broad categories, described in more detail below.

Table 10.2   LUML: types of attack reported (n = 385)

Type of attack	2000–2002		2003–2005		2000–2005	
	n	%	n	%	n	%
Sexual assault	48	20	16	11	64	17
Sexual assault & robbery/theft	23	9	16	11	39	10
Robbery/theft, no sexual assault	116	48	86	60	202	52
Violence/weapon	19	8	6	4	25	6
Other incidents	37	15	18	13	55	14
*All sexual assaults	71	29	32	22	103	27
*All robbery/theft	139	57	102	72	241	63
All reports	243	100	142	99	385	99

*Overlapping categories, not summed into total incidents.

- Sexual assault – includes everything from inappropriate sexualised behaviour to rape.

- Robbery/theft – includes forcing refunds after receiving a sexual service and attempts to do so, thefts of property, robbery or attempted robbery and obtaining sexual services fraudulently.

- Attacks which include both sexual assault and robbery/theft.

- Violence or threats with/use of weapons unconnected to sexual assault or robbery/theft.

- Other incidents – excludes incidents of sexual assault or robbery/theft; includes verbal aggression, nuisance, apparent intention to rob, damage to property and bizarre or disturbing behaviour.

Robbery, theft and other property crime

It is often assumed that violence against a sex worker means a sexual assault carried out by a client, but the most common type of attack reported by indoor workers was robbery, attempted robbery and forcing or attempting to force refunds after receiving a sexual service. In the first period 57 per cent of all incidents and 72 per cent in the second period involved robbery or other forms of theft. Only 30 per cent involved someone who had received a service and only 27 per cent described any kind of sexual assault. The majority described assailants who had no interest getting in a sexual service, some of whom imitated client behaviour to gain access to the premises; others posed as police officers or other officials; a few were groups which included women claiming to be seeking work. Having gained entry, such individuals or groups then usually robbed or attempted to rob the premises.

> The working woman answered the door to the first guy, who said that he had hit her car. She felt suspicious and said she would just go and get her car keys. As she went to close the door, the second man appeared and they both barged their way in.... They took money, jewellery and her mobile phone and threatened that if she reported it to the police they would kill her. (LUML 2000)

Only 44 per cent of incidents (169 out of 385) involved someone who may have paid for a service. Of these reports, 30 either did not specify whether payment had been made or described assailants who had paid on a *previous* occasion, but not when the attack occurred. These have been classed as 'paid'; if they had been classed as non-payers, the proportion of 'paid' would have been only 35 per cent. However, of the 169 here classed as 'paid', 93 (55 per cent) took or attempted to take their money back afterwards, often robbing other money and property as well. In the earlier period 48 per cent of assailants had paid for a service: this proportion fell to 37 per cent in the later period, while the proportion of those who paid but then committed robbery rose from 24 per cent to 50 per cent. Paying for a service did not always mean receiving a service: some clearly only paid to allay suspicions of intent to rob; others paid but did not get a service due to other conflicts. Of those who did receive a service, in the first period 30 per cent demanded or forced refunds and another 20 per cent robbed or attempted to rob other money or property as well. In the later period, two-thirds of those who had received a service refused to honour the bargain: 22 per cent demanded or forced refunds and 46 per cent also committed or attempted to commit robbery.

> [Several reports of an assailant who] would attend for a service and be well-behaved. He would then return a couple of days later and rob the flat, with increasing levels of violence. (LUML 2000)

In the earlier period, 21 per cent of robbery/theft incidents (30 out of 139) involved clients demanding or forcing refunds after paying for a service but not stealing other money or property as well. In the later period, only 9 per cent of robbery/theft incidents (9 out of 102) were of this nature. The proportion of those who complained about the service also fell from 21 per cent to 12 per cent. Since dissatisfaction with the service is the usual 'justification' given for demanding refunds, it appears that more attackers in the later period were cynically using the 'client disguise' as a precursor to robbery, were less willing to accept the client role and pay for sex, or were more desperate financially so more prone to commit money crime.

> The man had a service earlier that day. At 7pm he came back for what was thought another service.... When he came into the flat he produced a gun and took the whole day's earnings (LUML 2003)

Many robberies were extremely, unnecessarily violent, to sex workers, maids and clients. Many involved weapons and 15 per cent also involved sexual violence. Other 'money crime' incidents were non-violent, but with or without violence, stealing money or possessions earned through selling sex violates the basis on which those sexual services were given. Taking money back after a service and obtaining sexual services fraudulently, e.g. with bad cheques, forged notes or by conning women into giving free services, are all manifestations of men resisting the role of client. Even though their methods are less terrifying than rape at gunpoint, they are nevertheless asserting their right to take sexual services without paying.

> Gains access to the parlour legitimately then once in ... shows knife or handgun; several attacks on saunas – usually robbery. He has also raped a receptionist and indecently assaulted a receptionist. (North West 2002)

The propensity of groups to commit robbery appeared to intensify, robbery comprising 70 per cent of incidents involving groups in the first period, rising to 81 per cent in the second, but the biggest increase in robbery was seen among lone attackers. In the first period, a third of attacks by 'singles' involved robbery, but this rose to 53 per cent in the second period. Lone robbers also became more likely to use violence or weapons, rising from 57 per cent to 91 per cent of single-person robberies. The use of guns by lone robbers also increased dramatically, from 17 per cent of robberies in the first period to 42 per cent in the second, while 22 per cent of group robberies involved guns in both periods. Groups were more likely to use knives or other bladed instruments as their most dangerous weapons, although a variety of weapons was often used in the same incident.

Weapons included firearms, stun-guns, knives, machetes, meat cleavers, baseball bats, truncheons, hammers, CS gas, mace, bottles, shears and screwdrivers, but the increased use of weapons between the earlier and later periods was wholly due to the increased use of guns. Firearms were shown in 9 per cent of incidents in the first period, rising to 23 per cent in the second period. They were mainly used to intimidate, however: there is only one report of a gun being fired, at a chair. There were 23 incidents where sex workers, maids, security staff or clients were attacked with other weapons, and many more where, although it was clear that a weapon was shown, it is not clear if it was used.

Came in and had a quick service. He then wanted the money back and then wanted all the flat's money. The maid put up a strong fight ... (LUML 2004)

A minority of robberies were committed by people who had paid for a service. In some cases, it appears the assailant used the 'client disguise' to the extent of paying for and receiving a service without any resistance, only then taking back his money, or indeed all the money and items of value he could find. Accounts of this type of incident sometimes portray the offender as quite calm, suggesting that there was never any intention of paying for sex, that the aim was solely to get free sex or, to get free sex and rob the premises at the same time. One report describes two men visiting a flat, one of whom had a service while the other chatted to the maid. When the service was over, a gun was produced and money demanded:

After the men had taken the money they were very calm, opened a packet of crisps and offered them around. One man also told the other off for calling the women abusive names. (LUML 2003)

Sexual assaults and violations

Over the course of the project women have reported numerous incidents to me where they have been sexually assaulted. Usually this is expressed in terms of a client doing something to the woman during sex that she has not agreed to do. She has told him to stop and he has continued without her consent. The women who have reported these incidents to me have not usually perceived them as sexual assaults or rape even though they have been very distressed by them, are clear they have not consented and have sometimes been left with physical injury such as bruises or bleeding. (Ibbitson 2002)

Ibbitson's reflections on her interviews with indoor sex workers in Bolton and their perceptions of 'acts not agreed' are echoed in the language of reports to the LUML (see Table 10.3). Only 15 per cent of sexual assaults were described as 'rape', 'attempted rape' or 'sexual assault'; 32 per cent referred to men forcing or attempting to force 'acts that were not agreed', sometimes quite clearly such as 'he tried to force sex without a condom', and other times more obliquely,

Table 10.3 LUML: sexual assaults and violations (n= 103)

Sexual assaults and violations	2000–2002 n = 71		2003–2005 n = 32		All n = 103	
	n	%	n	%	n	%
Rape, attempted rape, sexual assault	9	13	7	22	16	15
Acts not agreed	27	38	6	19	33	32
Violence during or after sex	22	31	9	28	31	30
Other sexual violations	13	18	10	31	23	22
Total	71	100	32	100	103	99

such as 'he took an £80 service for £40'. A further 30 per cent of sexual assaults involved physical violence either before, during or immediately after sex. Twenty-three per cent of sexual assaults are categorised as 'other sexual violations'. This includes covert photography, peeping, groping, clients exposing themselves in public areas of the premises – one client began masturbating over waiting clients and was rapidly ejected from the premises with enthusiastic help from the other clients; another who badgered the sex worker into giving him free 'phone sex' and instances where robbers conducted strip searches of women.

In total 27 per cent of reports described sexual assault, which was more strongly associated with lone working than working with other people: 48 per cent of reports made by lone workers included a sexual assault, compared to 24 per cent of reports from those working with others.

Twenty-nine per cent of all attacks in the first period involved any kind of sexual assault, and 22 per cent in the second period, suggesting that the actual incidence of such events may have declined. This is largely accounted for by the decline in reports describing 'acts not agreed', such as overrunning on time, deliberately breaking condoms or forcing sex without them, or taking services which had not been paid for. An acute sense of what is and is not permissible, is more frequently associated with a professional approach to sex work and with experience. As with the decline in reports of suspect persons being excluded from indoor premises, it is possible that the decline in reports of 'acts not agreed' reflects a less experienced population of sex workers and perhaps increased pressure to tolerate obnoxious clients in order to maximise earnings.

... forcing uncomfortable positions; told to stop – punter got angry, said he was a regular, demanded money back, threatened to hit her. (LUML 2003)

Most sexual assaults – 87 per cent, were committed by lone assailants, a third of which also involved demanding or forcing refunds or robbery/attempted robbery. Only 13 per cent of sexual assaults were committed by assailants in groups, half of which were combined with robbery. The proportion of sexual assaults which were combined with robbery or theft rose from 32 per cent of all sex attacks (23 out of 71) in the first period to 50 per cent (16 out of 32) in the second. Over 30 per cent of all sexual assaults were committed by those who had not paid for a service, and of assailants who had paid, 38 per cent (27 out of 71) took or attempted to take their money back afterwards and one in seven committed robbery or theft as well. Therefore, only 43 per cent of sexual assaults (44 out of 103), 10 per cent of all incidents reported by indoor sex workers to the LUML, could be said to fit the stereotype of the client who thinks that paying for sex entitles him to commit any kind of sexual assault.

Lone sex workers

Only 33 reports over the whole period clearly indicated that the victim was alone when attacked, 22 from escorts or flat workers doing 'outcalls' and 11 from women working alone in flats. The numbers were too small to identify any changes over time, but, like those working in groups, those working alone from flats were most likely to be targeted for straightforward robbery (9 out of 11 reports), whereas attacks on escorts and flat workers doing outcalls were much more complex. The attackers were all people who refused to honour the 'client contract'. In 9 of the 22 reports relating to escorting or outcalls, clients refused to pay, demanded their money back, committed robbery or theft *and* committed a sexual assault, ranging from removing condoms to rape. There were 5 sexual assaults which did *not* include robbery or theft, and 5 reports of clients refusing to pay or demanding their money back which did *not* include a sexual assault. Altogether 23 out of 33 reports made by lone sex workers (70 per cent) involved non-payment or robbery, and 16 (48 per cent) involved sexual assault.

Other violence and other incidents

A small proportion of incidents (6 per cent) involved physical violence unconnected to robbery or sexual attacks. These included pushing, grabbing, punching, kicking and threats with or use of weapons. Some seem to have been attempts to intimidate sex workers as a precursor to robbery, although no overt attempt to rob was made; in one incident the owner of the premises was stabbed with threats to take over the business and/or burn down the property, and in others the aggressor seems to have been mentally disturbed or merely drunk. Others became aggressive because the women refused to do business with them, or because they did not want to pay or were dissatisfied with the service they had received: several of these were also drunk.

> He said he wanted a service and would pay after. If he was satisfied. If not, would not pay. Maid instructed working girl not to give any service. Man became abusive and threatening and refused to leave the flat. (LUML 2002)

Similar motivations or triggers were evident in some of the events categorised as 'other incidents' (14 per cent), but while verbal abuse and aggression were frequently used, doors kicked, cameras smashed or bricks thrown through windows, no weapons were used and no actual physical assault occurred. Many described suspicious behaviour, such as entering the premises as clients and then leaving without having a service, usually construed as 'checking out' the premises with the intention to rob it later. Other events caused anxiety and annoyance, such as anonymous threatening letters, visits from bogus officials and people impersonating police officers, to customers who behaved bizarrely, became obsessed, urinated on the floor, or screamed and threw their clothes about because the sexual interaction disappointed them.

Repeat attackers

Twenty-nine per cent of reports in the first period and 16 per cent in the second indicated that the person or group described were repeat offenders, known to have attacked other sex workers. It seems unlikely that the actual proportion of repeat offenders fell by such a large margin, so this difference may arise from other factors: the changing demographic profile of attackers from 2003 onwards (see below) suggests that offenders new to the London area began targeting sex work premises, and changing personnel in sex work premises may have meant that fewer assailants were recognised by fewer sex workers. There was also a marked difference between the two time periods in the proportion of reports which clearly indicated that the assailants were *not* known: 19 per cent in the first and 43 per cent in the second, which would tend to support the above interpretation.

Only 17 reports specified that the assailant had been a 'regular' client, 4 per cent of the total, although other information contained in descriptions of attackers indicated that 39 others (10 per cent) had been clients on at least one previous occasion.

Reporting to the police

> ... man rang the bell of the flat and was seen on camera ... two more sets of feet were seen on the camera. Two minutes later the camera was pulled down and left hanging. More than one man was then heard trying to kick in the front door ... police were called and said to be "brilliant". (LUML 2004)

Eighty-nine reports stated that the incident had also been reported to the police; 19 per cent of all reports (see Table 10.4). Other incidents may also have been reported to the police, but the information not recorded on the Ugly Mug reporting form. Ten were incidents where potential assailants were successfully excluded from sex work premises, 14 per cent of all 'not admitted' reports. The other 79 represented 1 in 5 incidents (21 per cent) where the assailants had

Table 10.4 LUML: types of attack reported to police (n = 89 – 19% of all reports)

Attacks reported to police	2000–2002 n = 60 (20%)		2003–2005 n = 29 (18%)		2002–2005 n = 89 (19%)	
	n	%	n	%	n	%
Sexual assaults	10	17	4	14	14	16
Robbery	27	45	24	83	51	57
Aggravation	17	28	1	3	18	20
Other	6	10	0	0	6	7
All reported	60	100	29	100	89	100

gained entry to sex work premises, or assaulted sex workers on outcalls or escort jobs.

In 2000/2, 38 per cent of incidents reported to the police involved individuals or groups who caused aggravation or anxiety either inside or outside the premises. Only one incident of this kind was reported to the police in the second period. This might indicate that before 2003, some sex workers felt confident in calling for police help to eject a client who was causing a nuisance, for example, but that this confidence had all but vanished in the later period. However, the rate of reporting to the police of more serious incidents rose slightly in the later time period. Nineteen percent of all robberies or attempted robberies were reported to police in the first period, and 21 per cent in the second; 13 per cent of sexual assaults were reported in the first period, and 15 per cent in the second.[4] From 2000 to 2002, 45 per cent of incidents reported related to robbery or attempted robbery and 17 per cent concerned sexual assault, while from 2003 to 2005 83 per cent involved robbery or attempted robbery and 14 per cent concerned sexual assault, but these differences reflect the changes in types of report made to the LUML over the two periods.

Over the four full calendar years, the proportion of incidents reported to the police fell slightly (see Table 10.5), but this fall was mostly accounted for by the decline in reporting of more minor incidents. Levels of reporting fell most markedly between 2001 and 2002, but remained fairly constant thereafter.

> ... he said he was from the police ... but he wanted to come to a financial arrangement with them ... woman told him to leave and that she knew the police would not do that. (LUML 2001)

Given the large influx of sex workers from overseas, it is interesting that the levels of reporting to the police did not change very much between 2001 and 2005. It is possible that incidents reported to the LUML by overseas sex workers were all among the 80 per cent which were not reported to the police, but as Ugly Mug reports do not include any personal details about the victims of attacks, this can only be speculation. Some reports in the LUML contain appeals from the police regarding attacks, including reassurances that investigating officers were not concerned with the immigration status of potential

---

[4]Reporting of sexual assaults by sex workers to Sexual Assault Referral Centres is believed to have been higher than the levels of reporting to police recorded in the LUML.

Table 10.5 LUML: change in rate of reporting to police over time

	LUML reports	Police informed	%
2001	143	34	24
2002	101	17	17
2003	82	14	17
2004	64	13	20
2001–2004	390	78	20

witnesses, which may have reassured some. However, the Home Office prostitution strategy which urges robust targeting of indoor premises was not published until January 2006, so if there has been any diminution of confidence in reporting attacks to police since then, these data will not show it.

There were five incidents of men apparently impersonating police officers and either robbing the premises or attempting to get sexual services for free. All these incidents were reported to the police, but reports of the conviction of Keith Foad for preying on sex workers while posing as a policeman (between December 2001 and February 2003) demonstrate that those with insecure immigration status may not report such incidents. Foad was only detected because he was in a brothel, posing as a policeman, when it was raided. He was convicted on four sample counts of blackmail and obtaining sexual services by threats against two victims, both being

> ... foreigners who lived or worked 'on the fringes of illegality', and were 'vulnerable to having their premises raided and closed down'. One, a Lithuanian, was even in the country illegally and risked being deported.[5]

On a couple of occasions clients phoned the police to complain they had had a bad service and wanted their money back: they did not get sympathetic responses.

Ethnicity and nationality of attackers

A description of the appearance of attackers is an essential element of the Ugly Mug report, and together with information about perceived

[5]'Phoney "vice cop" jailed', *Evening Standard*, 30 January 2004.

nationality, some very broad categories of ethnicity/nationality can be derived from these descriptions (see Table 10.6). This is a sensitive area; there is no intention to stigmatise or contribute to racist discourses about either new or old immigrant groups, and it should be remembered that London has the largest non-white population in the country, estimated to have reached 32 per cent of the total in 2006 (Bains and Klodawski 2006). However, there is evidence that the ethnic profile of attackers changed between 2000 and 2005 (see Table 10.7), and changed in different ways in relation to attacks motivated by robbery compared to sexual attacks.

Categorisation of ethnicity/nationality

- White: predominantly white British; also Irish, USA, and Europe.
- Black: Black British; Black Caribbean; Black African; also "black" and "mixed race".
- Asian: predominantly Indian sub-continent; also Middle East and far east.
- East European: former Soviet bloc countries and Balkans.
- Mixed Groups: containing different combinations of the above four groupings.

Both lone and group attackers are included in each ethnic category, except for incidents involving 'mixed groups', i.e. groups composed of individuals of differing perceived ethnicity. The proportion of attacks by white and black assailants fell over the two time periods, while those committed by 'Asians' rose somewhat, and those committed by assailants from Eastern Europe and the Balkans rose markedly.

Table 10.6 LUML: ethnicity or nationality of attackers (including 'not admitted' n = 441)

Ethnicity	2000–2 n = 284		2003–5 n = 157		All n = 441	
	n	%	n	%	n	%
White	87	31	33	21	120	27
Black	118	41	40	25	158	36
Asian	31	11	25	16	56	13
East European	12	4	40	25	52	12
Mixed groups	36	13	19	12	55	12
Total	284	100	157	99	441	99

A different picture emerges when looking at lone attackers and group attacks separately, however. The proportion of group attacks by those perceived as white (usually British) hardly changed, while 'Asian' groups almost disappeared. Incidents involving groups from the Balkans and former Soviet bloc countries rose dramatically, from 3 per cent of the total in 2000–2 to 42 per cent in 2003–5. This was in contrast to attacks from 'black' groups, which showed a marked decline both in absolute numbers and as a proportion of the whole.

Overall, one-third of groups were multi-ethnic, indicating that while inter-ethnic animosities may be evident in other areas of life, in the world of criminal gangs there is a veritable rainbow coalition, giving too many different combinations of perceived ethnicity and geographic origin to list separately. However, the proportion of attacks involving 'mixed groups' fell from 42 per cent to 26 per cent over the two periods. In the earlier period two-thirds of mixed groups (20 out of 30) contained white British members cooperating with members of all other ethnic groups, although this fell to a quarter (4 out of 15) in the later period. The proportion of robberies[6] committed by black groups fell from 33 per cent of group robberies to 21 per cent; those by 'mixed' groups fell from 45 per cent to 30 per cent, while those committed by east European groups rose from 2 per cent to 36 per cent.

The decline in attacks by 'mixed' groups might indicate a retreat by criminal gangs into tighter ethnic identities, but as the numbers are small and repeat attacks by groups (especially those intending to

Table 10.7 Ethnicity: groups (n = 129)

Ethnicity	2000–2 n = 72		2003–5 n = 57		All n = 129	
	n	%	n	%	n	%
White	8	11	6	10	14	11
Black	22	30	10	17	32	25
Asian	10	14	2	4	12	9
East European	2	3	24	42	26	20
Mixed groups	30	42	15	26	45	35
Total	72	100	57	99	129	100

[6]'Robberies' here excludes theft in the form of extorting refunds after a service.

rob) are common, the apparent changes could simply be the result of one or two gangs being broken up by police action. Also, in the period when LUML reports of robberies by both black and 'mixed' groups declined, similar reports of attacks on indoor premises outside London and the south-east became more common. It is possible that certain individuals or groups have been displaced from the London area, driven out by competition from East European gangs.

The ethnic profile of individual attackers differed from that of groups (see Table 10.8). The impact of immigration from former Soviet bloc and Balkan countries was less evident: although numbers increased they remained the least numerous among lone attackers. The proportion of attacks by both black and white individuals was very similar and both fell from around 40 per cent to around 30 per cent of the total, while the proportion of attacks by those classified as Asian rose. The propensity of both white and black lone attackers to commit robbery rose over the two time periods. Less then a quarter of lone white attackers committed robbery in the first period, but half did so in the second, and amongst lone black attackers robberies also rose from 54 per cent (37 out of 69) to 64 per cent (16 out of 25).

Table 10.8 Ethnicity: lone attackers (n = 253)

Ethnicity	2000–2 n = 170		2003–5 n = 83		All n = 259	
	n	%	n	%	n	%
White	68	40	27	33	95	38
Black	69	41	25	30	94	37
Asian	19	11	18	22	37	14
East European	6	4	12	14	18	7
Other/missing data	8	4	1	1	9	4
Total	170	100	83	100	253	99

*Including 'not admitted'; excluding 'other' (4) and missing information (5)

Sexual attacks and ethnicity

Overall sexual assaults were most frequently ascribed to white British assailants, although the proportion as well as the absolute numbers of such attacks fell markedly over the time period. Ninety sexual assaults were committed by lone attackers.[7] Half the reports about single white (34 out of 68) and Asian (9 out of 19) assailants in the first period included a sexual attack, compared to 25 per cent of reports about single black assailants (17 out of 69). In the second period, the proportions for white and black assailants fell to 43 per cent and 20 per cent respectively, but for single Asian attackers it rose to 14 out of 18. Only one sexual assault was reported by a lone attacker described as East European throughout the period.

Summary

- The number of reports from indoor sex workers to the LUML declined sharply from 2002 onwards. It appears this was mainly due to projects in south London either ceasing to work with indoor sex workers or ceasing to contribute to the list, although other factors may have contributed to the decline.

- Only one-third of incidents involved someone who had received a service and only 27 per cent described any kind of sexual assault. Many incidents involved those who paid but then forced or tried to force repayment, but only 12 per cent involved someone who paid and did not take back payment afterwards or did not attempt to do so.

- Only 4 per cent of reports specified that the assailant had been a 'regular' client, although other information indicated that a further 10 per cent had been clients on at least one previous occasion.

- In the earlier period 21 per cent of all 'money crimes' were incidents of clients demanding or forcing refunds after receiving a service, but not stealing other money or property at the same time. In the later period, only 11 per cent of 'money crimes' were of this nature.

- The proportion of those who took or attempted to take their money back after receiving a service rose from 40 per cent to 65 per cent, while the proportion of those who also committed or attempted to commit robbery rose from 11 per cent of those who had received a service to 43 per cent. At the same time, the proportion of those who complained about the service fell from 22 per cent to 14 per cent.

---

[7]There were only 13 incidents which involved sexual assaults by assailants in a group, too few to make any meaningful comparisons by ethnicity.

- The propensity of groups to commit robbery once admitted to sex work premises appeared to intensify, robbery comprising 70 per cent of incidents involving groups in the first period, rising to 81 per cent in the second.

- The biggest increase in robbery was seen among lone attackers. In the first period, one-third of attacks by singles involved robbery, but this rose to 53 per cent in the second period. Lone robbers also became more likely to use violence or weapons in the course of their attacks, rising from 57 per cent to 91 per cent of single person robberies. Single robbers became more likely than groups to use guns (42 per cent compared to 22 per cent).

- Twenty-nine per cent of all attacks in the first period involved some kind of sexual assault, and 22 per cent in the second period, suggesting that the actual incidence of such events may have declined during the period covered. It is also possible that sex workers became less likely to report some types of sexual violation and assault in the later period.

- The proportion of sexual attacks which were combined with robbery or theft rose from 32 per cent of all sex attacks (23 out of 71) in the first period to 50 per cent (16 out of 32) in the second.

- Attacks by groups from the Balkans and former Soviet bloc countries rose dramatically, from 3 per cent of group attacks in 2000–2 to 42 per cent in 2003–5. This was in contrast to attacks from 'black' and 'mixed' groups, which showed a marked decline both in absolute numbers and as a proportion of the whole. It is possible that indigenous criminal gangs have been displaced by competition from new immigrant groups, and may have moved their operations beyond the south-east.

- Twenty per cent of incidents reported as Ugly Mugs were also reported to police in the first period, and 18 per cent in the second. Although this fall is slight, the Home Office prostitution strategy which urged robust targeting of indoor premises to uncover trafficking and exploitation was not published until January 2006, so if there has been any diminution of confidence in reporting attacks to police since then, these data will not show it.

Chapter 11

Attackers: court cases

To explore the circumstances of attacks on sex workers while they are 'at work' and the characteristics of assailants, I have examined reports of judicial proceedings against 139 individuals for non-fatal attacks on over 200 sex workers between 1990 and 2007. My main source of information has been reports in newspapers or on the Internet which identify victims as sex workers. Initially I studied the collection of press cuttings and Internet news items that have come my way over the years, later expanding this collection by repeated Internet searches using a variety of key words such as 'prostitute attack'. It was noticeable that the search terms 'prostitute attack' often produced more reports on initiatives to attack prostitution than reports of violence against sex workers. I have not selected particular types of attack – my only criterion has been that the victim appeared to be at work when attacked, and I have included every case I have found.

Media reports of court cases are limited and variable in the details given about the circumstances of attacks: factors which might illuminate aspects of violence in the sex industry are not necessarily those which barristers deem important nor of interest to journalists. Often there are scant details about the victims, but unlike murder trials, in non-fatal attacks the victims do have a voice and, even if not ultimately believed, can describe events from their own perspective. Also, unlike Ugly Mug reports, assailants are no longer anonymous, so there may be details regarding their social background and attitudes, and details of any previous history of offending, all of which are relevant to understanding the characteristics of those who attack sex workers. Therefore, although these cases represent a tiny proportion of attacks on sex workers – and it is to be hoped that they also represent a small proportion of cases where a prosecution has taken place – they can nevertheless tell us a great deal about the nature of violence against sex workers and those who commit it.

Since this exploration is focused on perpetrators, I have analysed the attacks according to the individuals charged. Some of the suspects were also concurrently charged with attacks on non-sex workers, and some were known to have committed other attacks on sex workers with which they were not charged. In some cases prolific offenders were only charged with a small number of 'sample counts'; in others, evidence given in court acknowledges that there were other victims whose cases were not prosecuted for a variety of reasons.

The earliest cases occurred in 1990, the latest in December 2007. The distribution by year is strongly related to the advent of the Internet facilitating my data collection, with only 11 offenders charged prior to 1999, two of whom were not brought to court until recent advances in DNA technology allowed suspects to be identified. In the years 1999 to 2007, there were between 8 and 20 cases per year.[1]

Regional distribution of cases and working method of victims

The geographical distribution of cases (see Figure 11.1) may reflect the local incidence of violence, the readiness of sex workers to complain, the willingness of police to investigate and of the CPS to prosecute, but variations are perhaps as likely to be a function of the predilections of regional editors regarding what cases they cover, while the chances of my having accessed any report depends heavily on whether the case was covered by Internet news sites and the vagaries of Internet search engines. No cases have been found in Northern Ireland and only one in Wales.[2] It seems unlikely that either country offered a safer environment for sex workers than England or Scotland, and more likely that attacks in these areas have not been flagged up as involving sex workers in media reports. However, the possibility that Northern Ireland and Wales *were* safer places for sex workers could be explored to see if there are any useful policy lessons for other regions. There is also the possibility that attacks on

---

[1]The year in which the alleged attack took place, not the year in which it came to court.

[2]The Welsh case is included in reports from the South West.

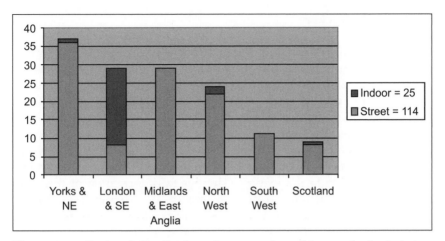

Figure 11.1 Regional distribution of cases and working method of victims (n = 139)

sex workers in these countries are not commonly prosecuted, which would be a matter of concern.

There are fewer cases from London and the South East than might be expected in terms of overall population distribution, but this may reflect the strong association of violence with street sex work, which is thought to be of proportionately less importance there than in the rest of the country. This supposition is supported by the working methods of victims in the sample. One hundred and fourteen suspects (82 per cent) were charged with attacks on street workers and only 25 (18 per cent) with attacks on indoor workers, 21 of whom operated in London and the South East, 72 per cent of all suspects in this area. This does not mean that the indoor sex industry is insignificant outside London and the South East, or that there is little violence at indoor premises elsewhere in the country. It may reflect the efforts that have been made over several years by sex work projects and the police to encourage reporting of crimes against indoor sex workers in the London area, and as the analysis of the LUML indicates, there are particular issues regarding indoor violence which may yet impact on other areas.[3]

---

[3]See Chapter 10, page 134.

Identity of attackers

There was no information about suspects' current or former employment in 99 cases (71 per cent); of the remaining 40 cases (29 per cent), 15 had various unskilled or semi-skilled jobs, of which eight involved driving; five were ex-soldiers, five worked for the police or fire service, four were students, four office workers, three had their own businesses, two were athletes and two were musicians.

The reports have been examined closely for details of the behaviour of the assailants to ascertain whether they were clients or had some other relationship to the victims. There is no information of this kind available regarding four suspects (3 per cent), although they appear to have attacked when their victims were working. These four cases have been excluded from this part of the analysis.

Non-clients

Of the remaining 135 suspects, 42 (31 per cent) were not clients.

One was apprehended for running around threatening women with a knife while declaring he would rid the streets of prostitutes. Two were partners of the victims, both of whom worked at indoor premises: one partner, having found out that his girlfriend was a sex worker, was arrested for creating a disturbance at her working premises; the other shot his partner outside her working premises for unknown reasons and was convicted of attempted murder. Sixteen were robbers who targeted indoor sex workers, all but one of whom carried out their attacks with accomplices; 12 committed sexual or physical violence in the course of robbing their victims. Another targeted indoor sex workers while impersonating a police officer: he was convicted on four sample counts – two of blackmail and two of procuring sexual intercourse by threats.[4]

One was a genuine police officer, accused of indecently assaulting four sex workers; one was a police community support officer, convicted of rape, false imprisonment and misconduct in a public office; one was a custody detention officer convicted of indecently assaulting four sex workers in the cells of a police station; and one was a transport policeman who was alleged to have used his position to demand sexual services.

---

[4]'Phoney vice cop jailed', *Evening* Standard, 30 January 2004 (see http://www.thisislondon.co.uk/news/articles/8895931?version=1).

One posed as a spurious 'Good Samaritan', enticing a woman who was being abused by a gang of youths into his car and then attacking her.

Seventeen merely dragged their victims into vehicles or attacked on the street, such as Matthew Smith, who grabbed a sex worker by the throat and hit her over the head with a bottle in Bradford in 2002. She bit him 'between the legs' and got away.[5] Smith had no previous convictions for sexual or physical violence, but four others did, although their previous victims are not known to have been sex workers. Others seem to have specifically targeted sex workers. Nine were charged with attacks on two or more sex workers and may be similar to homicide suspects classed as 'serial attackers':[6]

[He] 'dragged one woman into a churchyard and indecently assaulted her at knifepoint,' [then] 'attacked another woman ... after a long struggle in the secluded backstreets of Sheffield's red light district.[7]

[They] pulled up in the car but the woman could see the knife blade and tried to get away. She was forced into the car.[8]

'Clients'

In 93 cases (70 per cent), the approach seems to have been in the guise of a potential client.

However, of these 45 were 'non-payers' (33 per cent of all suspects and 48 per cent of 'client' suspects) (see Figure 11.2). Having approached as a client, the assailants then refused to pay or became violent as soon as payment was requested; 16 also robbed their victims of all other money they had on them. These men clearly did not meet the basic definition of a client, i.e. someone who pays for sex, and frequently violence seems to have been directly related to refusal to pay or intention to rob:

He agreed to pay her for a sex act and took her to the alleyway where he turned violent and demanded her takings. When she

[5]'Prison for man in prostitute attack', *Telegraph & Argus*, 3 September 2002.
[6]See Chapter 14, pages 191–4.
[7]'Evil sex fiend jailed for life', *The Star*, 14 March 2005.
[8]'Students jailed for prostitute attacks', *Telegraph & Argus*, 8 March 2005.

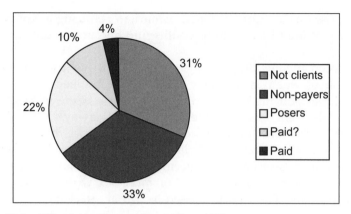

Figure 11.2 'Clients' and non-clients (n = 135)

said she had no money, she was knocked to the ground and raped[9]

... when the woman asked Howe for money, he threatened her with a wheel brace and raped her. When she asked Howe why he had raped her he replied: "You are all the same, now go and rip someone else off".[10]

The three-day trial had heard how the woman had approached 23-year-old Gurzynski and his friend offering them sex but said no when Gurzynski offered only £10. He then pulled her towards tennis courts and forced her to perform a sex act on him before making her have intercourse.[11]

Therefore, at least 64 per cent of assailants, 42 who were certainly not clients and 45 who did not pay or robbed the victims in the course of the attacks, cannot be described as clients, and it is doubtful whether 43 of the remaining 48 suspects qualified as clients either.

Thirty posed as clients (22 per cent of all suspects and 32 per cent of 'client' suspects), but having lured their victims into a position of vulnerability, then proceeded to attack them, and there is nothing to indicate that they paid:

[9]'Rapist jailed for "wicked" vice girl attack', *Bolton News*, 3 August 2007.
[10]'Wheel brace rapist jailed', *Daily Echo*, 30 September 2002.
[11]'Man guilty of raping prostitute in Hillfields park', *Coventry Evening Telegraph*, 3 April 2008.

Smith approached her and asked if she was doing business ...
[he] asked the woman to go back to his house.... The woman
refused but did agree to have sex with him. They went into
a nearby derelict building but, once inside, Smith became
aggressive, threatening the victim. He forced her to perform
sexual acts and violently and repeatedly raped her, telling her
that he would "batter her" if she screamed.[12]

He picked her up in his car and drove her to a remote part
of Hinton Parva. He assaulted her, he then raped her and he
further assaulted her.[13]

Andrew Humphris, who had previous convictions for sexual violence
going back 15 years, was convicted of attacking three women in the
north west on the same night in 2004. He bit off and swallowed a large
part of one victim's tongue, a sex worker whom he had enticed into
his car. He also forced his way into another woman's car, and chased
a third down the motorway before ramming her car, forcing her to
stop. The other women are not known to have been sex workers,
suggesting that he was not specifically targeting sex workers, merely
attacking any woman he encountered that night.[14]

Thirteen are reported as agreeing to pay (10 per cent of all suspects
and 14 per cent of 'client' suspects), but then attacked their victims,
and there is nothing to indicate that they did pay – indeed, the
accounts of these attacks suggest it is much more likely that they
did not:

[He] grabbed the woman's throat ... after they had agreed a
price for sex ...[15]

He offered her £150 to spend the night with him. But once at
the house he pinned her to a settee and raped her twice, while
threatening her with a screwdriver.[16]

---

[12]'Man sentenced after rape of sex-worker', Greater Manchester Police website,
22 November 2007 (see http://www.gmp.police.uk/mainsite/pages/be846d
ab73843a508025739b0062e319.htm).
[13]'Teenager is sent to prison for rape', *Swindon Advertiser*, 5 January 2002.
[14]'Life for tongue-bite sex attacker', *Manchester Evening News*, 13 April 2005.
[15]'"Decent" man jailed for prostitute attack', *Bradford Telegraph & Argus*, 22
December 2005.
[16]'Rapist used screwdriver to threaten prostitute', *Northern Echo*, 16 June 2002;
'Rapist given 10 years for second attack', *The Scotsman*, 1 July 2006.

The court heard she agreed to perform a sex act on him for £15 but, when they reached a car park, he locked the car doors and threatened to stab her.[17]

There are only five cases, 6 per cent of 'clients' and 4 per cent of all suspects, where the reports indicate that the assailants paid and do not state that they took the money back afterwards, although even in these cases it may be that this was a detail not thought to be sufficiently important to mention:

The 29-year-old woman ... said she would only have protected sex with him ... she offered him a refund but [he] began arguing and raped her twice.[18]

Age and ethnicity of suspects

Age when the offence took place is known for 134 suspects and ranged from 17 to 57 with a median of 27 years and an average of 30 years. Figure 11.3 shows suspects' age groups, comparing 'clients' with 'non-clients': four suspects whose client status could not be ascertained are excluded from this chart. The average age for 'clients' was 30, and 28 for non-clients, but there was a greater difference in the age distribution of 'clients' and non-clients. Among non-clients, 51 per cent were aged 16 to 24 compared with 33 per cent of 'clients'.[19] The British Crime Survey found that 44 per cent of violent offenders were aged 16 to 24 (Brookman and Maguire 2003), indicating that non-clients were more similar to violent offenders in terms of age than were 'clients'. However, 'clients' in this dataset were younger than clients not known to have attacked sex workers, among whom the under 25 age group varied from 12 per cent to 22 per cent in various different surveys (Kinnell 2006b). The age profile of 'client' suspects charged with homicide of sex workers is also older than those charged with non-fatal attacks.[20]

---

[17]'Jailed rapist "used violence for his own satisfaction"', *Liverpool Daily Post*, 9 September 2006.
[18]'Man, 38, jailed for rape', *Liverpool Echo*, 14 December 2006.
[19]Four suspects who could not be identified as 'clients' or non-clients had an average age of 37, range 20 to 57.
[20]See Chapter 14, pages 184–5.

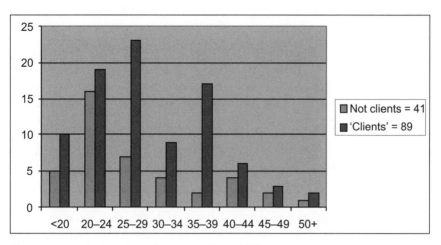

Figure 11.3 Age group of suspects (n = 130)

Ethnicity or cultural background has been identified by surnames, other information given in reports and photographs if available, but could not be determined for 50 suspects (36 per cent), all of whom had British names, except in three cases where the suspect's name was not publicised. Many of these are likely to have been white British, but others may have been from the Caribbean, Ireland or elsewhere. Of the 87 whose ethnicity could be identified, 37 were Asian (42 per cent); 34 were white, of whom nine were Eastern European and 25 are believed to have been British (39 per cent). Sixteen were black (18 per cent: seven African, six British and three Caribbean).

The ethnic-cultural profile of the suspects appeared to be strongly related to whether the attacks were committed by groups or by single assailants. Among the 40 suspects charged with group attacks, 22 (55 per cent) were Asian, 59 per cent of all Asian suspects, and seven (17.5 per cent) were Eastern European out of nine Eastern Europeans in the dataset. Four (10 per cent) were black, all believed to be British, but it is not known what proportion they represented of black British suspects in the dataset; one (2.5 per cent) was white British and the ethnicity of five suspects (12.5 per cent) is not known. In contrast, of the 99 'lone assailant' suspects, for 47 ethnicity is not known, although a high proportion of these are likely to have been white British. Of the remaining 52, 25 (48 per cent) were white, one of whom was Eastern European; 15 (29 per cent) were Asian and 12 (23 per cent) were black.

Group attacks

> Green ... was part of a group of up to six men who broke into
> the brothel in ... December 2004 ... [he was] found guilty of
> six counts of rape and two counts of robbery ... the gang had
> forced entry into the brothel threatening occupants with a gun
> and demanding cash and valuables.[21]

Forty suspects, in pairs or larger groups, were charged with attacks on
over 50 sex workers, having between one and seven known victims
each. In some cases not all members of these gangs were brought
to court or did not appear in court at the same time: numbers here
refer only to suspects for whom I have trial reports. Thirty of these
suspects were charged with rape or sexual assault; 23 with robbery
or conspiracy to rob; other offences included wounding with intent,
false imprisonment, kidnap, threats to kill, possession of firearms,
aggravated burglary and blackmail. Ten gangs (25 suspects) carried
out sexual attacks on street workers, often combined with robbery.
Seven gangs (15 suspects) targeted indoor sex work premises for
robbery, all in the South East; five of these gangs used sexual as
well as physical violence during their attacks; the other two used
extremely sadistic physical violence, during which one victim was
killed.

Offences

Attacks which resulted in a prosecution were overwhelmingly of
an extremely serious nature. Four suspects charged with non-fatal
attacks were concurrently charged with murder. Excluding these
homicide charges, the primary charges brought against 105 suspects
(76 per cent) were for rape or other sexual assault; 9 (6 per cent)
were charged with attempted murder, 15 for other physical assault
(11 per cent), and 10 (7 per cent) were charged with other offences
including robbery, false imprisonment, procuring and threatening or
disorderly behaviour (see Figure 11.4). These offences reflect most
kinds of attack that are reported via Ugly Mug schemes, with some
exceptions. Incidents which cause anxiety and distress rather than
physical harm, such as stalking and pestering, 'weird' behaviour,

---

[21]'Youth jailed for "horrific" rape', *BBC News*, 13 May 2005 (see http://news.
bbc.co.uk/go/pr/fr/-/1/hi/england/london/4545365.stm).

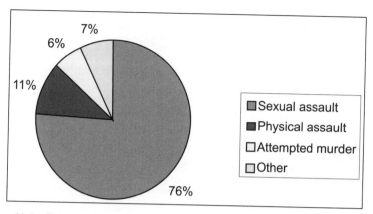

Figure 11.4 Primary charges against suspects

disputes over the use of condoms and disputes over payment, will rarely result in criminal proceedings unless they form part of a serious physical or sexual attack, but there are other categories of incident only minimally reflected in this dataset but regularly reported via Ugly Mug schemes. These include violence, abuse and harassment from the 'general public' (passers-by, residents, gangs of youths and vigilantes), 'clients' stealing back money after sex and robberies which are not accompanied by sexual assault, both on-street and off-street.

Where the 'primary offence' is listed as a sexual assault, there may also have been physical assault, robbery or false imprisonment charges as well, but where suspects were charged with attempted murder (nine suspects), in only one case was a suspect also charged with a sexual offence. Few suspects were charged with only one offence. For example, while 84 suspects were charged with rape, between them they faced 163 rape charges. Forty-seven were charged with one rape each, the remaining 37 were charged with between two and nine rapes each: 23 were also charged with robbery or theft; 20 were also charged with additional sexual assaults; 16 were also charged with kidnapping or false imprisonment, and 12 were charged with physical assault. One was also charged with the murder of a sex worker which had taken place three weeks before the rapes, and another was charged with the murder of a non-sex worker which occurred during the same episode as the rape. Sexual assault (usually rape) was the most common primary charge for all categories of assailant.

Figure 11.5 includes concurrent homicide charges, but excludes cases where the main charge was robbery (six suspects) and subsidiary or less serious offences.

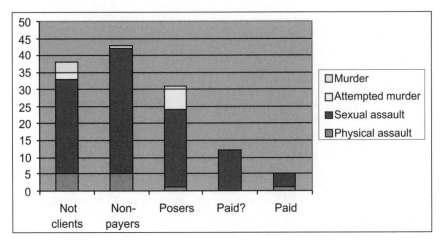

Figure 11.5 Primary offence by category of assailant (including murder charges)

Multiple victims and serial offenders

Sixty-three (45 per cent) of the suspects were charged with attacks on more than one sex worker. Thirty-six (26 per cent) were charged with attacks on two sex workers, and 27 (19 per cent) with attacks on three or more sex workers. Five were concurrently convicted of murder: three of the murder of two sex workers and two with the murders of a man and a woman who were not sex workers. Forty-two (30 per cent) were known to have been convicted of previous offences, ranging from drink-driving to murder; another two had previously been acquitted of murder. Thirty-six (26 per cent) were known to have previous convictions for violent or sexual offences. Several trial reports do not include sentencing, and those that do may not include details of previous convictions, therefore, the proportion of offenders with such convictions is likely to be even higher than these figures indicate.

'Clients' were much *less* likely than non-clients to have multiple sex worker victims: 39 per cent (36 out of 93) compared to 62 per cent (26 out of 42), but were only slightly less likely to have previous convictions of any kind (31 per cent compared to 36 per cent), and the level of previous convictions for violent or sexual offences was the same (27 per cent of clients; 26 per cent of non-clients). Even so, 'client' suspects were not 'typical clients'. The criminal careers of kerb-crawlers were explored by Brooks-Gordon (2006): under 6 per cent had a criminal record, and only eight out of over a thousand had convictions for sexual or other violence. Among kerb-crawlers in Southampton, only 8 per cent had previous convictions for violent and sexual offences (Shell *et al.* 2001). As in this analysis, both studies found that those with previous convictions were likely to be repeat offenders.

Outcome of court cases

Ten of the 139 suspects were acquitted on all counts. Several were acquitted on some charges but convicted on others. In a further 14 cases, the outcome of proceedings is not known. Excluding cases where the outcome of proceedings is not known, a conviction rate of over 90 per cent suggests that, even if it has been difficult to bring prosecutions against those who have harmed sex workers, juries *are* willing to convict if satisfied by the evidence. The success of prosecution illustrated by these figures may, however, paint an over-optimistic picture, since it is not possible to know whether the media are less likely to report on unsuccessful prosecutions or whether some media organisations filter out cases where suspects have been acquitted from their digital archives. It is somewhat concerning that eight out of the ten acquitted suspects were tried in Yorkshire and the North East, which *might* indicate regional bias against sex worker victims or witnesses, but it is also possible that this finding is merely an artefact of how the data was collected.

Because the cases were tried in both English and Scottish jurisdictions, and over a period of 18 years, during which time definitions of offences and sentencing guidelines have changed, it is not possible to derive any distinct patterns or trends in sentencing. However, some individual cases raise concerns around minimum periods of detention, particularly with regard to cases where an indefinite sentence for public protection (IPP) has been imposed. These issues will be explored further in Chapter 18.

Chapter 12

Motives for violence

The assumption that violence against sex workers nearly always comes from men who pay for sex has channelled deliberations over the reasons for this violence into theorising about the nature of the sex worker/client relationship, but the evidence presented thus far demonstrates that paying for sex is not commonly linked to violence, although *not* paying is. The LUML shows that 75 per cent of attacks on street workers were committed by those who did not pay; of those charged with non-fatal attacks on sex workers, 31 per cent were not clients or posing as clients and another 33 per cent posed as clients but then refused to pay and/or robbed their victims of all their money. Only 4 per cent were described as actually having paid.

If the radical feminist orthodoxy – that paying for sex is the ultimate expression of men's power to command the sexual subservience of women – were true, the frequency of violence from men who *refuse* to pay would be incomprehensible. But it is not incomprehensible: the explosions of anger that erupt when the sex worker insists on payment indicate that the problem is not that these men believe that paying for sex gives them the right to command women to obey their sexual demands or to inflict violence on them, but that they are insulted by the suggestion that they can only get sexual compliance if they pay, that they have the right to 'take' sex from these women and that refusing to pay asserts that right and demonstrates their power.

Hostile attitudes

The constellation of derogatory beliefs, contempt and hostility towards sex workers, expressed both physically and verbally by numerous attackers, is summed up by Miller and Schwartz (1995) as the 'fundamental belief that prostitutes are public property and that their bodies are open territory for assault'. Miller and Schwartz analyse the violence sex workers experience through the concept of 'rape myths', thus characterising that violence as predominantly sexual, and implying that assailants are usually clients. However, the same attitudes unite the man who uses brute force to drag a woman down an alleyway, the man who uses a uniform to intimidate a woman into compliance, the man who entices a woman with the promise of payment then rapes her and watches while his friends do the same, and the man who robs a woman of all her money, ensuring that she does not benefit from having been paid by others. They also frequently surface in the physical assaults, community violence, individual vigilantism, verbal abuse and general harassment which sex workers experience more often than they suffer sexual assault. Nevertheless, the four themes, which Miller and Schwartz describe as 'rape myths' – that 'sex workers are unrapeable', that 'no harm is done', that 'they deserve to be raped' and that 'all sex workers are the same' – do resonate with descriptions of attacks and justifications expressed by attackers in Ugly Mugs and trial reports, although rape is not necessarily, or even most frequently, the form of violence used.

Many reports indicate that attackers view sex workers as 'unrapeable' since, because they have previously consented to sex with multiple partners, they have given up the right to refuse other partners or other acts, sometimes with the variant whereby a sex worker, having agreed to sex with one man, can then be raped by his friends:

> Took her to his nearby flat ... arranged price outside and also said he would be alone. Once in flat man only had half the money so girl declined business. Man called out and 2 men appeared who held her down whilst the original man raped her. (Midlands 2002)

> Man approached and asked for business. Walking away from road he said he had lots of money but was going to rape her. (North 2003)

The belief that 'no harm is done' if a sex worker is raped seems based on the rationale that since the woman has frequent sex anyway, the event is no more than a 'bad business deal':

> He ... punched her and refused to pay, forced oral sex and then raped her. Asked why she was crying and asked personal details; when she managed to get away he walked off as if nothing had happened. (London 2004)

The 'no harm done' belief was also voiced in the trial of Christopher Savill for raping a Glasgow sex worker. Savill described sex workers as being on 'the lowest rung of the ladder', while his defence counsel 'stressed that ... she was uninjured afterwards.'[1] A variant of the 'no harm done' belief, 'that prostitutes' lives are not valuable enough for violence against them to be taken seriously' (Miller and Schwartz 1995), has sometimes characterised law enforcement attitudes in the past, and may still underlie assailants' expectations that they will not be punished for attacking sex workers:

> He said he could do anything he wanted to me because I was a prostitute and a smack head. He said 'if you disappeared, who would be bothered?'[2]

The belief that sex workers 'deserve to be raped', because they have violated the norms of behaviour for 'good' women leading to justifiable anger and moral indignation, sexual violence here being used as it is in war situations, as a weapon of punishment and subjugation, is also evident. A serial gang rapist 'told one of his victims that he "couldn't stand prostitutes" and threatened there would be vigilante-style "lynches" to rid the streets of them.' In this case, defence counsel appeared to echo his client's belief that the practice of selling sex justified rape, pointing out 'that the women would have been willing to have sex with them for money.' The judge, however, was not moved, saying, 'That does not provide anyone with a reason or excuse to attack them or terrify them. This was clearly the abuse and humiliation of prostitutes.'[3] Violence as a sign of moral superiority was also claimed by Crawford Nakasala, who said he had killed a parlour worker to 'show his contempt' for

---

[1] 'Man jailed for raping prostitute', *The Herald*, 17 April 2007.
[2] 'Rapist used screwdriver to threaten prostitute', *Northern Echo*, 16 June 2002; 'Rapist given 10 years for second attack', *The Scotsman*, 1 July 2006.
[3] 'Students jailed for prostitute attacks', *Telegraph & Argus*, 8 March 2005.

her. (She had accused him of stealing from the parlour.)[4] This reaction from a would-be client on being turned down by a sex worker also exemplifies a furious need to assert moral superiority and command subservience:

> Picked up girl, but girl did not want to do business so he beat her up very badly saying; "I AM NOT A BAD MAN, I AM A GOOD MAN". (Midlands 2002)

Victimising sex workers may also be seen as worthy of praise and fame: David Fairbanks, convicted of raping a sex worker in Stoke-on-Trent in 2001, said he wanted to 'go down in history',[5] and Rizwan Yaqub, convicted of raping two sex workers in Sheffield in 2004, was heard saying after his arrest, 'I'll be massive when I come out. I'll be the next serial killer.'[6]

Miller and Schwartz relate the fourth element, that 'all sex workers are the same', to the concept of 'collective liability', whereby all persons in a perceived group are held responsible for all others in the same category.[7] This attitude is most clearly expressed in revenge attacks by men who claim to have been 'ripped off' by sex workers in the past: 'She was viciously assaulted as the man demanded her money saying that another woman had robbed him and she would pay for it.'[8] Others also seem to regard sex workers as publicly available objects for anyone to vent their anger on, whether or not their anger has anything to do with individual sex workers or sex workers as a group: Robert Sinclair, already a convicted rapist, attacked a sex worker in Glasgow only two months after his release from his previous sentence; he told police he had planned the attack, saying 'I was having a bad day. I wanted to do it. I thought it out.'[9]

---

[4]'Parlour maid killed by her own thong', *icSouthLondon*, 18 July 2006 (see http://icsouthlondon.icnetwork.co.uk).

[5]Fairbanks was first convicted of rape ten years earlier, aged 18. 'Prostitute rapist jailed for life', *The Sentinel*, 28 April 2001.

[6]'"Naive" man jailed for raping two vice girls', *The Star*, 26 November 2004 (see http://www.thestar.co.uk/news/39Naive39-man-jailed-for-raping.895433.jp).

[7]Miller and Schwartz (1995), quoting D. Black (1983) 'Crime as social control', *American Sociological Review*, 48: 34–45.

[8]Ugly Mug report, North West 2003.

[9]'Rapist struck again weeks after release on licence', *The Scotsman*, 21 April 2006.

An extension of 'collective liability' is where the assailant regards sex workers as representing all women; attacks and murders have sometimes been explained by the assailant having a grudge against women or seeking revenge for rejection by another woman. Miller and Schwartz also suggest that some attackers are enraged by a 'new order' in gender roles, against which they 'fight back violently trying to reimpose the sexual order of a previous generation'. Dahir Ibrahim, convicted of raping street sex workers in Birmingham, expressed this clearly; when interviewed, he said 'that prostitutes were "dirty women" and that "a woman's place was at home, not on the street".'[10]

The influence of 'rape myths' on the behaviour of sex workers' clients has been explored extensively since Miller and Schwartz published their exposition, through questionnaires administered to men attending 'John Schools' in the USA and Canada. To the apparent surprise of some investigators, acceptance of 'rape myths' was found to be no more prominent among those who paid for sex than among those who did not (Monto and Hotaling 2001). This conundrum can be reconciled to the prominence of these attitudes among those who attack sex workers, because so many attackers are *not* clients and, therefore, perhaps not likely to have been surveyed in programmes aimed at clients.

Miller and Schwartz did not explore the identity of attackers in any detail; however, many descriptions of attacks on sex workers make clear that *not* paying is inextricably linked to the motivation behind the violence. For example, Duncan Smith, convicted of raping a sex worker in Norwich in 2005, had threatened her with an imitation gun, saying 'This time you're going to do it for free'. Four men convicted of gang rapes in Manchester in 2000 had 'lured [the women] into a car by one of the men posing as a 'punter' while the others hid nearby', and after one rape, 'one of the four men callously threw a 50p at her, saying: "Here's a tip"'.[11] A street worker in London was raped by a man who agreed to her price, but once out of sight of other people, started smashing her head against a wall, repeating 'I don't pay'. It is evident that such men do regard sex workers with contempt and do want to dominate, humiliate and hurt, but it is also apparent that they are *not* clients: they do *not* pay.

---

[10]'Serial rapist was given an ASBO to keep him off streets', *The Times*, 14 August 2006.
[11]'Gang is jailed after attacks on prostitutes', *Rochdale Observer*, 19 April 2000.

Some apparent motivations for violence are not fully represented in the 'public property' and 'open territory for assault' cluster of attitudes, although they are clearly part of the same spectrum. Dissatisfaction with sexual services – often the inability to achieve an erection or to ejaculate within the time limit – as a trigger for violence, was explored in Chapter 5 (see page 61), and it was noted that this is mentioned relatively infrequently in sex workers' accounts of violence. However, rage at being unable to perform sexually is one of the few 'reasons' for violence given by murderers.[12] This could be interpreted as the urge to punish and destroy the woman who has failed in her perceived fundamental responsibility to 'give satisfaction' and has witnessed his deficient manhood, but frustration and rage at more generalised impotence – incompetence as a sexual being – might also underlie other attacks, where the anger does not necessarily arise from failure to perform sexually, but from the inability to get sex without paying for it. This kind of motivation may also be behind attacks where the 'non-client excuse' is proffered, perhaps in the belief that violence will be regarded as an understandable reaction to being asked to pay, or to hide 'shame' at being obliged to pay.[13]

Monto and Hotaling (2001) found a small percentage of clients did subscribe to the hostile beliefs encapsulated in 'rape myths', which is reflected in the evidence from Ugly Mugs, that such clients do exist but constitute a small proportion of assailants; only 9 per cent of street workers' reports to the LUML were of sexual violence from a paying client, and 10 per cent of those from indoor workers. Sexual arousal through inflicting fear, pain and humiliation was evident in other attacks, but not associated with payment. This is not to argue that refusal to pay is worse than sadistic violence, but to demonstrate that sadism is not invariably or even commonly associated with paying for sex. For example, Frank Ormesher, who attacked and robbed two sex workers in Bolton within 75 minutes using a two-foot-long iron bar, had targeted them 'because they were prostitutes and were attacked for no other reason'. Prosecuting counsel said: 'Their money was taken but this was not motivated by robbery. This was gratuitous violence with a sexual motive.'[14] Arun Patnaik, 'who carried out a campaign of rape, sadism and degradation' against

---

[12]See Chapter 14, pages 190–3, and Chapter 17, page 248.
[13]See Chapter 5, page 63.
[14]'Life for prostitute attacks', *Manchester Evening News*, 13 December 2005; 'Attack horror', *Bolton Evening News*, 19 July 2005.

sex workers, acting out 'scenes from his depraved and sadistic pornographic library', was also a non-payer.[15]

Attackers may also target sex workers, not because they are sex workers, but simply because they are vulnerable, due to their unprotected situations when working.[16] Robbers who systematically target indoor sex work premises may choose to do so primarily because they assume that sex workers will not complain to the police, although the extremities of violence often used and the sexual assaults in the course of these attacks may reflect similar attitudes of contempt towards sex workers as is exhibited by those who approach in other guises. Although it is a mistake to assume that those who attack and murder sex workers are primarily motivated by a specific hatred for sex workers, it is also unquestionably the case that many assailants repeatedly target sex workers. Nearly half (47 per cent) of those charged with non-fatal attacks (Chapter 11) had multiple sex worker victims, and non-clients were more likely to have attacked multiple victims (62 per cent) than those who approached as clients (39 per cent).

Provocation

In homicide cases, assailants sometimes claim that the victim provoked the attack, through arguments over money, attempted robbery or verbal insults (Brewer *et al.* 2006), but in none of the cases examined in Chapter 11 was an excuse of this kind reported, perhaps because the victims were alive and able to dispute such claims. 'Arguments over money' can be interpreted in the light of numerous Ugly Mug and press reports as refusal to pay, and 'verbal insults' may be connected to the ubiquitous problem of impotence. Whether the victim has actually made some disparaging comment or not may be unimportant to the man who feels she is to blame for his detumescence. Robbery, however, may be a real grievance. As mentioned above, sex workers often report being attacked by someone who claims to have been robbed by another sex worker, and while robbing punters is recognised as likely to produce this kind of reaction, it does happen, especially if sex workers are under

---

[15]Mike Slingsby, 'Rapist gets 9 life sentences', *Manchester Evening News*, 17 November 2006; "Sadistic' rapist loses appeal bid', *Preston Citizen*, 13 July 2007.
[16]See Chapter 11.

pressure from lack of clients, low prices and the demands of drug dependence.

Homicide and non-fatal violence

> The difference between homicide and assault may simply be the intervention of a bystander, the accuracy of a gun, the weight of a frying pan, the speed of an ambulance or the availability of a trauma centre.[17]

This narrow margin between homicide and assault is evident in some of the cases of non-fatal violence analysed.[18] One offender was Noel Dooley, who stabbed a sex worker in Bradford 43 times in October 2000, while shouting, 'You bitches are all the same. Die bitch, die.'[19] He was confronted by passers-by, leading to his swift arrest and prompt attention for his victim, who survived. Another was Leigh Thornhill, who tried to strangle a sex worker in Croydon in 2003: she bit him in the neck, shouted and got away, but a few hours later Thornhill murdered another woman who was not a sex worker.[20] Both Dooley and Thornhill evidently intended to commit murder, but Dooley failed because passers-by intervened; Thornhill succeeded, but with a different victim. In their intention to kill, they may have been unlike the majority of assailants; as Dorling (2005) argues, most homicides are 'acts of sudden violence, premeditated only for a few minutes or seconds, probably without the intent to actually kill in many cases.' Brookman and Maguire (2003) also observe that the patterns of homicide and characteristics of suspects are very similar to those for violent crime in general. However, although it seems reasonable to suppose that the scenarios and motivations for sex worker homicide will be similar to those found in cases of non-fatal violence, there are differences between the datasets. Case inclusion in the analysis of non-fatal attacks was dependent on chance factors,

---

[17]Gottfredson, M.R. and Hirschi, T. (1990), *A General Theory of Crime*, Stanford, California: Stanford University Press.

[18]See Chapter 11.

[19]'Woman sobs as she recalls stab ordeal', *Yorkshire Post*, 17 October 2001.

[20]'CCTV bid to catch killer', *BBC News*, 27 August 2003 (see http://news. bbc.co.uk/1/hi/england/london/3184113.stm); 'Man gets life for murder', *Metropolitan Police*, 30 September 2004 (see http://www.croydonontheweb. com/mynews/news/).

whereas the number of homicide cases analysed is very similar to official figures.[21] The geographic distribution of the two datasets is also somewhat different, and there are differences in the demographic profile of suspects charged with homicide. These differences might also indicate differing motivations, which will be explored in the following chapters.

---

[21]See Chapter 13, page 163.

Chapter 13

Murder of sex workers

'And then the silly girl went and got herself murdered'

Gail Whitehouse was the 'silly girl'. She was 23 and the mother of two children. She worked the street beat in Wolverhampton until September 1990, when she was strangled. She was the first sex worker to be murdered about whom I knew something personally: she sometimes worked in Birmingham and was known to my outreach team, but she had also made the papers some months before her death for having all her fines written off at a court appearance before Wolverhampton magistrates. Her comments to reporters remain a succinct indictment of the criminalisation of sex work:

> I think the decision of the court was brilliant. It makes a mockery of the whole system. I was originally paying £4 a week in fines but because I have been arrested so often, they put up the payment to £30 a week. There was no way I could afford to pay over £4,600 in any case. It was pointless them fining me that amount in the first place. I have been a prostitute for two-and-a-half years and I suppose I have been arrested between 80 and 90 times. It is ridiculous to have fines like that brought against you. Nobody could possibly afford to pay them.[1]

---

[1]'Outcry as vice girl has fines written off', *Shropshire Star*, 13 February 1990.

She was then rearrested for loitering later the same day, which annoyed the police, who thoroughly disapproved of the magistrates' isolated attempt to break the cycle of arrest/fines/soliciting-to-repay-fines/arrest. It also annoyed the magistrates, and it was one of these magistrates who later called Gail a silly girl who got herself murdered. She was a well-meaning lady who attended the same meetings I did to discuss the problems of prostitution, which was where she made this remark. Perhaps it was just a figure of speech, like talking about girls 'getting themselves pregnant', but perhaps it betrayed how deeply even the well-meaning regard sex workers as being to blame for all their misfortunes, including being murdered. Gail's story also illustrates a recurring theme among street working murder victims: they are often deeply enmeshed in the institutions of the law, but these institutions seem able only to punish, not protect them.

In exploring sex worker murders, I have not dwelt on the stories of individual victims, partly to avoid creating the impression that their deaths were caused by their own difficulties, but mainly because the evidence overwhelmingly incriminates structural factors – legislation, law enforcement, and attitudes of contempt towards sex workers – as the causes of their vulnerability.

Perceptions of sex workers' risk of murder

> I would be happier if I knew whether she was working as a prostitute when she killed, because it does affect how you feel. Not being a prostitute myself, if she was working then I wouldn't feel as at risk myself, but if she was just walking along and someone pulled her into a back alley as a random thing then I would be very worried. I hope the police will be open with us and tell us what they know.[2]

There are a number of widely held assumptions about sex workers and the dangers they encounter which place their experiences into the realm of 'things that can't happen to me or to people I care about.' It is assumed that those who kill sex workers are motivated by a specific hatred of sex workers and/or have a perverted sexuality which can only be satisfied by killing; that their attacks are planned

---

[2]'Are sex workers killer's target?', *The Sentinel*, 27 March 2008 (see http://www.thesentinel.co.uk/).

and targeted; that sex workers' lives inevitably expose them to such killers; that people who murder sex workers do not murder other people, and, therefore, that the rest of us are safe. None of these assumptions is true. Sex worker murders rarely show any sign of premeditation; motivations – where they can be known or guessed at – are varied; many of those who attack sex workers also have a history of violence towards people who are not sex workers, including men, women and children. Also, sex workers' risk of encountering deadly violence is not uniform but strongly influenced by their working methods, which are in turn strongly related to legislation and law enforcement practice.

Sex worker murders are also quite rare, especially in comparison to murders in the context of domestic violence. Home Office figures show that 1,157 women in England and Wales were killed by a partner or ex-partner in the years 1995–2005/6 (Coleman *et al.* 2007), 40 per cent of all female homicides[3] and 19 times the number of female sex workers[4] (62) killed in the same period, 2 per cent of female homicides. Dorling (2005) analysed over 13,000 homicides from 1981 to 2000, finding that risk of murder was strongly correlated to poverty, with those living in the poorest neighbourhoods being six times more likely to be murdered than those in affluent areas. This factor alone is also likely to influence sex workers' risk of murder. Among adult victims in Dorling's analysis, working-class men were most at risk, but the following comment might also apply to sex workers:

> The rate of murder represents the tip of an iceberg of violence. It can be seen as a marker of social harm. For murder rates to rise in particular places, and for a particular group of people living there, life in general has to be made more difficult to live, people have to be made to feel more worthless. (Dorling 2005)

Potterat *et al.* (2004) have examined female sex workers' risk of murder in the USA, estimating that they were 18 times more likely to be murdered than women of similar demographic characteristics. More recent work by these investigators estimates that 2.7 per cent of female homicide victims in the USA were sex workers (Brewer *et al.* 2006). The only British study (Ward *et al.* 1999), which reports on

---

[3]That is, 'offences currently recorded as homicide' – see Coleman *et al.* (2007) for definitions of homicide.

[4]The two murders of male sex workers have been excluded from these comparisons.

mortality from *all* causes among female sex workers, estimated that the mortality rate was 12 times the normal rate for women in this age group, but Ward *et al.* do *not* compare the risk of murder in their cohort with the risk for all women in the same age range. Bindel and Atkins (2007) misreport their findings, saying the 'mortality rate for women in street prostitution in London equals twelve times the national average'. Ward *et al.* explicitly state that of the four deaths in their study two died of AIDS and two were murdered, neither of whom were street workers.

I hope to shed some light on the characteristics of both victims and killers, the circumstances in which homicides have taken place and the outcomes of homicide investigations. However, given the absence of firm estimates of the numbers of sex workers active in this country and the difficulties in obtaining accurate figures about numbers of homicides among this group, I shall not attempt to compare sex workers' risk of becoming the victims of homicide with any other group in society. Lack of access to official information means that this examination of sex worker homicides cannot be more than it is – a painstaking look at such information as is available to me. If others have more comprehensive information which supports different conclusions, let them publish and enlighten the rest of us!

Sources of information

Brookman and Maguire (2003), reporting on strategies to reduce the level of homicides, observe that sex worker deaths are likely to go unrecorded due to limitations in the coding systems for reporting. Forty per cent of homicide victims were categorised as unemployed, which, they acknowledge, may conceal deaths among sex workers. However, information obtained in February 2007 from the Home Office under the Freedom of Information Act includes a table relating to 'offences initially recorded as homicide where the victim was a prostitute' (England and Wales only), indicating that such information has become available, if only recently.

In the absence of official data, media reports and Internet searches have been an important source of information. I have also received information from local sources, from friends and colleagues close to the victims and occasionally from investigating officers. Most of this information is in the public domain, but in a few cases there are details about victims or suspects which are not public knowledge. I shall not be divulging any privileged information. Without access to police data, and because there are few reports relating to the early 1990s available on the Internet, it is likely that my figures under-represent the true scale of deadly violence against sex workers, especially in the years 1990 to 1998. This supposition is strengthened by the Home Office table referred to above, which records 40 homicides between 1990 and 1997, whereas I have recorded 34.[5]

Other sex worker homicides may be hidden among the figures for 'missing persons'. Tens of thousands of people go missing every year, sex workers among them. As Brookman and Maguire (2003) state, 'We do not know how many killers manage to dispose of the bodies of their victims without trace.' During 2007, the bodies of two young women (not sex workers) were discovered 16 years after they disappeared,[6] demonstrating the problem of determining whether 'missing persons' have or have not been murdered unless they turn up alive or their bodies are eventually discovered. Some issues around 'going missing' and homicide are explored below, but death by homicide may be inadvertently concealed in other ways. In my own experience there have been deaths among sex workers about which I and my colleagues had suspicions but were not investigated as possible homicides. One woman fell from the top of a multi-storey car park, another died in a fire. They were treated as suicide and misadventure – plausible explanations, but not the only possibilities. Another was the death of a young woman from a drugs overdose. She was not known to be a drug user, but her death was not treated as suspicious. A few months later another young woman, not known to use hard drugs, died from a heroin overdose. Two men were accused of giving her a large dose of unusually pure heroin and both were convicted of her manslaughter. There is no evidence to suggest any link between these two cases, but there may be other deaths from drug overdose for which third parties may be culpable.

It is not, therefore, over-melodramatic to suggest that there may have been many more homicides among sex workers where the victims were not identified as sex workers or where deaths were not investigated as homicides or where sex workers have simply

---

[5]Apart from this discrepancy, my figures per year are very similar to the Home Office figures in the table referred to, but this table does not sum the cases into an overall total because of a change in the reporting periods in 1997/8.

[6]'Second body is missing girl Dinah', *BBC News*, 16 November 2007 (see http://news.bbc.co.uk/go/pr/fr/-/1/hi/england/7099290.stm).

'gone missing', but between January 1990 and December 2006, 118 sex workers died or disappeared in circumstances that did lead to a homicide investigation: 104 in England, 13 in Scotland and 1 in Northern Ireland – an average of 7 per year.

Defining victims as sex workers

Brewer *et al.* (2006) use the term 'prostitution-related homicide' to include victims who were pimps and clients. I have not followed these authors' inclusion of pimps and clients, but I have included two victims who worked in the broader sex industry: a clip-joint hostess and a lap-dancer, and four who died in attacks at massage parlours who were not or may not have been selling sexual services personally, but were exposed to the same vulnerabilities as those whose involvement was more direct. There are also two male and one transgender sex workers in my analysis, and a bona fide masseuse whose killer is known to have attacked sex workers in the same locality. This case is included partly because the police force concerned includes it in their statistics of violence against sex workers, but also because the murderer may have applied to her the same attitudes he brought to his encounters with sex workers who operated in a similar way. These victims may not have been defined as prostitutes by the Home Office so not included in their data, but I have included them in mine. I also include the cases in Scotland and Northern Ireland.

Missing presumed dead

Street working women are often characterised as leading chaotic lives, estranged from their families, liable to take off without warning. If they vanish from their usual locations, it may be assumed they have gone to work in other towns – especially if there is a crackdown against prostitution on their usual beats or if they are subject to an ASBO or have warrants out against them – or that they are on the run from violent pimps or from dealers to whom they owe money. They 'go missing' too frequently for instant alarm bells to ring – except with those who are closest to them and are best able to judge.

I know of only three 'missing' cases where a homicide investigation is believed to be ongoing,[7] but at least 26 other victims went missing for between a week and over a year before a homicide investigation started. The body of Chantel Taylor, who went missing from her home in Birkenhead in March 2004, was never found, but 16 months later, a man responsible for an arson attack on a mosque the day after the London bombings of 7 July 2005 confessed to her murder. Chantel's family and friends had been convinced her disappearance was ominous from the start; the UKNSWP[8] sent out Chantel's description to all outreach projects within three weeks of her disappearance, but because she was a drug user, local police claimed 'no evidence had emerged that led them to believe a criminal act had taken place', and put her disappearance down to her 'chaotic lifestyle'.[9] The other 25 women had been missing between one week and four months before their bodies were found. Nine of these cases are currently unsolved (36 per cent), including one case which resulted in a murder conviction in 1998 but the conviction was declared unsafe in 2005.

The case of Donna Healey illustrates how investigations may continue for many years after the initial disappearance. She was last seen alive at Leeds magistrates court in 1988. Her mother told the Salvation Army of her disappearance in 1991, but the police did not record her as a missing person until 1997. Donna's body had been found in 1991, but was not conclusively identified until 2003. The uterus was missing and pathologists at first believed the victim was male.[10] The investigation of this case is ongoing, but it is not included in this analysis as it is assumed Donna died before 1990.

---

[7]Following the conviction of Steve Wright for five murders in Ipswich (February 2008), there is speculation that the disappearances of sex workers Amanda Duncan (Ipswich 1993) and Kellie Pratt (Norwich 2000) may be linked to Wright. These cases are not included in this analysis.

[8]UKNSWP – UK Network of Sex Work Projects.

[9]Kate Mansey, 'Killer chopped off Chantel's head', Liverpool Echo, 26 January 2006; 'End the soft-touch sentences for killers without a conscience', Liverpool Echo, 13 July 2006; personal communications to the author.

[10]'DNA link on 1980s body in garden', The Guardian, 24 October 2003; 'Prostitute's death still a mystery', Yorkshire Post, 5 May 2004; Crimewatch UK, BBC1 Television, 27 January 2004.

Gender

Only 2 of the 118 victims were male.[11] As male sex workers have the added risk of encountering homophobic violence, it is probable that others have been killed in the time period covered, but if so, their deaths have not been associated with sex work in media reports accessed, nor reported to me by agencies working with male sex workers. This in itself is interesting. There were male sex workers among the victims of Dennis Nilsen, who killed around 15 young men between 1978 and 1983 (Wilson 2007), but, as Alibhai-Brown noted, the press coverage of the Nilsen case was not 'smeared in drool', unlike media reactions to the Ipswich murders.[12] It may be that homicides of male sex workers are not publicised as such because, like Nilsen's crimes, they are recognised as homophobic, and any involvement of the victims in selling sex is not considered relevant to their vulnerability or to their killers' motivations.

The two known UK cases exemplify opposite ends of the spectrum of male sex work. One was a 15-year-old 'rent boy', killed by two other teenagers in what appears to have been a homophobic attack. He was punched and kicked before being pushed into a canal, where he drowned.[13] The second male victim was a 32-year-old masseur, killed by three extremely violent robbers who had also attacked several women at indoor sex work venues. One of the victims was a pre-operative transgender woman (Gilbert *et al.* 2007). It is possible that other victims were also transgender, whose identity as women was never publicly questioned. However, there does not seem to have been any overt targetting of trans sex workers by murderous attackers in Britain, in contrast to the USA, Canada and Portugal, where serial attacks and murders have been reported among this group.[14] All the other victims are listed as female.

---

[11]Male sex workers in other countries have experienced extreme violence, as illustrated by the massacre of nine male masseurs in Cape Town in January 2003; 'Eight killed in gay massage parlour', *The Guardian*, 21 January 2003.
[12]Yasmin Alibhai-Brown, 'Where are the men in this horrific story?', *The Independent*, 18 December 2006.
[13]'Thug guilty of rent boy murder', *Manchester Evening News*, 21 March 2001.
[14]See page 36.

Age at death

Age at death is known for 110 sex workers (see Figure 13.1): 55 (50 per cent) were aged under 25 years; eight were under 18 years (7 per cent). The mean age was 26 years, with a range of 14 to 55. My analysis of homicides up to May 2004 (Kinnell 2006a) showed an age range of 14 to 46, and 61 per cent were under 25 years. Since then, no victim was under 19 but five cases where the victims were over 40 have been added since my earlier analysis, whose average age was nearly 48, which will have pulled up the mean age of the dataset.[15] The average age of the 26 victims who died after May 2004 was 28 years. The age distribution is very similar to that found in most larger surveys of sex workers, and like such surveys reflects the preponderance of street workers among the victims, who tend to be younger on average than off-street workers. All victims under 18, and 80 per cent of those between the ages of 18 and 34, were street workers. Of those aged 35 to 55, 60 per cent were street workers and 40 per cent worked indoors.

The fact that no recent victim was under 19 may attest to the work which is being done to prevent young people becoming involved in the sex industry, but the older age profile of recent victims, one-third of whom worked in off-street settings, suggests that vulnerability is not so strongly associated with youth and street work as in the past.

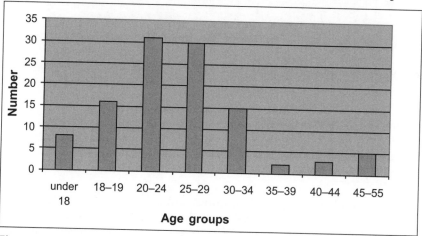

Figure 13.1 Age group of sex workers at death

---

[15]Three of these deaths occurred prior to May 2004 but were not then known to the author.

Geographical distribution of homicides

One hundred and four deaths occurred in England, 13 in Scotland and one in Northern Ireland (see Figure 13.2). I have not identified any cases since 1990 in Wales. The English cases seem to be distributed roughly as might be expected in relation to main concentrations of population, although difficulties in accessing information from the London area may have resulted in undercounting for this region. The Scottish situation is very different, with three cases in the east of Scotland and ten others in Glasgow and its environs. There have been significant regional differences in official attitudes to prostitution in Scotland, which may have impacted on sex workers' safety, although the current policy on sex work, approved by the Scottish Parliament, favours the Glasgow model over more tolerant and apparently safer strategies formerly adopted in Aberdeen and Edinburgh.

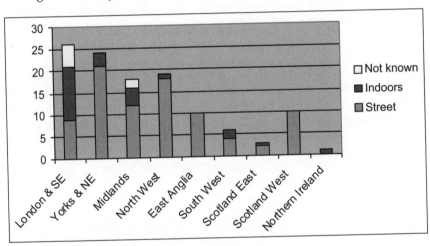

Figure 13.2 Region of deaths 1990–2006

Ethnicity and nationality

Ethnicity and cultural background impact on disadvantage and vulnerability in so many ways, it might be expected that these factors would be evident in the demographic profile of sex worker homicide victims. This does not appear to be the case. Surveys which have explored the nationality or ethnicity of sex workers in Britain have usually shown a distribution which reflects the local population characteristics, with a large majority being white British women in most areas (Hester and Westmarland 2004). This pattern is reflected in the ethnic profile of murder victims. Ethnicity has been determined by information about the background of victims in media reports and photographs where available. No such information is available for 15 victims (13 per cent), but among the rest 86 (83 per cent) were white British, 10 were non-white British (10 per cent), 4 were from Eastern Europe (4 per cent) and 4 were from elsewhere (4 per cent).

Drug use

Drug use is often assumed to be linked to risk of violence, since it can impair judgement in assessing potentially dangerous situations and reduce the ability to react to or escape from violence. Drug users may also work longer hours and service more clients to make sufficient money to pay for their own, and sometimes their partners' drug use. The individual circumstances of various homicides indicate how drug use may impact on sex workers' vulnerability: some victims had recently had their methadone prescriptions stopped or were known to be in debt to dealers, both of which situations may have pushed them into accepting clients they did not trust or working longer hours. However, it may be the drug use of the killer that is the precipitating factor, rather than that of the victim, and this question is explored further in relation to suspects charged with homicide.[16]

Sixty-six victims were known to use drugs, all of them street workers (56 per cent of all victims; 76 per cent of street workers), and this figure may underestimate the total with drug use problems. None of the indoor workers were known to use illegal drugs. Superficially it seems the link between drug use and risk of violence is self-evident. However, Barnard *et al.* (2001) concluded that working outdoors was the one significant risk factor associated with violence: drug use only appeared to increase risk because it is strongly associated with street work, which is the crucial risk factor. Since Barnard *et al.* collected their data, the association between street work and drug use has strengthened, and this is reflected in the known drug use of homicide victims. In the first half of the period (January 1990 to June 1998), 58 per cent of street victims were known to use heroin or crack; in the second half (July 1998 to December 2006), 87 per cent did so. However, the proportion of street victims in each period remained

---

[16]See Chapter 14, page 186.

the same, suggesting that increased drug use has not increased the relative risk of street work, despite its increased prevalence.

Other risk factors

There are other characteristics of victims, such as inexperience, working in unfamiliar locations and even physical stature, which might impact on their vulnerability, but my information is not sufficiently comprehensive to draw any firm conclusions about the influence of these factors. Several were small women, sometimes cited as a risk factor attracting aggression,[17] but others were of average height or over, and for most such information is not available. Some street workers were new to the area where they were killed and had not perhaps had time to link in to local networks through which they could have been warned of known serial attackers or 'dodgy punters'. Emma Merry, forced out of Wolverhampton by draconian policing in 1994, was working in Stoke-on-Trent when she was murdered by a man who was known to local women as a dangerous client, but Emma, as an outsider, did not know and she was killed. Another apparent casualty of anti-prostitution initiatives was Amanda Walker, killed by David Smith in London in April 1999. She was from Leeds, where West Yorkshire police were then implementing a vigorous anti-kerb-crawler policy in association with the Kerb-crawler Rehabilitation experiment run by Leeds Metropolitan University. The course organisers had already been warned that this approach would drive women to work in areas where they did not know the risks, including which clients to avoid.[18] Smith was a known 'Ugly Mug' in Paddington, and at 6ft 3" tall, weighing 19 stone and nick-named 'Lurch' after the Addams Family character, he would not have been hard to pick out. But as an out-of-towner, Amanda would not have known to avoid him.[19]

Some were inexperienced as sex workers: three of the eight sex workers who were killed in Glasgow between 1995 and 1997 had been working the streets for less than six months, but others had as

---

[17]Jean Rafferty, 'Double jeopardy', Guardian Weekend, 14 March 1998.
[18]Letter to Leslie Wagner, Vice Chancellor, Leeds Metropolitan University, 23 March 1999; c.c. Jalna Hanmer, Julie Bindel and others; from Hilary Kinnell, representing Europap-UK.
[19]'Killer beat earlier murder charge', BBC News, 8 December 1999 (see http://news.bbc.co.uk/1/hi/uk/556081.stm).

many as 20 years' experience, and for most there is no information about how long they had been working. Some, like one of Anthony Hardy' victims (London 2002), may have had experience of working indoors but not on the street. Elizabeth Valad had previously worked in sex flats in Soho but was forced into street work when Westminster Council adopted an aggressive cleansing strategy towards this traditional aspect of the area's economy.[20]

Several victims were homeless, of 'no fixed abode' or literally roofless. Research among homeless people in 2004 found that 52 per cent had experienced violence in the past year (Newburn and Rock 2004), and homeless sex workers' vulnerability may be increased by agreeing to go to clients' homes to do business.[21] Two of the Ipswich victims, Annette Nicholls and Paula Clennell, were of no fixed abode; Rebecca Stephenson was living in an old car (Doncaster 2005); Leona McGovern and Amy Anderson, (Glasgow 1995; Dunbartonshire 2002) were sleeping rough; Janet Rushby, aged 50, was of no fixed abode (London 2003); Nikola Higgins was sleeping on the streets with an abusive boyfriend who was barred from all housing registers, and as Nikola wouldn't leave him, no one was able to house her (Stoke-on-Trent 2001); Zoe Parker (London 2000), aged 24, of no fixed abode and with mental health issues and learning difficulties, would have sex in exchange for a meal or a bed for the night and craved warmth and affection ...

Several had suffered acute problems and personal tragedies, such as the death of friends or family members shortly before being killed, and others had had their children taken into care. It seems possible that grief and depression arising out of such events may have led to heavier than usual use of drugs, dulling their vigilance and self-preservation instincts, but it could be simply that so many street workers have multiple sources of pain and loss that such factors are no more likely to come up in the recent past of those who are murdered than those who are not.

The forensic psychologist, Paul Britton, enumerates several factors that he regards as likely to influence sex workers' risk of homicide, including their mobility, safety awareness and method of work, whether indoors or outdoors, alone or with others, all of which seem quite sensible. However, he also lists characteristics such as appearance, temperament – 'disdainful' or 'motherly' – and intelligence. He does not explain how these attributes might increase or decrease sex

---

[20]'Move to clean up Soho', *Evening Standard*, 7 June 2004. See pages 221–3.
[21]See pages 177–8.

workers' vulnerability, but their inclusion suggests he believes some sex workers may precipitate deadly attacks by a 'bad attitude' or lack the interpersonal skills to defuse homicidal tendencies (Britton 2001). I have no information that casts light on victims' temperament or intelligence, nor do I think it very likely that these factors have much importance in sex workers' overall risk of homicide, although they may influence the outcomes of confrontations at an individual level.

Working method

Working method is known for 111 victims (see Figure 13.3). Eighty-seven (78 per cent) were street workers, including three who worked from pubs or lorry parks, methods with similar location risks to street work,[22] while 24 worked indoors (22 per cent). Given that indoor sex workers greatly outnumber street workers, these figures alone indicate the far greater risk of deadly violence to which street workers are subjected. To ascertain whether this relative risk has changed over the past two decades, the cases were split into two equal time periods, January 1990 to June 1998 and July 1998 to December 2006, but the proportion of deaths in each period associated with either indoor or street work remained constant. Excluding cases where working method is not known, in the earlier period, 80 per cent of homicides

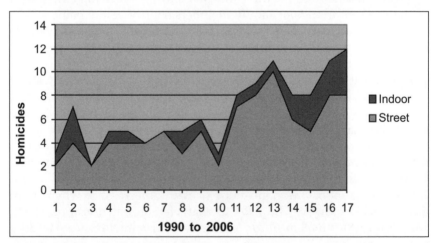

Figure 13.3 Homicides according to working method, 1990–2006

[22]The three victims working from pubs and lorry parks will be included with street workers in this analysis.

occurred among street workers; in the later period this figure was 79 per cent. However, of the 31 sex worker homicides that occurred in the three years January 2004 to December 2006, 21 (68 per cent) were street workers and 10 (32 per cent) worked indoors, suggesting that vulnerability in the off-street sex industry has recently increased. Half the deaths among indoor sex workers occurred in London and the South East.

Figure 13.3 suggests that the overall incidence of sex worker homicides is rising, and that the vulnerability of indoor workers is also increasing. Although the apparent increases may partly result from the difficulty in accessing data about homicides before 1998, the homicide rate certainly does not appear to be falling. Dorling (2005) found that the murder rate between 1981 and 2000 fell or remained constant for all females (apart from infant girls), particularly in the context of domestic violence. He suggests that this finding 'implies that when a group gains more self-worth, power, work, education and opportunity, murder falls.' Assuming these trends have continued, it appears that gains made by women in other walks of life have not been shared by sex workers.

Ethnicity and working method

Before 1999, no victim is known to have been born outside the British Isles, but over the past decade, increasing numbers of sex workers from overseas have been found at indoor venues, initially in London and the South East and subsequently more widely dispersed. From January 1999 to December 2006 there were eight victims from overseas: four from Eastern Europe, and one each from China, Somalia, Jamaica and Thailand, 11 per cent of all deaths in this period. Only one of the overseas sex workers was engaged in street sex work at the time of her death; the others worked in off-street situations, nearly half of the 15 deaths among indoor workers that have occurred since January 1999. This reflects reports that non-British sex workers are mainly located in the off-street sex industry, but there is no clear indication that their national origin increased their vulnerability. Four overseas victims appear to have died as a result of sexually motivated violence and two in the course of robberies. In only one case, that of Qu Mei Na (Belfast 2004) has there been any claim that trafficking issues were relevant. Chang Hai Zhang, who was convicted of her murder, said she was his girlfriend and that he had killed her after discovering her involvement in prostitution. Anti-trafficking organisations claimed

Na was trafficked into prostitution and was trying to escape, but the accusation that Zhang was involved in trafficking seems to be based on his having a hairstyle common among 'snakeheads'.[23] The case of one overseas sex worker is unresolved.

White British sex workers were most likely to do street work, and less likely to do off-street work than non-white British sex workers (see Figure 13.4).

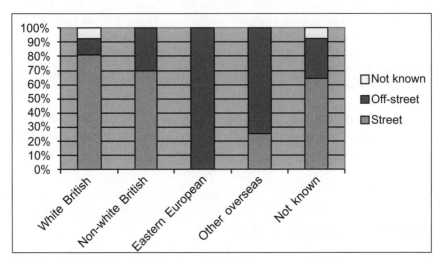

Figure 13.4 Ethnicity and working method

Working when attacked?

The working method of victims clearly has a strong influence on vulnerability, with street work the most obvious risk. Street workers are almost always alone when they are servicing clients, and even staying within sight of colleagues when soliciting has become difficult with the relentless dispersal of street beats. Indoor sex workers have more choice over whether to work alone or with others, although the effect of prostitution law is to make the safer option – working with others – the most heavily criminalised. The risks of working alone, even if indoors, are widely recognised, as one of Sanders' interviewees recalled:

[23]'Chinese man jailed for life after murder of prostitute', *Belfast Telegraph*, 6 February 2008; 'MLA and Women's Aid voice suspicions over "trafficking ring"', *Newsletter*, 6 February 2008 (see http://www.newsletter.co.uk/news/MLA-and-Womens-Aid-voice.3751911.jp).

I have a friend who was murdered ... in a building where there
were other clients downstairs and the clients thought she was
having kinky sex. This is one of the dangers of working alone,
she was and it killed her. She should have been working with
other people. (Sanders 2005)

Sixteen victims (14 per cent) were not working when they were
attacked, so any relationship between their vulnerability and their
role as sex workers was not as a result of location risks.[24] In 24 cases
(20 per cent) there is no information to indicate whether they were
working or not when attacked. The working environment is clearly
the most dangerous for street workers, 76 per cent of whom were last
seen alive while working or on their way to work. Among lone indoor
workers, 57 per cent (8 out of 14) were working when killed, whereas
only 30 per cent of those working indoors with other people (3 out of
10) were at work when they were attacked (see Figure 13.5).

Of the 24 who worked indoors, 13 were killed in their own homes
where they were alone when attacked, but only three of these were
killed by 'clients'; four were killed by partners, three by robbers,
and in three cases the relationship between the victim and killer is
not known. Three were killed at the homes of men subsequently
convicted of their murders, two of whom were clients and the other
a partner. Three were killed at working premises where they were
alone at the time of their death: one died in an arson attack on a
massage parlour which was closed at the time of the attack; one was
killed by a drunken client and the third case is unresolved.

Only three indoor sex workers were killed at premises where
co-workers were present at the time of the murder. The murders
of two women at a massage parlour in Shrewsbury in July 2006
demonstrated that working with others is not risk-free. It is possible
that workers at a discreet parlour in a small county town did not
expect to have to protect themselves with the armoury of security
devices now installed at similar premises in big cities, but this case
is unique.[25] The only other indoor sex worker to be killed when
working with other people was a clip-joint hostess who was close
to the door when a disgruntled customer ran in from the street

---

[24]Classification of homicide by occupation does not require the victim to
have been engaged in that occupation when killed (Brookman and Maguire
2003).
[25]See Chapter 15, pages 224–5.

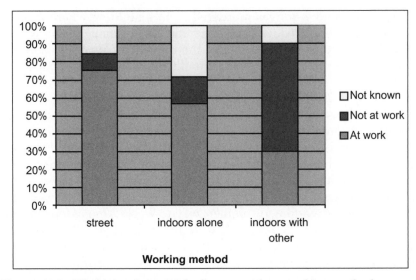

Figure 13.5 Working when attacked compared to working method

and attacked her, apparently because he was angry at having been fooled by the nature of the establishment. Of the remaining two victims who worked indoors, one was killed outdoors by two other sex workers although no clear motive was ever discovered for the attack, and the other, who did both parlour and escort work, was found dead in her car, but other circumstances of her death are currently unknown.

Deaths among indoor workers are few and six of the cases are unresolved so it is impossible to draw any firm conclusions, but the available information suggests that their risk of homicide is not related to their involvement in sex work in quite such a straightforward way as among street workers. Only 40 per cent are believed to have been killed by clients, but their risk of being killed during robberies is not shared by street workers: as has been suggested in earlier chapters, they may be targeted for robbery purely because they are assumed to earn enough to attract the interest of career robbers, although the gratuitous violence frequently meted out by these offenders may also indicate hatred and contempt for those who make their money in this way. Indoor workers also seem rather more at risk of being killed by non-commercial partners than street workers.

Where homicide took place

There is no obvious relationship between the vulnerabilities of indoor sex workers and the place where they were killed, but among street workers, in 22 per cent of cases (19 out of 87) it is not known where the homicide took place. Of the rest, 43 (63 per cent) occurred outdoors, including in cars or derelict buildings (see Figure 13.6). The proportion of deaths that occurred outdoors fell from 76 per cent (19 out of 25) of street worker homicides in the earlier period to 59 per cent (25 out of 42) in the second, which may reflect intensified policing of street work in the past decade. In only 22 of these cases (51 per cent) is there evidence that the suspects approached their victims as clients; in ten, suspects had a variety of relationships to the victims but were not clients; in nine cases no suspect has been identified and in two, although suspects have been identified, their relationship to the victim is not known.

Nearly a third of deaths among street workers occurred at the homes of the suspects charged with their homicide (21 out of 68; 31 per cent), and the proportion rose from 16 per cent (4 out of 25) of street worker homicides in the first half of the period (January 1990 to June 1998), to 38 per cent (16 out of 42) in the second half (July 1998 to December 2006). This would appear to reflect the rise in homelessness among street workers, as well as intensified policing. Sex workers who are roofless, or fear eviction for using their premises for prostitution, and want to avoid heavily policed outdoor locations, may agree to do business at the client's home, but it is not necessarily

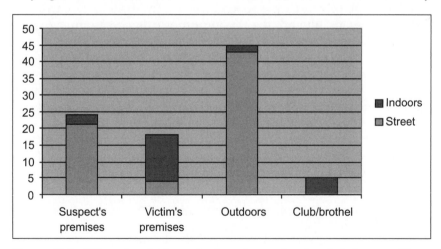

Figure 13.6   Where homicide took place, by workstyle of victim: n = 92

a safe option. Although it is not known where Steve Wright killed his victims, he was known to bring sex workers to his home, and after his conviction for the five Ipswich murders, it emerged that he had twice tried to persuade a sixth woman to go to there, refusing to go to her house: she was not suspicious but refused for unrelated reasons.[26] Homicides at the suspect's home are, however, likely to be solved: suspects were identified in all cases, although two were acquitted.[27] In 16 of these cases (76 per cent) the suspect appears to have approached the victim as a client; in four the suspect had a private relationship to the victim, and in one the relationship between the victim and suspect is not known.

Only four street workers were killed in their own homes throughout the period, two by 'clients', one by her partner and in one case no suspect was identified.

Summary

It is absolutely clear that sex workers' risk of homicide is primarily determined by location and isolation when engaging in sex work, with street soliciting the most obvious risk factor, and working indoors but alone the next most risky environment. The marked rise in homicides occurring at the home of the killer illustrates new levels of vulnerability arising out of increased homelessness and hostile policing of outdoor environments. Drug use is currently the overriding factor leading women to engage in street work and is sometimes perceived as the root 'cause' of any risks they encounter there. However, although the proportion of drug users among street victims rose from 58 per cent in the first half of the period studied to 87 per cent in the second half, the proportion of street victims compared to indoor victims remained the same. Changes in the relative risk of street and indoor working seem to be going in the other direction, with an increased proportion of homicides among indoor workers in the last three years studied. The numbers involved are still very small, however, and the individual circumstances of indoor homicides indicate that robbery and violence in private relationships are more important risks for indoor sex workers than are violent clients. This

---

[26]'How two brutal killers fuelled the DNA debate', *The Observer*, 24 February 2008.
[26]On appeal one suspect had her conviction for murder overturned and replaced with a 'Not Proven' verdict.

apparent rise in risks of indoor work has only been discernable since 2004, thus coinciding not with increased numbers of overseas sex workers at indoor premises, which has been evident since the mid-1990s, but with increasingly hostile enforcement policies towards indoor sex work.

Dorling (2005) demonstrates that structural conditions – the social and economic environment in which homicide takes place – rather than individual risk factors, account for the overall patterns of homicide, and examination of the patterns of sex worker homicides demonstrates that risky scenarios also arise out of 'structural conditions'. The actions of social institutions, the criminal justice system, housing authorities and social care agencies impact on sex workers' vulnerability by forcing them to work alone with no one to intervene in violent situations, making them homeless if they take clients to their own premises and forcing them to do business in the most dangerous and unmonitored places, as well as by failing to identify, apprehend or monitor the violent individuals who threaten them. The characteristics of those violent individuals will now be explored.

Chapter 14

Killers and suspects

Charges are known to have been brought or suspects identified in 94 (79 per cent) of the 118 deaths among sex workers referred to in the previous chapter. Information about suspects has been derived from the same sources mentioned above (Chapter 13, pages 162–4) and is available for 100 suspects in relation to the 94 deaths. Some of these suspects have been acquitted of homicide or not brought to trial, and it should be remembered that convictions referred to below may be overturned in future.[1] In three cases, although the identity of the suspects is not known, it is known that they were clients and descriptions are available for two of them, which allows for their inclusion in aspects of the following analysis.

Relationship of victims to suspects

Suspects have been categorised according to their believed relationship to the victim (see Table 14.1), but these categories are not necessarily mutually exclusive. For convenience, the term 'client' will be used for those thought to have approached their victims as clients, and the extent to which they deserve to be called clients will be further explored. 'Robber' refers to those whose primary motivation appears to have been robbery, although some approached their victims in

---

[1]Since I last reported on sex worker homicides (Kinnell, 2006b), two murder convictions have been overturned on appeal. One was replaced with a 'Not Proven' verdict under Scottish law.

Table 14.1 Relationship of victims to suspects

Relationship of victim to suspect*	Working method of victims				
	Street	Indoor	Not known	n*	%
'Client'	48	8	1	57	65
Partner	7	5	1	13	14
Acquaintance	7	1	0	8	9
Robber	0	5	0	5	6
Other	4	1	0	5	6
Total	66	20	2	88	100

*Figures relate to the number of victims of each type of suspect, not to the numbers of suspects.

the guise of clients. 'Partner' refers to current or former boyfriends, husbands, etc, and 'acquaintance' refers to people with whom the victims had private relationships but were not partners: some partners and acquaintances may also have been drug dealers or clients of other sex workers, if not of their victims. 'Other' includes drug dealers, those motivated by business rivalry, homophobic and other 'hate' attacks.

The relationship of victims to suspects has been ascertained from local knowledge and reports of court proceedings in 88 cases. In 30 cases no information of this kind has been found, and in 24 of these cases no charges are known to have been brought or suspects identified. Information in the public domain has not made clear the relationship between victims and suspects in six cases.

Excluding the cases where there is no information about the category of assailant, 57 (65 per cent) were victims of men who seem to have approached as clients; 13 (14 per cent) of partners; eight (9 per cent) of acquaintances; five (6 per cent) of robbers and four (5 per cent) of 'other' types of assailant. The vulnerability of sex workers to different types of assailant varied with their working method. Street workers were more vulnerable to clients and to acquaintances than indoor workers: 73 per cent of street workers (48 out of 66) were killed by clients and 11 per cent by acquaintances (7 out of 66), while 40 per cent of indoor workers (8/20) were killed by clients and only one (5 per cent) by acquaintances. Five indoor workers (25 per cent) were killed by partners, more than double the proportion among street workers, of whom only seven (11 per cent) are thought to have been killed by partners. All of the homicides by robbers were among indoor workers.

One of the complicating factors in trying to relate characteristics of suspects to victims, is that some victims were killed by more than one person, and some killers were responsible for more than one death. Consequently, the profiles of suspects in relation to types of homicide are different from the profiles of victims. For example, while only five victims were killed by robbers, there were nine suspects involved in these deaths. Nine victims were killed in circumstances involving more than one suspect: 25 suspects have been identified in relation to these nine deaths. Conversely, six suspects have been charged in relation to 16 deaths. The differing characteristics of those involved in group homicides and those responsible for multiple homicides will be explored below.

Cause of death

The cause of death ascribed (see Table 14.2) follows court or press reports. Some bodies had been dismembered or burnt, some were too decomposed for a cause of death to be established. Strangulation or asphyxiation are often associated with sexually motivated homicide, and 47 per cent of homicides by 'clients' were attributed to this cause, but so were 48 per cent of homicides by non-clients. In comparison with all female homicides in 2005/6 in England and Wales (Coleman et al. 2007), sex workers appear much more likely to be strangled or asphyxiated (45 per cent compared to 17 per cent) and less likely to be killed with a sharp instrument (16 per cent compared to 23 per

Table 14.2 Cause of death

Cause of death	Client	Acq*	Partner	Robber	Other	NK**	n	%
Asphyxia/strangulation	27	3	7	3	2	11	53	45
Sharp instrument	12	1	4	0	0	2	19	16
Beaten/head injuries	5	0	0	2	1	5	14	12
Other***	4	2	0	0	2	1	8	7
Not known	9	2	2	0	0	11	24	20
Total	57	8	13	5	5	30	118	100

* Acquaintance
** Relationship between victim and suspect not known
*** Includes overdose, drowning, falling, smoke inhalation

cent). However, many victims had been attacked by more than one method and/or with a variety of weapons, so the differences with the methods for all female homicides may be partly due to different approaches to assigning causation for the purposes of analysis.

Gender, ethnicity and age of suspects

Seven suspects charged in relation to five deaths were women. Four of the female suspects were acquaintances of the victim; two of them were sex workers who carried out one murder together. Another was also acquainted with the victim, but her motive was robbery. Two women were charged in the case of a sex worker who died in an arson attack on a brothel, one being a rival brothel owner who instigated the attack.[2]

Ethnicity is known for only 67 of the suspects (67 per cent). Of these 44 were white (67 per cent), one of whom was from Eastern Europe; all the rest are believed to have been British.[3] Ten (15 per cent) were Asian (nine from the Indian sub-continent and one from China), nine (13 per cent) were black, of whom three were believed to be British, and four were Turkish (6 per cent). As with suspects charged with non-fatal attacks,[4] those of Asian or Middle Eastern origin are easily identifiable by their names, whereas those of Irish, Caribbean or other origin may be indistinguishable from white British suspects without additional information. The ethnic profile of suspects charged with homicide is different to that for suspects charged with non-fatal attacks. There is a high proportion of 'missing data' in both data sets (33 per cent of homicide suspects; 39 per cent of suspects in non-fatal attacks), but among those where ethnicity is known, homicide suspects were more than twice as likely to be white British compared to those charged with non-fatal attacks (66 per cent compared to 30 per cent), and much less likely to be Asian (15 per cent compared to 42 per cent). The geographical distribution of homicide cases also differs from the non-fatal attacks, which may affect this variable.

---

[2]'Brothel madam jailed over fatal arson attack on rival premises', *Yorkshire Post*, 1 August 2007 (see http://www.yorkshirepost.co.uk/news?articleid=3075527).
[3]'British' may include those of Irish nationality.
[4]See Chapter 11, page 145.

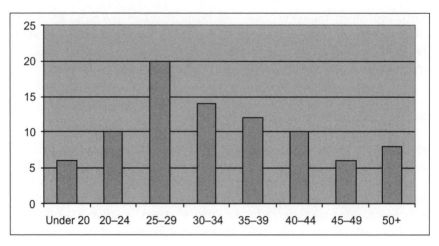

Figure 14.1 Age of suspects (n = 86)

Age at the time the victim died is known for 86 suspects (see Figure 14.1).[5] Forty-four were clients, 34 non-clients and 8 whose relationship to the victim is not known. Brookman and Maguire (2003) quote the British Crime Survey figures,[6] showing that in 44 per cent of violent incidents, the offenders were aged 16 to 24, observing that the patterns and characteristics of homicides are, 'to a large extent typical of *violent crime in general*', with significant proportions of offenders being in the 16 to 24 age group. This is not reflected in the age characteristics of those charged with sex worker homicides. Although 40 per cent of those prosecuted for non-fatal attacks on sex workers were in the 16 to 24 age range,[7] among those charged with homicide only 19 per cent were aged 24 or younger and 57 per cent were over 30. Suspects were most likely to be aged between 25 and 29, but there was a difference in the age distribution depending on the relationship of suspect to victim. The average age was 35 for clients (range 18 to 55) and 30 for non-clients (range 15 to 55): 39 per cent of clients (17 out of 44) were aged over 40 compared to 9 per cent of non-clients (3 out of 34). Among clients, only 6 out of 44 (14 per cent) were in the 16 to 24 age range. Among non-clients, 10 out

---

[5]One suspect has been counted twice because he was twice charged with murder, six years apart.
[6]Brookman and Maguire (2003) refer to Kershaw *et al.* (2000) *The 2000 British Crime Survey*, Home Office Statistical Bulletin 18/00. London: Home Office.
[7]See Chapter 11, page 144.

of 34 (29 per cent) were in the 16 to 24 age range, suggesting non-client suspects are more similar to violent offenders in general than are client suspects.

Among client suspects, 27 per cent were aged 18 to 26 (see Figure 14.2), a larger proportion than among general surveys of clients, although lower than among offenders in general. Shell *et al.* (2001) found that the age profile of their sample of kerb-crawlers was older than other offenders, with only 22 per cent being aged 18 to 26, compared to 53 per cent of other offenders under the supervision of Hampshire Probation. Other client surveys have found even smaller proportions in this age group: 12 per cent of clients interviewed in Birmingham were aged 18 to 26, and only 13 per cent of kerb-crawlers attending the West Yorkshire rehabilitation scheme were aged 18 to 25. A third of client suspects were aged 20–29, again a noticeably higher proportion than that found in three general client surveys: 16 per cent in Middlesbrough were in this age group and 21 per cent in both Southampton and Birmingham (Kinnell 2006b). These data suggest that client homicide suspects are more similar to other offenders than are clients in general, at least regarding age characteristics – not as young as most offenders, but younger than most clients.

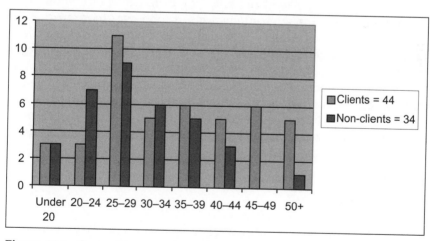

Figure 14.2 Suspects' age groups: clients and non-clients (n = 78)

Group homicides

Twenty-five suspects had participated in 'team' homicides, in which nine sex workers were killed. There were various motivations for these homicides: three were primarily motivated by robbery; one was a homophobic attack; one may have been arisen from drugs debts; one resulted from an arson attack at a massage parlour, the motive for which was alleged to be business rivalry and not directed at the woman who died; one was an unexplained attack by other sex workers; one was a premeditated, sadistic sexual murder; and for one, where the victim died of a drugs overdose, no motivation was established. One case is currently unresolved.

Alcohol and drug use by suspects

Brewer *et al.* (2006) suggest that cocaine use by victims might increase their irritability and propensity for violence, thus precipitating attacks, but they make clear that these factors may also influence the behaviour of the perpetrators. Crack use by a perpetrator was suggested in only two of the British homicides, and although 15 other suspects were known to use drugs, usually heroin, in only a few cases does there seem to have been a direct link between the homicide and either the killer's or victim's drug use. In some unresolved cases it is thought that the victims may have been killed by drug dealers to whom they owed money, but among client suspects, alcohol was more frequently mentioned as a contributory factor in their violence. Thirteen client suspects (28 per cent) were said to have been drunk at the time of the homicide, and two were using drugs as well as alcohol. In all seven clients (15 per cent) were known to use illegal drugs. It is likely that the alcohol and drug use of suspects is under-reported in the sources accessed, but on the evidence available, it seems that alcohol is more frequently associated with deadly violence than illegal drug use among those approaching as clients.

'Client' suspects

Of the 88 deaths where information is available, in 57 (65 per cent) it is assumed that suspects approached their victims as clients.[8] The

---

[8] Three other victims were killed by people approaching as clients, but as

proportion of murders of sex workers ascribed to clients is similar to that found in Canada – 64 per cent – between 1992 and 1998 (Lowman 2000), and in the USA, where between 60 per cent and 77 per cent of sex worker homicides were attributed to clients in different data sets (Brewer *et al.* 2006). Excluding three cases where the killer is known to have been a client but has not been identified, there were 47 suspects who appear to have approached as clients (54 victims).

The assumption that suspects approached their victims as clients is based primarily on the belief that the victims were 'at work' when they were killed. However, the analysis of non-fatal attacks resulting in a prosecution found that 30 per cent of attackers did not exhibit any 'client behaviour', even though their victims were 'at work' when attacked: they either approached in some other guise, or simply attacked on the street or dragged their victims into vehicles, or forced their way into indoor premises brandishing weapons.[9] It seems reasonable to suppose that the scenarios for homicide will be similar to those found in non-fatal attacks, but because the victim is dead and suspects charged with homicide are even less likely to describe their actions honestly than in non-fatal prosecutions, using the term 'client' in respect of these suspects is not necessarily an accurate description of their behaviour. Forensic evidence may establish that some sexual event has taken place between the suspect and victim, but this does not prove that the assailant approached as or behaved as a client.

Exploring the 'client behaviour' of homicide suspects indicates that paying for sex is not a very useful predictor of murderous violence. For 29 of the 47 'client' suspects (62 per cent), no evidence has been found to confirm that they had paid for sex, either with their victims or with other sex workers, although 14 ('serial attackers') were known to have attacked sex workers other than the victims who died. Fifteen ('client approach') appear to have approached their victims as clients but were not known to have paid for sex or to have attacked sex workers previously, although several had previous convictions for attacking people who were not sex workers. Nine suspects (19 per cent) are known to have paid for sex frequently ('regulars') and nine (19 per cent) claimed to have paid for sex with their victims ('paid') but were not known to be either regular clients or serial attackers of sex workers. These categories of 'regular', 'paid', 'serial attacker'

it appears that their motivation was robbery these cases are explored with 'non-client' homicides.
[9]See Chapter 11, pages 140–1.

and 'client approach' are shown in Figure 14.3, compared with the number of victims of suspects in each category.

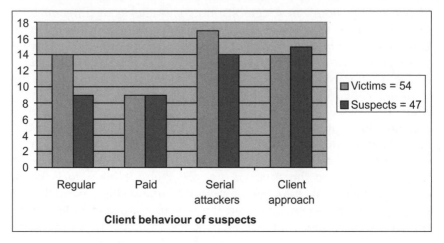

Figure 14.3 'Client' suspects and their victims

'Regulars'

Nine suspects (19 per cent of 'clients') charged with 14 murders were 'regulars', believed to have made a habit of paying for sex.

Steve Wright was convicted of five of the murders in this group, which gives the 'regulars' category the appearance of being the most dangerous. However, only one other 'regular', David Smith, had been charged with more than one sex worker homicide. Smith had a long history of violence against women, including sex workers; he was acquitted of one murder which took place in 1991 and convicted of another in 1999. Two other 'regulars' had previously been convicted of the manslaughter of their wives. Three 'regulars' are not known to have previous convictions for violence: Steve Wright, Crawford Nakasala, who murdered a parlour worker in London in 2005, and George Johnstone, tried for the murder of a sex worker in Glasgow in 1996. Johnstone had convictions for other types of offence, including causing death by dangerous driving. Wright had a conviction for theft, is suspected of having committed other homicides and is alleged to have been violent towards private partners. Three others had a history of violent or sexual offences, or were known to have attacked other sex workers. One of these was Daniel Archer, a 55-year-old crack user. Although press reports do not mention his having any previous convictions, after the murder several other sex workers reported having been attacked by him.[10] Another was Geoffrey Porter, 40 when he killed a 17-year-old in Bolton in 2002. Porter had previous convictions for sexual assault, including on children, but there is no mention of him being under any kind of supervision. He was described as 'inadequate' and frequently drunk; he also had non-commercial relationships with sex workers, driving them around, lending them money and allowing one to move into his flat. This arrangement led to him being evicted shortly before the murder; he began sleeping in his car and then lost his job. It was suggested he had 'snapped' under the pressure of 'a bad week'.[11]

'Regulars' were markedly older than other client suspects. Only one was under 30, and their average age was 43 (range 24 to 55). Nine of the 14 victims had been strangled or asphyxiated,[12] three were killed with sharp weapons and the bodies of two were too decomposed for a cause of death to be established. Four suspects had left the bodies in their homes and gone 'on the run' after the murder. Three bodies were left at the place the murder occurred and two others were dumped outdoors. The only bodies posed or placed in water were the five Ipswich victims.

Only two 'regulars' are reported as offering any explanation for their actions. Archer claimed his victim had attacked and tried to rob him, although there was no forensic evidence to support this claim. Nakasala claimed that the victim had accused him of stealing from the parlour where she worked and had killed her to 'show his contempt' for her.[13] The others either denied the charges, blamed their mental health problems or offered no explanation at all for their actions.

Eight 'regulars' were convicted of murder (12 victims); David Smith was also acquitted of murder and George Johnstone was acquitted on a 'Not Proven' verdict.[14]

---

[10]'Brutal killer guilty' *Dorset Echo*, 24 November 2005.

[11]'Pervert killer's obsession with young vice girls', 'Why police started to quiz Porter', *Bolton Evening News*, 3 December 2003.

[12]The five Ipswich victims are assigned to this category.

[13]'Parlour maid killed by her own thong', *icSouthLondon*, 18 July 2006 (see http://icsouthlondon.icnetwork.co.uk).

[14]'Not Proven' – a verdict available under Scottish law which implies that there is grave doubt as to the defendant's innocence, but effectively it amounts to an acquittal.

'Paid'

Nine suspects (19 per cent of 'clients') claimed to have paid for sex with the victims at the time of their deaths, but none were known to be habitual clients, nor to have attacked sex workers previously. Their average age was 34 (range 18 to 50). None had previous or multiple homicide victims; three were known to have committed other violent offences but their victims in these offences were not known to be sex workers, and one was on the DNA database for unknown reasons. Suspects in this group were more forthcoming with explanations for their actions than other homicide suspects, reflecting scenarios for violence mentioned in Ugly Mug reports and in media reports of non-fatal attacks.

Stephen Wynne, a former soldier discharged from the army for using cannabis, had also committed arson, on a Merseyside mosque, the day after the July bombings in London in 2005. After his arrest for arson, police searched his home and found notes referring to the death of Chantel Taylor, whom he had known since childhood. He had used alcohol, cocaine, cannabis and heroin that night, and claimed he killed her because she tried to steal his heroin.[15] John Law, who beat a woman to death with a car-jack, claimed she had mocked him after he failed to get an erection.[16] Shaun Tuley claimed he had paid for unprotected sex; that the victim attacked him when he ejaculated inside her, but believed she was alive when he left her. Forensic evidence showed she had fought for her life before being asphyxiated.[17] The money Tuley said he had given her was not on her body when it was found, which leaves doubt over his claim to have paid. Wakil Sahebzadeh claimed his victim had stolen his wallet, provoking him to stab her in the buttocks, arm and chest and wrench out some of her hair.[18]

Despite the categorisation of these suspects as 'paid', the key importance of money in the escalation of violence is illustrated in several cases including that of Stuart Milsted, who bludgeoned a sex worker to death in 2002. She was 21 and five months pregnant;

---

[15]Graham Davies, 'Protest at cut in killer's sentence', *Daily Post*, 10 July 2006; Kate Mansey, 'End the soft-touch sentences for killers without a conscience', *Liverpool Echo*, 13 July 2006.
[16]'Ten Scottish prostitutes murdered, but only three men are convicted', *The Scotsman*, 14 December 2006.
[17]'Vice girl bit man, murder trial told', *Northern Echo*, 19 July 2001.
[18]'MURDER: Zelia's killer was here illegally', *Evening Telegraph*, 27 May 2006 (see http://www.peterboroughnow.co.uk).

he had been drinking heavily on top of taking anti-depressants. He attacked her 'after paying £40 for sex. He failed to get aroused and demanded his money back.' Prosecuting counsel said, 'She lost her self-control and began to fight with him. He took back the £40. He admitted that he grabbed her by the throat then hit her on the head ...'[19]. Note that the prosecution (not the defence) emphasised that *she* lost her self-control, not the man who beat her to death with a house brick, even though he had already retrieved his £40.

One admitted paying for sex with the victim, but denied murder.

Paul Hiscock was convicted of preventing a lawful and decent burial and sentenced to 21 months in prison, after the body of Aleesha Nedic was found dumped under a pile of rubbish, over 40 miles from where she was last seen soliciting in Wolverhampton, in January 2004.[20] Police launched a homicide investigation; Hiscock was tracked via DNA and admitted to being her last punter. He said she had choked during sex; he panicked, bundled her body into the boot of the car he was driving while disqualified and then dumped it. Aleesha suffered from asthma and deep vein thrombosis and it was not possible to establish how she died.[21]

Two victims were strangled or asphyxiated, four killed with sharp weapons, two beaten with blunt instruments and one died from head injuries. This victim was leaning through the suspect's car window, arguing about payment, when he drove off. She fell, hitting her head on the pavement, which caused her death. Seven victims were left where they died, and one was dismembered – only fragments of body tissue were recovered.

One 'paid' suspect was acquitted of manslaughter; seven were convicted of murder.

Serial attackers

Fourteen suspects (30 per cent of 'clients') charged with 17 homicides were known to be serial attackers of sex workers who posed as clients, but whether they had ever paid for sex is not known. Eight had other convictions for violence against both sex workers and non-sex workers, including convictions for homicide. Their average age was 34 (range 22 to 55).

[19]'Danielle killer is jailed for life', *Manchester Evening News*, 17 October 2005; 'Family say killer should never be let out of prison', *Liverpool Echo*, 18 October 2005.
[20]'Race to trace steps of tragic teenager', *Express & Star*, 15 January 2004.
[21]'Man jailed for dumping body', *BBC News*, 30 April 2004 (see http://news.bbc.co.uk/1/hi/england/coventry_warwickshire/3674943.stm).

Edward Akester, a former soldier who had been discharged from the army for violence, was convicted of murdering a sex worker in Hull in 2006. He had a history of violence towards women and a previous conviction for attempting to strangle a sex worker. He was said to associate with sex workers and, according to him, invited women to his house to smoke drugs. At his trial it was alleged that he would offer women large sums of money to go back to his home, but he also told colleagues 'he never paid for sex'.[22]

Alun Kyte, convicted in 2000 of murdering two sex workers in the Midlands in 1993 and 1994, was in prison for rape when DNA connected him to the murders.[23] He conceded he might have had sex with one of the victims but denied murder. At his trial fellow prisoners testified that Kyte claimed both murders began when he argued with the victims over payment for sex, that one of the victims laughed at him for his lack of sexual prowess and that he strangled her to shut her up.[24] With reference to one of the victims, he is alleged to have said, 'you don't pay for that sort of girl' (Britton 2001).[25]

Albert Webb, convicted of murdering a sex worker in Bristol in 2003, had many previous convictions, including for indecent assault on a sex worker in 1997.[26]

Paul Brumfitt had previously been convicted of killing two men before he killed a Wolverhampton sex worker in 1999. He also twice raped another sex worker, three weeks after his third homicide. The surviving victim testified that she had been raped at knifepoint, which does not suggest that Brumfitt was a paying customer.[27] Multiple killers Anthony Hardy and George Naylor have also been assigned

---

[22]'Prostitute murderer jailed for 30 years', 4 July 2007; 'Fantasist with a long history of violence towards women', 5 July 2007; 'He is one of the most dangerous men I have ever met', 5 July 2007, all on http://www.thisihullandeastriding.co.uk; 'Vice girl strangler may have struck before', *Yorkshire Post*, 5 July 2007.

[23]'Prostitute killer jailed', *BBC News*, 14 March 2000 (see http://news.bbc.co.uk/1/hi/uk/664746.stm).

[24]'Prostitutes killed in money rows – court', *The Sentinel* [Stoke-on-Trent], 7 March 2000.

[25]See Chapter 15, pages 219–21.

[26]'Man guilty of prostitute murder, *BBC News*, 18 October 2004 (see http://news.bbc.co.uk/1/hi/england/bristol/3752668.stm).

[27]'Chief Constable attacks jail system', *The Guardian*, 22 July 2000; 'Life for vice girl's killer', *Shropshire Star*, 21 July 2000; 'Brumfitt the serial killer', *Newsquest Media Group*, first published 27 July, 2000 (see http://archive.thisistheblackcountry.co.uk/2000/7/27/64765.html).

to the 'serial attacker' category, as their homicide victims were all sex workers and there is no evidence that they ever paid for sex. Hardy was known to have attacked other sex workers, and both he and Naylor were also known to be violent towards other women.[28]

Alan McLaren, convicted of raping one sex worker in 1999 and murdering another in 2001, both in Stoke-on-Trent,[29] was described as 'a prolific liar and womaniser, duping women by falsifying his name and being involved in several relationships at the same time as well as using prostitutes in Manchester and Stoke'.[30] His dishonesty in his private relationships does not suggest a man who would be honest in his dealings with sex workers, hence his inclusion in the category of 'serial attacker' rather than 'regular'.

Only two 'serial attackers' offered an explanation for the homicide: Alan Duffy, who was convicted of murdering a 17-year-old in 1993, said he had choked her and smashed her head onto a concrete floor in frustration at not being able to reach a climax.[31] Steven Smith, who was convicted of murdering a sex worker in Bournemouth in 2005 and had a previous conviction for assaulting a sex worker, claimed to have 'lost it' while having sex with the victim, due to personal problems that were preying on his mind.[32] All others either denied the homicide, claimed they 'could not remember' or offered no explanation.

Eleven victims had been strangled or asphyxiated (65 per cent), several of whom had also been beaten, one was killed with a sharp instrument, one beaten, one drowned and for three the cause of death is not clear. There was no overall pattern as to where the murder took place or how the bodies were treated after death. Some suffered post-mortem mutilation; three were dismembered; three were placed in water; six were left where they died – three in the victim's home, three outdoors; three were dumped outdoors after being killed elsewhere; one died of her injuries some days after the attack, and one was found at the suspect's home.

Two serial attackers were acquitted of murder: both went on to attack other sex workers after their acquittals. One was also believed

[28]See Chapter 15, pages 217–19 and 221–3.

[29]'Man jailed for killing prostitute', *BBC News*, 17 February 2006 (see http://news.bbc.co.uk/1/hi/england/staffordshire/4724420.stm).

[30]*Chief Constable's Certificate of Commendation*, Staffordshire Police, 13 June 2006 (see http://www.staffordshire.police.uk/news/2006/06_jun/13_citation.htm).

[31]'"Life" for callous killer', *Doncaster Advertiser*, 16 February 1995.

[32]'Blind rage', *Dorset Echo*, 16 March 2006.

to be responsible for numerous violent robberies from sex flats; there was DNA and photographic evidence against him, but he was acquitted of murder, even after admitting to repeatedly lying in court. He continued to menace indoor workers in the same area after his acquittal. Gary Allen, acquitted in 2000 of the murder of a sex worker in Hull in 1997, was arrested within six weeks for attacking sex workers in Plymouth.[33] Ugly Mugs about Allen warned that he attacked as soon as he was asked for money. Allen was described as 'a psychopath with a dangerous aversion to women',[34] but was released early from prison on a curfew tagging scheme, removed his tag and went on the run in 2004.

One serial attacker was not charged; all others were convicted of murder.

'Client approach'

Fifteen suspects (32 per cent of 'clients', 14 victims), are believed to have approached their victims as clients, but were not known to have paid for sex, nor to have attacked sex workers previously. Seven were known to have a history of violence against both men and women. Their average age was 32 years (range 18 to 53).

Michael Sams, convicted of the kidnap and murder of sex worker Julie Dart in Leeds in 1991 (charges which Sams denied), was better known for kidnapping estate agent Stephanie Slater in 1992.[35] Britton (2001) claims that Sams used Julie to practise his plans for abduction and ransom, suggesting that he chose a sex worker because it would not create much fuss, then killed her to 'convince the police that he was to be regarded as a serious adversary.' If this summary of Sams' motives for killing Julie is correct, he was clearly using the 'client disguise' to take advantage of her vulnerability in terms of her location and marginalised social status.[36]

Adam Bowler, convicted with Deepak Bouri of murdering a sex worker in 2003, was said to be fascinated with Peter Sutcliffe, and their

[33]'Sex attack man goes on the run', *Yorkshire Post*, 11 March 2004.
[34]'Murder-case police hunt for hammer', *Yorkshire Post*, 28 November 2001; 'Sex attack man goes on the run', *Yorkshire Post*, 11 March 2004.
[35]'Life in jail's so good, who needs a pension?', *The Times*, 19 April 2007 (see http://www.timesonline.co.uk/tol/news/uk/article1673821.ece).
[36]Britton does not state that he gave police assistance as a forensic psychologist on the Sams case, nor does he give a source for his insights into Sams' motives for targeting Julie Dart.

victim was killed using a hammer and knife, as did Sutcliffe.[37] Bouri had been convicted of indecent assault aged 14. Bouri and Bowler were both only 18 when they committed murder: their age and the fact of their having worked as a 'team' in planning and executing the murder make them highly unusual for 'client' suspects. Only one other homicide where the offenders appear to have approached as clients was committed by a 'team', although a third case, currently unresolved, may have been of this kind.

Philip Stanley, convicted of murdering a sex worker from Norwich in 2001, had a history of extreme domestic violence and was a convicted rapist. Stanley admitted the woman died while they were having sex, but claimed it was from 'natural causes'. Reports of the trial suggest that the victim lived with Stanley for some weeks after she disappeared, but also that she met him while she was soliciting, hence the inclusion of this case under the 'client approach' section.[38]

Mark Corner was alleged to have enticed two Liverpool sex workers back to his home on consecutive nights, killing and dismembering both. Corner was suffering from untreated schizophrenia at the time of the killings and was found guilty of manslaughter due to diminished responsibility.[39] Peter Slack also had mental health problems and was also convicted of manslaughter due to diminished responsibility, after killing a sex worker in Nottingham in 2001; he said he was afraid she was going to rob him. He had been convicted of two previous stabbings, 20 years earlier, for which he had been detained in a secure hospital for several years. John Nixon had served 21 years for the manslaughter of a woman in County Durham in 1979. He was convicted of murdering a sex worker in Northampton in 2005; he claimed they had argued over money.[40]

Three denied being clients. Stuart Burns (Leeds 2004), Matthew Rounce (Hull 2001), and Joseph Harrison (Aberdeen 2005), all stated that their rage was provoked by their victims' request for payment. Perhaps these three should not be described as 'clients' at all, but the circumstances described in reports suggest that their approach had

---

[37]'Life for pair over burning body' BBC News, 23 March 2004 (see http://news.bbc.co.uk/1/hi/england/london/3562025.stm).

[38]'Life term for prostitute's killer', BBC News, 11 November 2005 (see http://news.bbc.co.uk/1/hi/england/4428720.stm)

[39]See Chapter 15, pages 223–4; 'Why was schizophrenic allowed to kill Hanane?', Chester Chronicle, 12 December 2003.

[40]'Woman was killer's second victim', BBC News, 8 August 2005 (see http://news.bbc.co.uk/1/hi/england/northamptonshire/4132770.stm).

been indistinguishable from that of a client. For example, Harrison was seen on CCTV chatting to his victim while withdrawing money from a cash machine.[41] Rounce's victim was actively soliciting when he picked her up; the judge at his appeal against sentence also inferred that Rounce had stolen her money and her earrings.[42]

Five victims of this group had been strangled, four killed with a sharp instrument, three beaten, one died from an overdose, and in four cases the cause of death is not known. Ten bodies had been dumped outdoors, two dismembered and two found in the home of the suspect. Apart from the explanations given in the cases above, suspects either denied being involved in the deaths, offered no explanation, or no relevant information is given in media reports.

One of the 'client approach' group was acquitted of murder on a 'Not Proven' verdict. Four were convicted of manslaughter, one of culpable homicide (Scotland). Nine were convicted of murder.

Previous and multiple offences

In the 17 years from 1990 to 2006, 54 deaths have been attributed to 47 'clients', but only 40 were convicted of murder or manslaughter, relating to the deaths of 46 victims, giving less than three deaths a year apparently caused by clients. Given the very large numbers of men who pay for sex every year (Kinnell 2006b), it is safe to say that only a tiny proportion of clients are potential murderers. However, 36 per cent (17 out of 47) of 'client' suspects were known to have committed non-fatal attacks on sex workers; 45 per cent (21 out of 47) were known to have previous convictions for violent or sexual offences, and 17 per cent (8 out of 47) had a history of violence, but no known previous convictions. Previous violence was not necessarily against sex workers nor even against women, demonstrating the inaccuracy of the assumption that those who attack and murder sex workers do not pose a threat to other people. Another 15 per cent (7 out of 47) had convictions for other offences or were on the DNA database for unknown reasons. Altogether 77 per cent of 'client' suspects

---

[41]Tanya Thompson, 'Asking for it?', *The Scotsman*, 3 March 2007. He was convicted of culpable homicide and sentenced to six years imprisonment. Harrison's sentence was confirmed on appeal by the Crown against its leniency: 'No extra time in jail for killer', *BBC News*, 14 December 2007 (see http://news.bbc.co.uk/go/pr/fr/-/1/hi/scotland/north_east/7144048.stm).

[42]Trial Judge Report 2004/320/MTS, Matthew Leslie Rounce, in High Court judgment rejecting Rounce's appeal for reduction of sentence, 4 November 2005 (see http://www.hmcourts-service.gov.uk/cms/144_7503.htm).

(36 out of 47) were either known to the police or known as 'Ugly Mugs.' Only half of the previous attacks on sex workers are known to have been prosecuted, indicating the scope for improvement in prosecuting non-fatal violence against sex workers, and in restraining those already known to be violent. Previous and multiple violent offences by category of 'client' are shown in Figure 14.4.

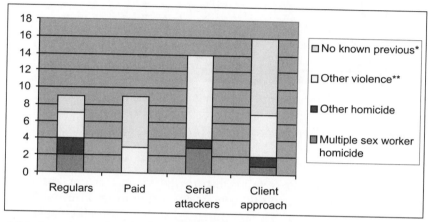

* 'No known previous' refers only to violent offences.
** 'Other violence' includes violence against non-sex workers

Figure 14.4 Clients: previous and multiple offences

Non-client suspects

There were 31 homicides where the victims are believed to have been killed by people who were not clients, with 41 suspects in all (see Figure 14.5). Thirteen suspects were partners or former partners of the victims; eight deaths were attributed to acquaintances with various relationships to the victims (nine suspects), five were killed in the course of robberies (nine suspects) and five were killed in other circumstances (ten suspects).

Among non-client suspects, 35 per cent (12 out of 34) were in the 18 to 26 age group, making them more like offenders in general than 'client' suspects. However, there were age differences between the sub-categories of 'non-client'. The average age of those classified as 'other' was 25 years (range 15 to 32); the average age of robbers was 24 years (range 19 to 30); of partners, 32 years (range 27 to 44); and acquaintances had an average age of 36.5 years (range 20 to 55).

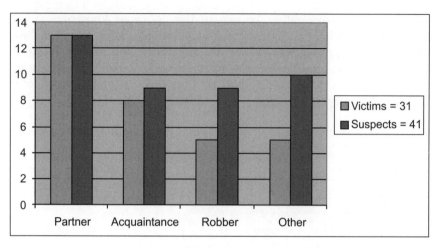

Figure 14.5 Non-client suspects (n = 41) and their victims (n = 31)

Among those whose relationship to the victims is not known at present (six of these suspects were due to come to trial during 2008), the average age was 41.5 years (range 31 to 58). Non-client suspects' age groups are shown in Figure 14.6.

Partners

Thirteen deaths (14 per cent) were attributed to partners, a low figure considering the extremes of violence sex workers are commonly believed to face in their private relationships, although it is possible that others have been killed by their partners, but were not publicly identified as sex workers. Five indoor workers, 25 per cent of all indoor cases, were killed by partners, all being convicted of homicide, more than double the proportion among street workers, of whom only seven (11 per cent of street workers) are thought to have been killed by partners, and of these, three were not convicted.

Six partners were known to be drug users. One was said to have publicly assaulted and abused his partner for not making enough money.[43] Another victim had left her drug-using partner in the process of exiting from sex work and giving up drugs herself. He threatened to kill her for leaving him and carried out his threat shortly afterwards.

---

[43]'Prostitute was "scared" of man', *This Is Hull and East Yorkshire* website, January 1999.

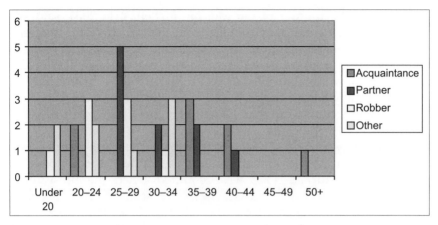

Figure 14.6 Non-client suspects, age groups (n = 34)

In three cases, deadly violence seems to have arisen because the suspect objected to his partner's involvement in sex work. George Tayali, a Zimbabwean national serving in the Household Cavalry, strangled his girlfriend when he found out she worked at a brothel. He left a note admitting to her murder, saying, 'I found out my girlfriend is a prostitute so I killed both of us'. Instead of killing himself, he attempted to flee the country and had boarded a plane for South Africa when he was arrested. At trial he said he 'couldn't live with the embarrassment' of having a girlfriend who was a sex worker, even though he had asked a friend to visit the brothel to see if she really was working there. His defence claimed he had post-traumatic stress disorder (PTSD) after serving in Iraq, but he was convicted of murder.[44] Derek Barron was convicted of killing his ex-wife, a massage parlour worker, in 1994. The prosecution alleged that he was jealous of her relationships with other men and had stalked her before the murder. Barron admitted he had gone to her house on the day she died to see if she 'entertained clients' there, but he denied killing her and has mounted various legal challenges against both conviction and sentence.[45] Chang Hai Zhang,

---

[44]'Killer wanted to go home to die', *Dorset Echo*, 15 March 2006; '"Cruel" murder soldier jailed', *BBC News*, 21 March 2006 (see http://news.bbc.co.uk/1/hi/england/dorset/4830476.stm).

[45]Case No: 2006/2/MTR, 11 May 2006, High Court of Justice, Queen's Bench Division, Royal Courts of Justice, Strand, London WC2A 2LL, before The Hon. Mr Justice Gray.

convicted of the murder of Qu Mei Na in Belfast in 2004, said she was his girlfriend and that he killed her after discovering that she was involved in prostitution. Anti-trafficking organisations asserted his victim was trafficked, and that Zhang was covering up for the traffickers. However, this allegation does not seem to have been put to the court at Zhang's trial.[46]

Six partner victims were strangled, five killed with sharp instruments and in two cases the cause of death could not be determined.

Of the 13 cases, eight resulted in a conviction for murder and one for manslaughter, although one of the murder convictions has since been overturned. One was acquitted when the prosecution offered no evidence: in this case, the police seem to have mistaken the dead woman's partner for someone else of the same name; one was acquitted on a 'Not Proven' verdict (Scotland); one was named as chief suspect but not brought to trial;[47] and in the last case, the outcome of judicial proceedings is not known.

Acquaintances

Eight deaths were attributed to acquaintances (nine suspects) who were thought to be neither commercial nor private sex partners. Four of the suspects were women. A Doncaster sex worker was killed in a prolonged attack by two other working women in 1993. Although it was suggested that they were involved in an 'underworld feud', no clear motivation was established.[48] Another sex worker was beaten and kicked to death in her front garden by a neighbour, Angela Walmsley, who had already caused a great deal of distress by informing the victim's boyfriend and grandmother that she was working as a prostitute. Walmsley was convicted of manslaughter.[49] One 'acquaintance' was a vagrant, convicted of killing and dismembering a woman who occasionally sold sex: she was also homeless and drug-dependent. Two of the 'acquaintances' had also

---

[46]'Chinese man jailed for life after murder of prostitute', *Belfast Telegraph*, 6 February 2008; 'MLA and Women's Aid voice suspicions over "trafficking ring"', *Newsletter*, 6 February, 2008 (see http://www.newsletter.co.uk/news/MLA-and-Womens-Aid-voice.3751911.jp).

[47]This person is currently in prison for the attempted murder of another of his former partners.

[48]'Prostitute's murder "may be part of underworld feud"', *Yorkshire Post*, 30 October 1993.

[49]'Woman denies vice girl murder charge', *Bolton Evening News*, 19 April 2006.

killed women who were not sex workers: as multiple killers, these cases will be explored further in the next chapter.

Three victims were strangled, one stabbed, one beaten, one fell from the twentieth floor of a tower block and in two cases the cause of death is not known. Six acquaintances were convicted of murder and two of manslaughter, although one of the murder convictions was overturned on appeal and replaced with a 'Not Proven' verdict. Another was also acquitted on a 'Not Proven' verdict.

Robbers

Five indoor sex workers were killed in the course of robberies, involving nine suspects. Three victims were killed in group attacks involving at least nine people, although one of these was never identified. As illustrated in Chapter 10, indoor sex work premises have become highly vulnerable to career robbers, often working in gangs, and many such robberies are extremely violent, possibly indicating vehement contempt for the people whose money they steal and for the way in which the money has been made. While their primary motivation may be acquisitive and their choice of victims influenced by assumptions that sex workers will not report such crimes to the police, some of these offenders evidently share the hatred displayed by other assailants for those who sell sex.

Two victims were killed by a single assailant, Garry Harding, in Shrewsbury in 2006. Harding had been a client at the massage parlour where they worked on previous occasions, but on this occasion he beat them both to death with a hammer in the process of stealing £330.[50] Equally vicious, if less baffling, was the sadistic murder of a 32-year-old male sex worker by a gang of three robbers in London in 2004. They also posed as clients to gain access to the victim's flat and murdered the victim in the course robbing him. The gang had previously targeted several female sex workers, whom they bound, gagged and humiliated in the course of the robberies. The gang leader, Darren Johnson, had been acquitted of a previous homicide, in which a male victim had been 'pelted with stones and bricks and then "cremated" in his own car in a gangland-style killing'.[51] Johnson was sentenced to 35 years, the longest sentence handed down for a sex worker murder before Wright was given a whole life sentence for the five Ipswich murders. Johnson's accomplices, who had many

---

[50]See Chapter 15, pages 224–5.

[51]'Sadistic gangster gets life sentence', *South London Press*, 7 July 2006.

previous convictions, including convictions for robbery and firearms offences, were also convicted of murder. In all, four robbers were convicted of murder, three of manslaughter and two were acquitted of homicide but convicted of conspiracy to rob.

Other

Five sex workers are believed to have been killed by other types of assailant. One was killed in an arson attack on a massage parlour; three suspects were convicted of manslaughter and one of conspiracy to commit arson and perverting the course of justice. In one case two drug dealers were charged with homicide but lack of witnesses led to the charges being dropped. Another, a 15-year-old 'rent boy', was killed by two other teenagers in an apparently homophobic attack, one being convicted of murder, the other of manslaughter.

Hate of sex workers probably underlies many homicides and was made explicit by the murderer of an Ipswich sex worker who was killed by a local resident in December 2003. Darren Brown, a security guard, objected to her working near his house. He punched her, kicked her and stamped on her so hard the imprints of his shoes were left on her head. He dragged her down an alleyway and dumped her under some bushes, where she died of her injuries. The judge commented that throughout the course of the trial, Brown's 'views about prostitutes had become clear'.[52]

Non-clients: previous and multiple offences

As a group, those who were not clients appear much less likely to have a history of violence than 'clients', (27 per cent with known 'previous', compared to 62 per cent of 'clients'), although two acquaintances and one robber had been charged with other homicides, and one robber committed two sex worker murders (see Figure 14.7).

Outcomes of homicide investigations and judicial proceedings

Wilson (2007) has stated that between 1994 and 2004 about 60 sex workers were murdered in England and Wales, with just 16 convictions. Wilson seems to have misread a paragraph in *Paying the Price* (Home Office 2004: para. 5.22), referencing an article I

---

[52]'Guard kicked prostitute to death', *BBC News*, 11 October 2004 (see http://news.bbc.co.uk/1/hi/england/suffolk/3733984.stm).

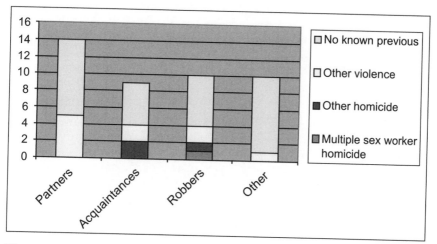

Figure 14.7 Non-clients: previous and multiple offences

wrote in 2001 referring to 51 homicides, 29 prosecutions and 16 known convictions for homicides committed between January 1990 and March 2001 (Kinnell 2001). Harrison and Wilson (2008) repeat this assertion several times and at some length in their book on the Ipswich murders (Harrison and Wilson 2008). However, while the success rate in sex worker homicide investigations is lower than among other victim groups, the situation has improved greatly over the period studied. Dividing the years 1990 to 2006 into two periods of 102 months each, there were 45 known homicide cases in the first period, January 1990 to June 1998, and suspects were brought to trial in 25 cases (56 per cent). In the second period, from July 1998 to December 2006, there were 73 homicide cases, and in 58 suspects were brought to trial (79 per cent). Coleman *et al.* (2007) report that at least one suspect had been identified in relation to 84 per cent of all homicides in England and Wales in the year 2005/6, showing that sex worker homicide investigations are now nearly as successful as for other categories of victim, although identification of suspects may take longer.

Figure 14.8 and Table 14.3 show the relative success of homicide investigations, up to the point of bringing a case to court, compared to the working method of the victims. Although the greatest number of unresolved cases are among street workers, the proportion of solved and unsolved cases is almost identical for both street and indoor workers, which challenges the assumption that the 'chaotic lives' of street workers materially impede investigations, although the criminalisation of sex work, both street and indoor, may do so.

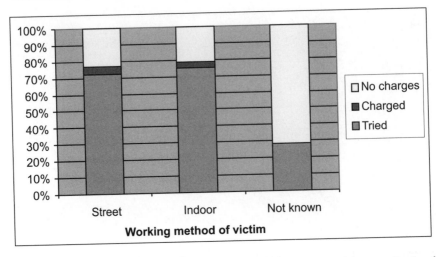

Figure 14.8 Outcome of homicide investigation by working method of victim (%)

Table 14.3 Outcome of homicide investigation by working method of victim

	Working method of victim				
Outcome of investigation	Street	Indoor	Not known	All	%
Suspect tried	63	18	2	83	70
Suspect charged*	4	1	0	5	4
No charges	20	5	5	30	25
Total	87	24	7	118	99

*Suspect charged – includes two cases where it is believed a trial has taken place but no information has been found to confirm this, and cases which have not yet come to trial.

Judicial outcomes

Police success in finding suspects to charge in sex worker homicides has improved greatly in the past decade, and the proportion of cases resulting in a homicide conviction has also increased. Of cases from the first period (January 1990 to June 1998), 16 led to homicide convictions, 36 per cent of homicides and 64 per cent of cases tried.[53] Of those from the second period (July 1998 to December 2006), 50 led to homicide convictions, 68 per cent of homicides and 86 per cent of cases tried. These improvements may arise from changed police attitudes, improvements in forensic science and more willingness on the part of juries to convict.

Over the whole period 1990 to 2006, 67 per cent of cases brought to court resulted in a murder conviction, 10 per cent for manslaughter or culpable homicide and 17 per cent were acquitted. Compared to the outcomes for all homicide prosecutions in England and Wales (2005/6; Coleman *et al.* 2007), a higher proportion of sex worker killers were convicted of murder – 67 per cent compared to 53 per cent, and fewer for manslaughter/culpable homicide – 10 per cent compared to 28 per cent, but acquittals were similar, 17 per cent and 16 per cent.

No difference in investigation success rates can be seen in cases involving either street or indoor workers. Neither is there any difference between street and indoor cases in the proportion which resulted in a conviction for homicide: 69 per cent of street cases led to homicide conviction and 68 per cent of indoor cases. 'Clients' were more likely to be convicted of homicide than other categories of assailant, 85 per cent of those brought to trial being convicted of murder, manslaughter or culpable homicide, while 66 per cent of the 'non-clients' were convicted of homicide.

Acquittals and failure to identify suspects

> There seem to be a lot of people who were around at the time but when it comes to the crunch not that many people have been willing to come forward.[54]

No charges are known to have been brought in 30 homicides, a quarter of the total, although suspects have been identified in two but not brought to trial. The majority of homicide cases resulting in acquittals or where no suspect was identified occurred before July 1998. There are also regional differences in the proportion of cases without a satisfactory outcome. Of eleven cases where no suspect

---

[53]Three cases which occurred between 1990 and 1997 have recently been reopened and arrests made in two of them.
[54]'Gun victim fights for life', *Crewe Chronicle*, 13 March 2002.

has been identified since July 1998 (up to December 2006), four were in London, four in Yorkshire and the North East, and one each in East Anglia, the Midlands and the North West.[55] The London cases included two homeless women who sold sex occasionally, a clip-joint hostess and a woman working from private premises. Four of the seven 'no suspect' homicides outside London were women regularly engaging in street work, two in Middlesbrough and one each in Bradford and Sheffield. All four occurred in situations where vigorous anti-prostitution tactics were being pursued at the time of the homicides, which may have increased the victims' vulnerability as outlined in Chapter 6 and reduced the likelihood of potential witnesses cooperating with investigations.

In November 2000, when Middlesbrough sex worker Vicky Glass was found dead, the robust enforcement approach towards kerb-crawlers, which had resulted in 300 prosecutions in two years, continued unabated, with kerb-crawlers brought to court in the week before Christmas. The police announced, 'We have repeatedly warned that men who come to Middlesbrough looking for prostitutes will be prosecuted. I accept that their families are also victims and it is a terrible thing to happen in the run-up to Christmas, but kerb-crawlers must accept the consequences of their actions.' At the same time, detectives from the same force complained about lack of public cooperation in the murder enquiry: 'A Cleveland Police spokeswoman said: "Officers are dismayed yet again at the lack of response to pleas for help. This latest appeal ... has not resulted in a single call to the incident room".'[56] Middlesbrough police have continued to promote their anti-kerbcrawler strategy, but the murder of Vicky Glass and the subsequent disappearance of Rachel Wilson in May 2002 are still unsolved. Also unsolved are the murders of Rebecca Hall in Bradford (2001) and Michaela Hague in Sheffield (2001), where similarly hostile policing was practised at the time of their deaths and during the initial stages of the murder enquiries, and remain in place. Suspension of 'zero tolerance' during the investigation of the Ipswich murders suggests that this lesson has been learned, if only in this extreme context.[57]

Figure 14.9 shows the regional variations in the outcome of

---

[55]Including one case where a suspect who had been charged was formally acquitted because he had made a false confession.

[56]'Kerb crawler GP tells of regret', *Teesnet news*, December 2000; 'Family's plea met by silence', *Teesnet news*, 23 December 2000.

[57]See Chapter 6, pages 73–7; see also Chapter 16, pages 239–42..

homicide investigations, excluding cases where the outcome of judicial proceedings is unclear and where suspects have been identified but not brought to trial. London and the South East had the highest proportion of cases where no suspects have been identified, although difficulties in obtaining information from the London area may have led to an overstatement of the proportion of cases unsolved. Scotland had the lowest proportion of 'no suspect' cases, but the west of Scotland had the highest proportion of acquittals. Comparing outcomes in England with those in Scotland, a slightly higher proportion of cases in Scotland, 10 out of 13 (77 per cent) have resulted in charges being brought than in England, 77 out of 104 (74 per cent), but the rate of conviction for homicide was conspicuously lower.

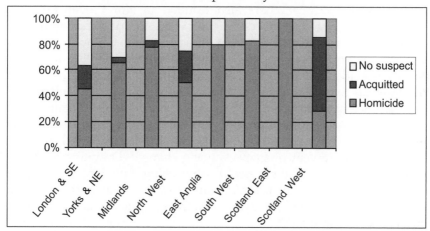

Figure 14.9 Outcome of homicide investigations by region (per cent): England and Scotland only

Commenting on murders of drug-using street workers in Glasgow in the 1990s, Rafferty expressed the common view that drug use increases the risk of violence, but also argued that it hampered investigations after attacks:

> ... by far the biggest reason for the deaths is the prevalence of drugs. It's not just that the men around them press the girls to make enough money for two habits, or that using drugs can cloud the girls' own instincts for self-preservation. They cloud the memory too .... "They're hopeless as witnesses," says DCS Fleming. "They're wanting to help you, but they're drugged up to the eyeballs and they just don't know".[58]

---

[58]Jean Rafferty, 'Double jeopardy', *Guardian Weekend*, 14 March 1998.

Police in the west of Scotland may have blamed the failure of prosecutions on the victims' drug use, making them 'hopeless witnesses', but in England prosecutions in relation to drug using victims have been much more successful. In England, 55 victims were known to be drug users out of 104 (53 per cent), resulting in 35 homicide convictions (65 per cent) and four acquittals (7 per cent). Of the thirteen Scottish cases, eleven were drug users (85 per cent), resulting in three homicide convictions (27 per cent) and four Not Proven verdicts (36 per cent). All three cases in the east of Scotland resulted in a homicide conviction, but of the ten in the west of Scotland, only six went to trial, with three murder convictions, one of which was overturned on appeal and replaced with a Not Proven verdict. Three others also resulted in Not Proven verdicts. To have four out of nine cases that went to trial ending in this verdict – all in Glasgow – might indicate some regional prejudice against sex worker victims or witnesses.[59] However, failure to gather sufficient evidence has also caused problems in Glasgow. In three of the four cases which have not been tried, suspects were identified, but insufficient evidence found to bring prosecutions to court. One was the case of Emma Caldwell, murdered in 2005. Four suspects were charged in August 2007, but under Scottish law a trial date has to be set within a year of suspects being charged. Despite three years of investigations, and there presumably being sufficient evidence to charge the men in August 2007, in July 2008 the Crown Office stated that it had insufficient evidence and proceedings against the four suspects were dropped.[60]

[59]Jean Rafferty, 'Murder in limbo', *Guardian Weekend*, 29th January, 2005.
[60]Stephen McGinty, 'Four men accused of killing Emma go free – but case not closed', *The Scotsman*, 9th July 2008.

Chapter 15

Multiple killers

Most sex worker homicides are committed by people not known to have killed anyone else. However, as the Ipswich murders of 2006 demonstrated, it takes a 'serial' killer to interest the media. At least seven other sex workers died in other places around Britain during 2006, but their deaths went largely unnoticed. At least 118 died between 1990 and 2006, but their deaths had no such impact, except for brief ripples of media excitement when it seemed possible that one killer was responsible for several murders.[1] Multiple sex worker murders, because they receive the most attention in popular culture, inevitably exert a disproportionate influence on public perceptions, not just of violence in the sex industry but of the sex industry itself. At the beginning of this book I challenged the conceptual orthodoxies that have arisen around Peter Sutcliffe and I end this section with a rather different perspective on Steve Wright than emerged at his trial, or in the immediate aftermath. First, however, I will look at all the cases involving multiple killers between 1990 and 2006.

Wilson's study of serial homicide in Britain (Wilson 2007) highlights sex workers as a group most likely to be targeted by 'serial killers', which unfortunately is likely to fortify assumptions that most sex worker homicides are committed by multiple murderers. In fact of 94 sex worker homicides[2] between 1990 and 2006, only 24 (25.5 per cent) are believed to have been committed by people who have

---

[1]Natasha Walter, 'All victims of murder should be treated equally', *The Independent*, 9 January 2003.
[2]That is, those where a suspect has been identified.

killed more than once. Seventeen are believed to have been killed by suspects charged with previous or multiple homicides of sex workers (seven suspects) and another seven were killed by men previously or concurrently charged with the homicide of non-sex workers. There were nine non-sex worker victims of these killers: two were wives of the killers, four were women not known to have been sex workers and three were men. In the USA, Brewer *et al.* (2006) estimated that 35 per cent of sex worker homicides were committed by 'serial perpetrators' but it is not clear whether this figure (which they regard as an underestimate) may include 'single homicide' offenders who were known to have also committed non-fatal attacks on sex workers but not necessarily other homicides. In the UK, 36 per cent of the 'client' suspects charged with sex worker homicides are known to have committed non-fatal attacks on sex workers, but in this chapter I refer only those who are known to have been charged with more than one homicide.

> To be labelled as a "serial killer" a murderer would normally have to have killed three or more victims in a period of greater than 30 days (Wilson 2007)

Between 1990 and 2006, only three murderers of sex workers – Steve Wright, Anthony Hardy and Paul Brumfitt – could be classed as 'serial killers' by Wilson's definition, and he specifically excludes Brumfitt as there was a gap of nearly 20 years between his first two victims, both of whom were men, and his murder of a female sex worker. Criminologists do not agree on how a serial killer should be defined, however. Dr Keith Ashcroft of the Centre for Forensic Neuroscience in Manchester referred to Steve Wright as a 'spree' not a 'serial' killer because the intervals between his murders were so short. Rather than trying to fit sex worker killers into arbitrary categories, I will review the cases where suspects have faced multiple charges of homicide, to see if there are any common factors, examine their behaviour as 'clients' to see if there are any markers that sex workers should be wary of, and ask whether the policing of prostitution had a specific impact on the victims' vulnerability or whether intervention agencies (e.g. police and mental health services) had any prior knowledge of the suspects which might have been used to restrain their activities.

Suspects charged with both sex worker and non-sex worker homicides

Seven of those charged with sex worker homicides had also been charged with the homicide of nine non-sex workers, three of whom were men. One was Darren Johnson, 24, the gangster convicted of murdering a male sex worker in 2004, who had previously been acquitted of murdering a man in 2000.[3] Apart from Johnson, all suspects in this group were white British. One murdered three women in four days, but his other victims are not known to have been sex workers, and his relationship to the victim is thought to have been as an acquaintance, not a client. He was 35, had no previous convictions and was the only killer in this group who was not known to the police. All the others in this group were over 40 when they murdered a sex worker, their average age being 46 (range 41 to 54). In three cases their age is related to the fact that they were detained for many years after their previous homicides, but two had served less than five years. Two, Brumfitt and Leighers, had had psychiatric diagnoses but were deemed safe to live in the community.

Kenneth Valentine (a.k.a. Anness) was neither a client nor the partner of Bradford sex worker Caroline Creevy whom he killed in 1996. Valentine had many previous convictions, including two indecent assaults and the robbery and burglary of an 89-year-old woman, for which he received a seven-year sentence in 1985. In 1991 he killed a woman in Leeds by sexually assaulting her with a pool cue, and successfully pleaded guilty to manslaughter, claiming that it was 'a sex game gone wrong'. On his release in 1995 he moved into Bradford's street soliciting area, where he befriended sex workers, encouraging them to take clients to his flat, either charging them £5 a time or taking drugs as payment. When Caroline and her boyfriend became homeless, Valentine allowed them to stay with him, but shortly before she was killed, her boyfriend was imprisoned for theft. It was said that Valentine was obsessed with Caroline but that she was not interested in him, and police speculated that he killed her because she rejected him. Valentine hid her body in a storm drain but his movements were caught on CCTV, and when police went to arrest him they discovered another sex worker locked in his flat.

Valentine's case exemplifies the inadequacies of the criminal justice system in identifying, restraining or monitoring highly dangerous

---

[3]See Chapter 14, pages 201–2.

individuals. It also illustrates some of the vulnerabilities imposed on sex workers. Vigilantism had driven sex workers out of Bradford's traditional soliciting area the year before Caroline was killed, but violent incidents had continued, so the apparent safety of Valentine's flat must have been appealing. Homelessness and isolation after her boyfriend was imprisoned clearly increased her vulnerability. [4]

Paul Brumfitt, convicted of murdering a Wolverhampton sex worker in 1999, had an offending history which began at the age of 12. In 1979 when he was 23, after a row with his 15-year-old girlfriend, he broke into the home of an 85-year-old woman and attacked the woman's daughter who was seven months pregnant. He then fled to Tilbury, where he attacked a 59-year-old gents' outfitter with a claw hammer, leaving him to bleed to death. Brumfitt escaped abroad, travelling around Europe before strangling a bus driver in Denmark after a night's drinking. He was arrested on his return to England and in August 1980 successfully pleaded guilty to manslaughter on the grounds of diminished responsibility. According to Wilson (2007), Brumfitt claimed the two male victims had made homosexual advances to him: like killers who claim to have been enraged by their victims' request for payment, this looks like an excuse designed to elicit sympathy. Brumfitt was given a life sentence and was told by the judge: 'You suffer from psychopathic disorders, a permanent disability of mind which results in abnormally aggressive and seriously irresponsible conduct.' Brumfitt served 15 years but was released in 1994 when two psychiatrists said he had no evidence of a mental disorder.

In February 1999, 19-year-old Marcella Davis disappeared from the street beat in Wolverhampton. Three weeks later two other sex workers were attacked at knifepoint. Brumfitt was charged with three counts of rape. While in custody, traces of Marcella's blood were discovered in his flat and fragments of her bones and teeth were found at a scrapyard he had rented. Brumfitt claimed he had been 'set up', but was convicted of her murder and received two further life sentences for rape.[5] After his conviction the Chief Constable of West Midlands

---

[4]'Party horror after vice girl is attacked', *Telegraph and Argus*, 6 February 1996; 'Knifeman chased vice girls, court told', *Telegraph and Argus*, 25 March 1998; 'Minimum of 22 years for prostitute's killer', *Yorkshire Post*, 27 March 1998.
[5]'Brumfitt the serial killer', 'Cops in call for inquiry', 'Boozy night led to death', 'Mum weeps in court', 'Blood clue led to arrest', Newsquest

police said: 'Apart from the massive cost of police investigations, it seems inconceivable a man who has been convicted of a litany of offences since 1968, including two counts of manslaughter and wounding for which he received three life sentences, can still be allowed to wander the streets.' He called for an 'urgent review into decision-making' in light of the case. The Prison Service said it was reviewing 'the effectiveness, efficiency and fairness of the procedures for the review, release and recall of life sentence prisoners. This will include consideration of the effectiveness of risk assessment at all stages of the process.'[6]

George Leighers had previously been convicted of the manslaughter of his wife whom he had stabbed to death in 1986. He spent over ten years in mental institutions and then lived independently but under the supervision of community mental health personnel. During this time he became a 'regular' of two sex workers. He received regular anti-psychotic injections from his GP and was deemed no longer in need of close supervision less than six months before his second homicide, of a street sex worker in Middlesbrough, in 2003. She was also stabbed, with a bayonet.[7]

Daniel Collins was convicted of manslaughter for beating his wife to death with a tyre wrench in 1994; he then killed a sex worker in London in 1999. It is not known how long he had been imprisoned for killing his wife, but it appears that the gap between his release and his second homicide was extremely short. The victim usually worked at a sex flat, but had agreed to do an outcall because Collins was a known client at the flat. Her co-workers raised the alarm as soon as she failed to phone in as arranged. Her body was found under Collins' bed: she had been strangled.

John Nixon, an alcoholic, had served 21 years for the manslaughter of a woman in County Durham in 1979, and had been on parole for five years before killing a street sex worker in Northampton in 2005. He

Media Group, 27 July 2000 (see http://archive.thisistheblackcountry. co.uk/2000/7/27/).
[6]'Chief Constable attacks jail system', *The Guardian*, 22 July 2000; 'Life for vice girl's killer', *Shropshire Star*, 21 July 2000.
[7]'Wife-killer was freed only to stab teenager to death', *Northern Echo*, 11 February 2004.

said there had been an argument about money, and that he stabbed her twice. She had actually been stabbed nearly 50 times.

One feature common to Valentine, Brumfitt, Leighers, Collins and Nixon was that they all committed their second homicide in their own homes. Both Leighers and Collins then went 'on the run' abandoning the bodies where they were killed; Valentine and Brumfitt tried to dispose of the bodies, while Nixon called the police to his house.

Offenders convicted of homicide for a second time

Home Office data on homicide distinguishes those charged with more than one homicide at the same trial (such as Steve Wright) from those charged with homicide on more than one occasion (such as Paul Brumfitt). It is this last category of killer that is the most unusual. The Homicide Index shows that repeat homicides, whatever the characteristics of the victims, are extremely rare. Between 1995 and 2005/6, of 5,733 people convicted of murder or manslaughter, only 25 (0.4 per cent) had been convicted of homicide on a previous occasion (Coleman *et al.* 2007). Under 1 per cent of the victims of these 5,733 killers were sex workers, but 6 of the 25 (24 per cent) who had been convicted of homicide more than once were killers of sex workers: Paul Brumfitt, Daniel Collins, George Leighers, John Nixon, Kenneth Valentine and George Naylor. It is not necessarily the case that such repeat killers move on to targeting sex workers after their first homicide, as a case from an earlier era illustrates. George Unsworth, given a life sentence in 1970 for the manslaughter of a sex worker in Hong Kong when he was 21, had 'brain surgery to try to cure his behaviour', and was released on licence in 1979. Eight months later, he killed an eight-year-old boy in Huddersfield.[8] These cases might indicate that there is something highly atypical about some of the people who kill sex workers. It could also show that sex workers are extremely vulnerable to highly dangerous people.

Multiple sex worker homicides

Two offenders were charged with sex worker homicides on separate occasions: David Smith, acquitted of one murder in 1991 and convicted

---

[8]Andrew Baldwin, 'When killers strike on being set free', *Huddersfield Daily Examiner*, 24 January 2008, referring to C. Rickell (2007) *Yorkshire's Multiple Killers*. Barnsley: Wharncliffe Books.

of another in 1999, and George Naylor, who committed one homicide in 1985 and another in 1995.[9] Five were charged simultaneously with between two and five sex worker homicides each: Alun Kyte, two victims over three months between December 1993 and March 1994; Anthony Hardy, three victims over eleven months in 2002; Mark Corner, two victims in two days in 2003; Garry Harding, two victims in one episode in 2006; and Steve Wright, five victims over seven weeks in 2006. None of these offenders are known to have killed non-sex workers. In all cases, suspects are believed to have approached their victims as a client, although Harding was said to have been motivated by robbery.

Of those charged with multiple sex worker homicides:

- Fifteen of the 18 victims[10] (six suspects) were street workers whose vulnerability may have been increased by anti-prostitution policing or community hostility.

- Three – Kyte, Corner and Harding – were under 30 at the time of the homicides, and the other four were over 40, although two of those over 40 had been previously charged with a sex worker homicide when they were in their mid-thirties. Their average age was 38, range 22 to 52.

- Two – Hardy and Corner – were said to use illegal drugs; Hardy was also an alcoholic and Corner was said to drink heavily. Alcohol was mentioned in reports about Wright and Naylor, but not in a context which suggested they were drunk at the time of the homicides.

- Two – Corner and Hardy – had a diagnosed severe mental illness; Harding had a 'borderline personality disorder' and Naylor was described by his ex-wife (a psychiatric nurse) as a 'psychopath'.

- Five – Wright, Hardy, Smith, Naylor and Kyte – had strangled or asphyxiated their victims; three – Hardy, Smith and Naylor – had committed post-mortem mutilations; two, Corner and Hardy, had dismembered the bodies.

---

[9]Naylor's 1985 victim is not included in the analysis of sex worker homicides in Chapter 13.
[10]Including Naylor's 1985 victim.

- All four men over 40 but none of those under 30 had a history of domestic violence. None of the men under 30 was married or known to have had any long-term relationships with women.

- Two – Smith and Naylor, had previous convictions for violence; Kyte had been convicted of rape after committing murder, but before he was charged with murder. Three – Hardy, Smith and Naylor – were known to have been violent towards other sex workers, and six out of seven (all except Harding) either had convictions or had previously been investigated for serious offences but not charged.

- All suspects were white British.

Six out of seven, therefore, had 'come to notice', i.e. were known in some capacity to the police. This was the most common shared characteristic, but in three cases (Kyte, Corner and Wright) their known previous offences were minor.

David Smith was convicted of murdering Amanda Walker in 1999 when he was 43. He had previously been acquitted of murdering Sarah Crump in 1991 when he was 35. He had numerous previous convictions, including convictions for violence against women. In 1976, aged 18, he raped a woman at knifepoint in front of her children and was jailed for four years. In 1987 he attacked a woman in his car: she escaped by kicking out the windscreen; he received a two-year suspended sentence. A year later he confronted a sex worker in a hotel room wearing surgical gloves and armed with a knife. She escaped but was too frightened to give evidence so an attempted murder charge was dropped. He was acquitted of an attack on another sex worker days before Sarah Crump was killed. Sarah's body was found at her home in August 1991. At the trial in 1993, Smith admitted paying her for sex but denied murder. Defence counsel accused police of suppressing evidence, an allegation rejected by the senior investigating officer, but Smith was acquitted. After his acquittal police confirmed they were not looking for anyone else in connection with the case.

Six years later, Smith was said to be spending two-thirds of his wages on sex, even starting his own escort agency, but it was also alleged that his 'anger against women was fuelled by humiliating experiences at the hands of prostitutes and by his feelings of rejection when his wife ... ran off with their lodger.' [11] He then killed 22-year-old Amanda Walker in late April 1999, after meeting her in the street soliciting area of Paddington. Two days later her bloodstained clothing was found not far from Smith's home. As a convicted rapist, he was on a database of sex offenders who lived in the area and an aggravated missing persons enquiry began. In June Amanda's body was found in a shallow grave at Wisley, Surrey: she had been mutilated in the same way as Sarah Crump. As with Sarah, Smith admitted paying Amanda for sex but denied murder. However, his fingerprints were on her handbag and his blood was on her clothes, suggesting she had put up a desperate fight. He was convicted of her murder in December 1999.[12]

As outlined in Chapter 13, page 170, Amanda Walker's vulnerability may have been exacerbated by working in an unfamiliar area, indicating how the anti-prostitution policies of one area can have repercussions in others. However, the criminal justice system had also placed her in jeopardy. Smith was known to be dangerous; his history of violence against sex workers and other women was appalling; the judicial process had utterly failed to restrain him, yet the role of the police was not to monitor his actions or of those like him. Their priority was chasing sex workers and kerb-crawlers. Days after Amanda's body was found, London officers crowed about their ferocious approach to street prostitution at the National Vice Conference.[13] Amanda had been arrested herself the night she died, but the arrest had no deterrent or protective effect. When released from the police station, she went straight back to the beat and it is believed her next client was Smith.

After Smith's conviction, it was said that police 'across the country are examining details of unsolved murders involving prostitutes amid fears that he may have struck a number of times',[14] but no further homicides have been laid at his door.

---

[11]'Prostitute murderer gets life', *BBC News*, 8 December 1999 (see http://news.bbc.co.uk/1/hi/uk/552350.stm); 'The Nineties Ripper', *Evening Standard*, 8 December 1999 (see http://www.findarticles.com/p/articles/mi_qn4153/is_19991208/ai_n11915550); Justin Davenport, 'Life jail for new Ripper', *Evening Standard*, 8 December 1999; 'Killer beat earlier murder charge', *BBC News*, 8 December 1999 (see http://news.bbc.co.uk/1/hi/uk/556081.stm).
[12]'Killer beat earlier murder charge', *BBC News*, 8 December 1999 (see http://news.bbc.co.uk/1/hi/uk/556081.stm).
[13]National Police Vice Conference, Portishead, Bristol, 29 and 30 June 1999.
[14]Justin Davenport, 'Life jail for new Ripper', *Evening Standard*, 8 December 1999.

George Naylor was convicted of murdering Maureen Stepan in 1995 when he was 48. Ten years earlier he had been convicted of the manslaughter of Deborah Kershaw, both victims being sex workers in Bradford. Prior to Kershaw's death in 1974, shortly after his first wife left him, Naylor had burgled and raped a 61-year-old neighbour. He got a 15-year sentence, of which he served ten years, and was released in October 1985. Eight weeks later he killed Deborah Kershaw: her body was found wedged behind the front seats of his car after a police chase. He had choked her with his forearm and then strangled her, but nevertheless successfully pleaded guilty to manslaughter, claiming self-defence. His sentence was reduced to eleven years on appeal, and eventually he served only seven years. Two years later, in June 1995, he strangled Maureen Stepan, then stripped and abused her body with a lighted cigarette.

None of the reports I have accessed mention any parole conditions imposed on Naylor after completing his sentence for killing Deborah, but he was well-known to the police. After his conviction for Maureen's murder, they said Naylor had a long history of violence and that many of his attacks had never led to judicial proceedings, but they did not say why not, nor whether any of these attacks were on sex workers. They had been obliged to give Naylor's ex-wife protection whenever he was out of prison, ever since she left him in 1973, but it was not, evidently, their job to stop him being violent to anyone else. They also had a major community conflict to negotiate in the Bradford soliciting area. On 29 May 1995, eleven days before Maureen was killed, *The Independent* reported on local vigilante activity that was chasing Bradford sex workers away from their traditional spots in Lumb Lane. One of the women was quoted as saying: 'This used to be a safe place to work …. We've been here years, we know the punters, which ones to avoid.'[15] Whether or not the vigilantism influenced Naylor's behaviour – the worthlessness of sex workers was being proclaimed on all sides – the crowds of demonstrators and outbreaks of violence would have certainly heightened adrenaline levels and absorbed the attention of police. Maureen Stepan was killed after taking Naylor back to her flat for business, perhaps, like Caroline Creevy 17 months later, to avoid the hostility on the streets.

Police described Naylor as both 'cold and calculating' and 'unable to control himself', speculating that he had 'snapped' on the night he

---

[15]'Bradford's moral guardians', *The Independent*, 29 May 1995; see also page 106.

killed Maureen because he had failed to reach his (second) wife by phone after making repeated calls to her during the night. The officer leading the investigation commented, 'George has a problem with women who seek to control him', although, to an outsider, Naylor's behaviour suggests that his 'problem' was more to do with his need to control women than vice versa. Naylor's first wife, a psychiatric nurse, told the Bradford *Telegraph & Argus* that she had suffered six years of physical and sexual attacks before she left him and believed him to be a psychopath.

Naylor was sentenced to life imprisonment in February 1997, with the recommendation that he should serve a minimum of 20 years. The verdict was confirmed in two retrials and the minimum sentence confirmed in February 2006.[16]

Alun Kyte was 29 when he murdered two sex workers in the Midlands, in December 1993 and March 1994. The first was Samo Paull, who worked in Birmingham; her body was found over 40 miles away, near a motorway junction in Leicestershire. She was reported missing to Sandwell police as soon as she failed to return home. The second was Tracey Turner who lived in Stoke-on-Trent and worked from motorway service stations. Her body was found a few miles from where Paull had been dumped, the day after a television programme appealed for help with solving Paull's murder.

In the six months after Paull's death, four other sex workers, including Turner, were murdered in other parts of the country, and the senior detective in Leicestershire wanted a cross-force investigation. This would have been costly in terms of police time and resources and was not agreed by all forces involved (Bilton 1995). Instead, Leicestershire police investigated Turner's death, but because she lived in Stoke, Staffordshire police were also involved; because Paull had been reported missing before her body was found, her death was investigated by Sandwell police, and Birmingham police were also involved because that was where she worked. As the outreach project manager in Birmingham at the time, the upshot of this from my

---

[16]'The nearest thing to a serial killer', *Telegraph & Argus*, 1 February 1999; 'Maureen could have been alive if only they'd listened', *Telegraph & Argus*, 4 February 1999; High Court setting of minimum terms for mandatory life sentences under the Criminal Justice Act 2003, Case No.: 2004/32/MTS, Neutral Citation Number: [2006] EWHC 178 (QB), in the High Court of Justice, Queen's Bench Division, Royal Courts of Justice, Strand, London WC2A 2LL, 14 February 2006, before the Honourable Mr Justice Owen.

perspective was that we had repeated visits from officers of different forces, all asking for the same information, none of whom seemed aware of each other's visits. Within three months of Turner's death, street workers and their clients in Birmingham, who might have been able to assist the investigations, were driven in all directions by the anti-prostitution demonstrations of local residents.[17] Whether or not these factors made any difference, Kyte was not identified until he was arrested in 1997 for a subsequent rape and was in prison when DNA connected him to the murder of Tracey Turner. Before his arrest for rape, he had committed various minor offences, mainly theft. He was convicted of both murders in 2000.

Descriptions of his 'client behaviour' come from the testimony of fellow prisoners at his trial, and from a surviving victim, who identified Kyte as the man who attacked her shortly before Turner was murdered. Kyte picked her up in his car in Birmingham, took her to her usual place for business, then produced a knife, using it to nick her skin and to force her to hand over her purse. She kept calm, talked to him and told him she was pregnant. He eventually let her go, and she immediately ran to the nearest police station to report him. No accounts of Kyte's case say whether Birmingham police pursued the attack on the surviving victim.

Fellow prisoners testified that Kyte had boasted of killing both Paull and Turner and of attacks on other sex workers. He was alleged to have said 'you don't pay for that sort of girl' (Britton 2001), that both murders began with arguments over payment for sex, that one of them laughed at him for his lack of sexual prowess and that he strangled her to 'shut her up'.[18] The version of events Kyte gave his fellow prisoners is similar to the explanations and excuses given by other attackers, where the victim is portrayed as having provoked the violence by arguing over money or mocking her assailant. The version given by the surviving victim is one of sadism and robbery. Both show that not paying for sex was integral to Kyte's violence.

After Kyte's conviction, various newspapers announced that his possible involvement in many unsolved cases would be explored, but

---

[17]See Chapter 8.
[18]'Prostitute killer jailed', *BBC News*, 14 March 2000 (see http://news.bbc. co.uk/1/hi/uk/664746.stm); Nick Paton Walsh, 'Midlands Ripper unmasked', *The Observer*, 9 March 2000; 'My unborn child saved me from a horrible death', *Sunday People*, 26 March 2000; 'Prostitutes killed in money rows – court', *The Sentinel* (Stoke-on-Trent), 7 March 2000.

he has not been charged with any of the other homicides with which he was linked.

Anthony Hardy, the 'Camden Ripper', was aged 52 when he murdered three sex workers during 2002. He was an alcoholic and drug user who had a history of mental illness and of violence towards women, both sex workers and others. In the 1980s, in Tasmania, he tried to murder his wife: he spent two weeks in psychiatric care, then became homeless and began stalking his wife, but his only arrest was for car theft. By the 1990s, he was in Britain, homeless and abusing alcohol. He was investigated over a number of rapes, but the Crown Prosecution Service did not consider the evidence against him strong enough to bring into court. The body of his first victim was found when he was arrested for pouring battery acid through a neighbour's letterbox in January 2002.[19] Sally White was naked, dead and in a locked room, with a wound at the back of her head. Despite this, the pathologist concluded she had died of a pre-existing heart condition, so the police were not able to follow up her death as a homicide.[20] Hardy was in a mental health institution for most of 2002 but was discharged shortly before killing two more sex workers, Bridgette MacLennan and Elizabeth Valad, in December of that year. It was reported that several professional staff opposed Hardy's release, believing he posed a serious risk to others, especially women, but he was nevertheless allowed to leave. Hardy kept appointments with mental health personnel, including one on 30 December, when body parts of his victims were found by a homeless man searching the rubbish bins for food.

Camden and Islington Mental Health Trust conducted an internal inquiry into why Hardy was released, but its conclusions were somewhat Orwellian: the Chief Executive of the Trust, Erville Millar said: 'he was transferred following a crime of criminal damage to property including other non-violent offences.' This would be pouring battery acid through a neighbour's letterbox, though not, perhaps, having a naked dead woman in his flat. Mr Millar also declared,

---

[19]Matthew Taylor and Rebecca Allison, 'Life for killer who mutilated women', and 'Health chief defends handling of the case', *The Guardian*, 26 November 2003; Graham Coutts, 'The lives of three offenders', *The Guardian*, 5 July 2004.

[20]Julie Bindel, 'These deadly sins', *The Guardian*, 11 August 2004; Matthew Taylor and Rebecca Allison, 'Life for killer who mutilated women', *The Guardian*, 26 November 2003.

'he was well enough [to be discharged] but he was not discharged from the hospital .... He continued to remain in hospital under a detention order and continued in contact with the services right up to his arrest.' How he was 'in hospital under a detention order' and yet also in his flat, killing, mutilating and dismembering women, is not explained. Millar then complained, 'at no time did he declare his crimes. Therefore we could only deal with what we knew in terms of our contact with him.'[21]

Only two weeks before the remains of Hardy's victims were found, the BBC had highlighted the use of ASBOs against sex workers in King's Cross, where all the victims worked. One resident told the BBC, 'I don't care if these people want to kill themselves but I don't see why it should be in my face,' while a spokesperson for the English Collective of Prostitutes pointed out, 'because of these ASBOs [sex workers] are driven into unfamiliar areas. Their regular, safe clients can't find them and they take more risks ...'. It seems likely that the women Hardy murdered would have been more easily persuaded to do business at his flat, where they were all killed, rather than risk outdoor encounters in the local context of draconian policing and community hostility towards them. One of his victims was described as 'the neighbour from hell' because men came to her flat at all hours: by going to Hardy's flat, she might have thought she was avoiding trouble.[22] Another, Elizabeth Valad, had previously worked from indoor premises in Soho, but had been driven onto the streets when Westminster Council enforced closure orders on premises used as brothels.[23]

The mental health procedures which failed to identify the danger Hardy posed to women were publicly criticised after the trial, but the judicial procedures which failed to bring him to court before he murdered three women were not, and the anti-prostitution policies

[21]Martin Bright and Jo Revill, 'Secure unit freed "body bags" suspect', *The Observer*, 5 January 2003. *Note*: The hospital referred to was not a 'secure unit', but a 'general acute mental health service' (see http://www.guardian.co.uk/uk/2003/jan/05/politics.ukcrime); Rebecca Allison and Matthew Taylor, 'Health chief defends handling of case', *The Guardian*, 26 November 2003 (see http://www.guardian.co.uk/uk_news/story/0,3604,1093120,00.html).
[22]Natasha Walter, 'All victims of murder should be treated equally', *The Independent*, 9 January 2003.
[23]Chris Summers, 'Cleaning up King's Cross', *BBC News*, 12 December 2002 (see http://news.bbc.co.uk/1/hi/england/2550709.stm); Jon Silverman, 'Sex workers say "let us stay"', *BBC News*, 18 February 2003.

pursued in Westminster against both indoor and street sex workers remain in place.

After Hardy's conviction, it was announced that he would be investigated in connection with unsolved cases, but he is not known to have been charged with any other attacks or homicides.

Mark Corner, a bodybuilder aged 26, took two Liverpool sex workers, Hanane Parry and Pauline Stephen to his home on consecutive nights in July 2003, where he killed and dismembered both. Corner had only one previous conviction, for being drunk and disorderly, but had been known to mental health services since the age of 12. He was sectioned under the Mental Health Act in the summer of 2002 after threatening to kill a female neighbour, and told doctors he had 'an abnormal interest in girls who died and were dismembered'. Nevertheless, he was released three weeks later, only two weeks after a tribunal ruled he was a risk to others. Within ten days he had threatened another female neighbour with a knife, while drinking heavily, using cocaine, cannabis and ecstasy and failing to take his medication. He was then given outpatient appointments which he failed to keep. He was readmitted to hospital after taking an overdose in April 2003 but because emergency staff were unaware of his psychiatric history he was discharged the next day.[24]

At the time of the killings Corner was suffering from untreated schizophrenia and, therefore, found guilty of manslaughter due to diminished responsibility. In welcome contrast to their counterparts in Camden, the Mersey Care NHS Trust apologised for their failures in Corner's case, including failure to identify or act on warning signs that his condition had seriously deteriorated. Corner's psychiatrist, Eric Birchall, was criticised for failing to use 'approved monitoring systems' and reported to the General Medical Council. The GMC, however, declined to declare Birchall unfit to practice.[25]

---

[24]'Bin bag killer detained in hospital', *BBC News*, 10 December 2003 (see http://news.bbc.co.uk/1/hi/england/merseyside/3306841.stm); 'Killer's care slammed by probe report', *Daily Post*, 2 October 2006; 'Released killer dismembered women', *BBC News*, 8 April 2008 (see http://news.bbc.co.uk/go/pr/fr/-/1/hi/england/merseyside/7337181.stm); 'Psychiatrist "let crazed bodybuilder free to kill and dismember two women," tribunal hears', *Daily Mail*, 9 April 2008.

[25]Jessica Shaughnessy, 'Why was schizophrenic allowed to kill Hanane?', *Chester Chronicle*, 12 December 2003; 'Failings in double killer's care', *BBC News*, 29 September 2006 (see http://news.bbc.co.uk/1/hi/england/

The community context in Liverpool at the time had some similarities to that in King's Cross when Hardy committed his murders. Having been driven out of the traditional soliciting area around Liverpool's cathedrals, street sex workers had dispersed into neighbourhoods where they encountered frequent violence from gangs of youths and others who resented their presence. These factors may have influenced Corner's victims, like Hardy's, to agree to do business at his home, where they were killed.

Garry Harding killed two women at a massage parlour in Shrewsbury in July 2006. This case is unique for several reasons: Harding was 22, with no previous convictions; it is the only case where two victims were killed in a single episode, and one of only two cases involving the death of indoor workers at premises where co-workers were present. Harding was said to have been motivated by robbery to pay gambling debts, hoping to get about £2,000, but he had visited the parlour as a client on previous occasions, so he must have known that there was only one sex worker on the premises,[26] and that the standard charge was £50. To have made £2,000, the sex worker would have had to have seen 40 clients by mid-afternoon, in a small county town, on an afternoon when England was playing a World Cup football match. He found only £330, for which he battered both women to death with a hammer. Harding had researched murder (and suicide) on the Internet; he left no forensic evidence at the scene, but walked past several CCTV cameras in the town, wearing a heavy coat and gloves on a day when the temperature was above 30°C.

When the bodies were discovered, the local community, including a Shrewsbury councillor who also ran a business in the area, stubbornly refused to condemn the establishment: '[the parlour] ... has not given a moment's grief to anyone. The girls come and go, shop in various shops in the area and go home in the evening. There are no pimps – it's run by the women ...'. The landlady of a nearby pub commented: 'I saw girls arrive in the morning and leave at night, with gentlemen arriving during the day. There was never any trouble.'[27] These local responses offered no scope for 'seedy vice racket' stories, nor the

---

merseyside/5392032.stm); 'Doctor in "murderer release" will not be struck off, GMC rules', *Liverpool Daily Post*, 17 April 2008.
[26] The second victim was the receptionist.
[27] 'Shock at brothel double murder', *BBC News*, 18 April 2007 (see http://news.bbc.co.uk/go/pr/fr/-/1/hi/england/shropshire/6548413.stm); 'Police hunt man in pirate garb over double murder', *The Guardian*, 4 July 2006 (see http://www.guardian.co.uk/crime/article/0,,1812221,00.html).

blighting effects of such premises on respectable neighbourhoods. Neither were there any dark stories about trafficked women being held captive in brothels and forced to submit to dozens of customers every day, nor claims about 'massage parlours masquerading as bona fide businesses'. Within a week 250 calls had been made to West Mercia police, many of them by clients of the parlour volunteering information.[28]

Harding pleaded guilty on the first day of his trial, so no evidence was aired which might have shed light on his horrific actions and many questions remain unanswered by the motivation suggested for such unprecedented violence. Are there unscrupulous casinos in Harding's home town of Welshpool or did he gamble online? Had he perhaps ventured beyond the Welsh borders in his relatively short life? Are there unreported cases of hammer-wielding robbers at other parlours? Were his earlier visits to the parlour only to establish a 'good client' identity? His planning was as patchy as his arithmetic was poor, which does not suggest a sophisticated manipulator of interpersonal dynamics. Was he also addicted to computer games where digital sex workers can be killed without compunction and reappear in the next game unharmed?

In court he was said to have a borderline personality disorder but insufficiently debilitating to support a plea of diminished responsibility. He was sentenced to a minimum of 25 years: the judge said it would have been a 'whole life' sentence had it not been his first offence.[29] There was no media frenzy, no examination of the implications for sex work law and policy, no fountains of print demonising clients or ranting about 'tragic vice girls' – the case drew one sentence in the main BBC news, a couple more in the regional news and disappeared from the national press overnight.

Steve Wright, born 1958, was convicted of killing five women in Ipswich between 30 October and 10 December 2006: Tania Nichol, Gemma Adams, Anneli Alderton, Annette Nicholls and Paula Clennell. Wright's case is examined in detail in Chapter 16, but did he have anything in common with the other suspects charged with multiple sex worker homicides?

---

[28]'Murder helpline caller is traced', BBC News, 6 July 2006 (see http://news.bbc.co.uk/1/hi/england/shropshire/5154640.stm).
[29]'Double killer gets 25 years', Shropshire Star, 19 April 2007; 'Massage parlour murderer jailed for life', Birmingham Post, 20 April 2007.

He was over 40, like Anthony Hardy, David Smith and George Naylor, but both Smith and Naylor had previously been charged with killing a sex worker when they were in their thirties. Like the other men over 40, Wright was said to have a history of domestic violence, but unlike them, not of violence towards sex workers.[30] Hardy killed two women in a very short period, but his third victim was eleven months earlier, and there were several years between the homicides attributed to Naylor and Smith. Harding killed two in one episode and Corner's two victims were killed on consecutive nights, but both Harding and Corner were in their twenties; Corner was schizophrenic and Harding allegedly motivated by robbery.

Hardy, Smith, Naylor and Kyte all used strangulation or asphyxiation, but Hardy, Smith and Naylor also degraded and mutilated their victims; Harding beat his to death with a hammer and Corner's victims were too mutilated for a cause of death to be ascertained. Corner and Hardy both dismembered the bodies and dumped them in rubbish bags; Harding, Smith, Naylor and Kyte either left them where they died or moved them after death, but none were placed in water or posed, as were four of Wright's five victims.

Smith and Naylor both had previous convictions for serious offences, and though Hardy had escaped previous prosecution for violence, he was 'on the radar', while Wright was not. Neither were Harding, Corner or Kyte, but all three were under 30 when they committed homicide. Wright had, however, spent long stretches of his life abroad. Is it possible that he had 'come to notice' in another country? The American serial killer, John Armstrong, killed five sex workers in eight months (1999 to 2000) in Detroit, having killed at least 11 more in several countries around the world while serving in the US navy.[31] Could Wright have been among the 27,500 British criminals convicted abroad whose records were not entered on the criminal records database because of lack of Home Office funding? Or on the mislaid disc recently found at the Home Office?[32] Would we be told if he was?

---

[30] A former sex worker has claimed she was attacked by Wright in the 1980s, but he was not a known threat to sex workers in Ipswich. 'Wright "attacked ex-prostitute"', BBC News, 28 February 2008 (see http://news.bbc.co.uk/go/pr/fr/-/1/hi/england/hereford/worcs/7265501.stm).
[31] 'International serial killer suspect charged', BBC News, 14 April 2000 (see http://news.bbc.co.uk/1/hi/world/americas/713972.stm).
[32] 'Police chiefs take Reid to task in records row', The Guardian, 11 January 2007; Nicolas Watt, 'CPS admits disc of suspects' DNA was "mislaid" for a year', The Guardian, 20 February 2008.

As with Kyte, Hardy, Smith and Valentine, there has been speculation that Wright will also be charged with other unsolved murders. He knew the missing estate agent, Suzy Lamplugh, when they both worked on the QE2 cruise ship in the 1980s; there are two unsolved sex worker murders in Norwich, a third missing presumed dead, a fourth also missing presumed dead in Ipswich, and a fifth murdered young woman who was not a sex worker, also from Ipswich, all dating back to between 1992 and 2002. Police forces far from East Anglia also want to see if they can link Wright to yet more unsolved cases. However, none of the other multiple killers have faced further murder charges and the possibility of them receiving a fair trial if they did seems doubtful, which may be why they have not been so charged. It might also be that following up old cases of sex worker murders is not a priority for either the police or the judiciary. It will be interesting to see if we hear anything more about the outstanding cases to which Wright has been linked.

Chapter 16

Steve Wright: a passing nightmare?

Unanswered questions

The murders of five women in Ipswich in the last weeks of 2006 was the most extreme manifestation of violence against sex workers for 30 years, but the rapidity with which the case has vanished from public debate suggests that few want to discuss the difficult questions that remain, or to acknowledge the continuing shameful vulnerability of sex workers to extreme violence.[1] Neither did the trial of Steve Wright acknowledge the vulnerabilities imposed on his victims by the criminalisation of street prostitution.[2] Extensive information was aired about the victims: their backgrounds, drug problems, height and weight were deemed sufficiently relevant to their deaths to constitute legal evidence, but no attempt was made to explore other reasons for their vulnerability nor Wright's motivation. After Peter Sutcliffe's trial, feminists castigated the judicial process for its unrealistic separation of a 'sexual' motive from Sutcliffe's alleged 'divine mission', but at

---

[1]Harrison and Wilson (2008) are the first to turn the Ipswich tragedy into a book, which recycles journalistic coverage and extracts from Wilson's exposition on serial killers (Wilson 2007), including its serious inaccuracies regarding unsolved cases of sex worker homicide (see Chapter 14, page 203). It ends by endorsing the very policies against street prostitution which were being pursued with great vigour in Ipswich before the murders, placing all the women in jeopardy.

[2]I have used the comprehensive trial reports published on the *East Anglia Daily Times* website (http://www.eadt.co.uk) and other local insights.

least Sutcliffe's motives were explored. Because his guilt was not in doubt, the whole trial was about the cause of his behaviour. At Wright's trial, all the evidence was about fibres, DNA traces, CCTV images and ANPR,[3] backed up with the times his partner was on night shifts. No motivation – beyond the need to murder as an aid to sexual stimulation – was suggested, and no experts were wheeled into court to explain how such an unusual sexual perversion might suddenly manifest itself in this unprecedented fashion.

Before forensic science reached its present state of seeming infallibility, establishing a motive for murder was an important element of a prosecution, but, as the spokesman for the Crime Prosecution Service in Wright's case remarked, 'Quite often in a murder case we do not know the motive or understand it if we do. The evidence leads us to who did it and that's more important.'[4] Indisputably, but the need for a convincing explanation of *why* such terrible crimes were committed was reflected in every media report of Wright's conviction. The traditional alternatives of mental illness and sexual gratification appeared; his problematic relationships with other women in his life were cited as evidence of his misogyny; for those who regard paying for sex as intrinsically abusive, no other cause for Wright's behaviour was needed. Forget that no such killer has been seen for a generation, or ever if one takes into account the lack of frenzy that seems to have accompanied these acts of murder: Wright was a punter, no need to say more.

However, three out of six of the Ipswich residents interviewed for the BBC after Wright's conviction were unconvinced by the verdict,[5] and many of those who knew him remained baffled. It may be that in future more light will be shed on the mystery of why a man of 48, with no previous convictions for violence, should suddenly decide to kill five women in under seven weeks. It may be too soon to make any sense of Wright, but it is possible that tension arising at the interface between sex and money, as in many other less publicised cases, may also underlie the sudden outburst of extreme homicidal behaviour in this 'good punter'.

---

[3] ANPR – automatic number plate recognition.
[4] 'Steve Wright found guilty of murdering five Ipswich prostitutes', *Times Online*, 21 February 2008 (see http://www.timesonline.co.uk/tol/news/uk/crime/article3410456.ece).
[5] 'Ipswich reacts to Wright verdict', *BBC News*, 21 February 2008 (see http://news.bbc.co.uk/go/pr/fr/-/1/hi/england/suffolk/7257339.stm).

Possible motives

> One of the girls might have ripped him off or was trying to blackmail him. It's also possible he fell in love with one of them. Punters do that all the time and they take it badly when they get rejected.[6]

This was one sex worker's attempt to make sense of Wright's actions, and her guess may be as near the truth as any made by more exalted commentators. The prosecution, however, contented itself with declaring that 'we may never know' what motivated Wright, claiming that his killing spree was triggered solely by his move to London Road in the soliciting area of Ipswich, and that he murdered them for sexual gratification because mere sex was no longer enough for him. But we now know that his switch from model client to multiple murderer was not provoked by changing from indoor to street sex workers – according to those who survived, he had been using street workers in Ipswich for three years before moving to London Road, and regularly drove to Norwich to do business with street workers there too. What is more, they consistently described Wright as a trouble-free client.

So what else could have precipitated his killing spree?

Wright admitted paying for sex frequently, and one sex worker who knew him said, 'You would often see him driving round looking for girls, even if he had picked you the night before.' This suggests Wright was paying for sex every day of the week, although perhaps only when his partner was on night shifts. Such frequency is unusual – most client surveys find that once a week is common, and the average time gap between episodes of paid sex longer still (Kinnell 2006b). It would also have been expensive. Wright claimed that since his partner had been working night shifts, their sex life had become almost 'non-existent',[7] with the inference that his use of sex workers increased because of lack of sex with his partner – but his partner had been working night shifts for several months before they moved to London Road, raising the possibility that, by time he moved into the soliciting area, his frequency of paying for sex had caused him serious financial difficulties. Wright boasted in court that he always haggled over the price – commonly a precursor to violence,[8] but

---

[6]'Street girl felt comfortable with Wright', *Evening Star*, 22 February 2008.
[7]Trial evidence, 7 February 2008.
[8]See Chapter 5, page 57.

none of the sex workers who knew him confirmed this. Admitting to paying for sex may be humiliating, and Wright's offensive claim that he never paid the asking price may have been a twisted way of portraying himself as a less pitiful figure, but whether he paid £20 or £60 a time, a daily habit would have cost him between £140 and £420 per week. Yet the Wright household was apparently short of cash. One item found in his house was a demand regarding an unpaid bill of £272, and though golf was his passion, his golf club membership was about to be suspended because he had not paid the fee of £47.50, suggesting his financial affairs were in crisis.

Inability to live within his income seems to have been a recurrent theme in Wright's life, and various media reports attributed this to his addiction to paid sex, heavy drinking and gambling. None of his recent associates mentioned him drinking to excess, but at some point in the 1990s,[9] having sold his furniture and a car he didn't own and maxed-out his credit cards, he fled the country, and went to Thailand. There he 'lavished expensive lingerie and gold jewellery on a Thai girl', who, according to his brother, 'ended up scamming him for everything he had'. When he returned to England he had to declare himself bankrupt. His brother pinpointed this experience as one which hit Wright very hard and preceded one of his suicide attempts.[10] His past crises therefore seem to have arisen because he could not stop himself spending money he didn't have on sex. This time, instead of trying to kill himself, perhaps he decided to kill the temptresses who had caused his difficulties, or perhaps it was simply a way of avoiding payment. You don't have to pay a corpse. By killing five, Wright had saved himself up to £300, plus getting whatever other money they had on them when they died.

The relationship of non-payment to violence against sex workers has been referred to many times in this book, but it is usually ignored in discussions of serial killers, for whom far more complex and mysterious motives are usually suggested. However, an explicit acknowledgement of the intimate connection between not paying for sex and murder was given by Robert Hansen, who killed many sex workers in Alaska in the early 1980s. He admitted to being a

---

[9]No consistent date has been found for this episode.
[10]Sean O'Neill, 'Profile: Steve Wright, taciturn golfer with deadly secret', *Times Online*, 21 February 2008 (see http://www.timesonline.co.uk/tol/news/uk/crime/article3411602.ece); Karen McVeigh, 'He came out of nowhere', *Guardian Online*, 21 February 2008; Nick Allen and Gordon Rayner, 'Steve Wright: a real Jekyll and Hyde', *The Telegraph*, 21 February 2008.

lifelong thief, and that taking something without paying produced sexual arousal: 'I hate to spend money ... I damn near ejaculate in my pants if I could walk into a store and take something ... I got a lot the same feeling I did with a prostitute' (Wilson and Seaman 2007). Gary Ridgway, who killed dozens of women in the USA, was also explicit in his hatred of sex workers and his determination not to pay for sex: 'I hate most prostitutes and I did not want to pay them for sex ... they were easy to pick up without being noticed. I knew they would not be reported missing right away and might never be reported missing ... I thought I could kill as many of them as I wanted without getting caught.'[11]

The possibility that Wright's murder spree was a planned strategy to deal with his problem of wanting paid sex but not being able to afford it fits with his move into the Ipswich soliciting area. It was a move he chose to make, and the murders began within a month, apparently as soon as his partner worked a night shift. It looks as if he had deliberately given himself a blameless reason for being in the area if stopped by the police, which he was, and surrounded himself with opportunities, not to pay for sex, but to commit murder.

Wright also seems to have targeted women he had used before, but he did not kill every sex worker he picked up during that time. One wondered, 'Why wasn't I killed as well? ... because within the time that the killings were taking place I was going to the house ... and doing business with him ...'[12]. It seems possible he had identified those he wished to kill: a report in *The Observer* implies that Wright was working through a list of mobile phone numbers, one belonging to a woman he tried to persuade to go to his house immediately after Paula Clennell, his last victim, disappeared.[13] He admitted to knowing all the victims, and one survivor described his relationships with some of them: 'He was Annette's regular ... I think he picked up Tania once before but she didn't like him. She said "I'm never seeing him again." I don't know why she said that ... Paula saw

---

[11]'Defendant pleads guilty to 48 murders in Green River case', *New York Times*, 5 November 2003. Canter compared Wright to Ridgway, but does not mention the aspect of non-payment. David Canter, 'Comment: killed because they could be', *Times Online*, 22 February 2008 (see http://www.timesonline.co.uk/tol/news/uk/crime/article3412923.ece).
[12]'The "lucky girl" who knew killer', *BBC News*, 21 February 2008 (see http://news.bbc.co.uk/go/pr/fr/-/1/hi/england/suffolk/7248779.stm).
[13]Mark Townsend and Anushka Asthana, 'How two brutal killers fuelled the DNA debate', *The Observer*, 24 February 2008.

him. I think she stole his phone once.'[14] Joan Smith found humour in the suggestion that the 'Ipswich killer hates prostitutes because he's been swindled by one of them' (Smith 2006), but contemptible and inadequate as such an explanation might be, Sutcliffe seems to have developed his hatred for sex workers after being swindled out of £10, and revenge for being 'ripped off' is mentioned regularly in Ugly Mug reports. Paula's reputation for stealing was also mentioned by others; a boyfriend 'claimed she had taken £1,000 from a client.'[15] Could this client have been Wright? Had any of the others stolen from him? Anneli Alderton's mother said Gemma Adams taught her daughter to be a 'clipper', although devoted clients of Gemma's did not complain of her using this trick on them.[16] Another sex worker claimed Annette Nicholls, believed to have been Wright's favourite, also robbed clients and had stolen a client's phone shortly before she was killed (Addley 2006). The observation that Tania Nichol did not like Wright may also be significant. If Wright had shown her a side of himself he was usually able to suppress, it might be why Tania was the first to be killed, before she could warn others to be wary of him. Alternatively, it could simply have been because she refused to do business with him. The last time she was seen alive, she was talking to a man in a car, who Wright admitted might well have been him, shaking her head, as if refusing a suggestion made by the driver. If Tania was refusing his business, was this too much for Wright's self-esteem? As Ugly Mug reports demonstrate, turning clients down can provoke rage.[17]

And yet, the condition of the bodies did not suggest rage, but controlled, painless execution. The prosecution's opening statement at Wright's trial confirmed that there were 'no obvious signs of gratuitous violence, no significant injuries, no defence wounds, no signs of sexual assault.'[18] Even Paula's body, which showed some signs of struggle and appeared to have been dumped hurriedly, did not bear obvious signs of frenzy or contempt. This aspect of the murders

---

[14]Mark Bulstrode (Press Association), 'Wright: prostitute "saved by unexpected noise"', *The Independent*, 21 February 2008 (see http://www.independent.co.uk/news/uk/crime/wright-prostitute-saved-by-unexpected-noise-785174.html).

[15]Mark Townsend and Anushka Asthana, 'The killer of Handford Road', *The Observer*, 17 December 2006.

[16]Trial evidence, 22 and 24 January 2008.

[17]See Chapter 12.

[18]Prosecution opening statement, 16 February 2008.

more than anything else sets Wright apart from all the other British multiple killers. Several used strangulation or asphyxiation but also degraded and mutilated their victims; bodies were dismembered, burnt, dumped in rubbish bags or left where they died, but none were placed in water or posed, as were four of the five Ipswich victims. Few suggestions were made by external commentators about the significance of this treatment of the bodies. One dismissed it as a conscious attempt to leave a 'trademark', indicating a desire to acquire notoriety as 'the Crucifix Killer',[19] another speculated that it might have some religious significance. With bodies placed in water, suggesting post-mortem baptism, and others apparently arranged to signify the crucified Christ, some religious theme seems possible. Harrison and Wilson (2008) dismiss this possibility; they portray Wright as highly forensically aware, placing the first two bodies in water to minimise forensic evidence, and suggest he adopted the cruciform arrangement of the next two in response to media suggestions of a religious motive, thus ignoring the fact that Anneli and Annette both died before Tania Nichol's body was found, so before any association could be made between the disposal of her body with that of Gemma Adams.

Wright himself did not seek refuge in a Sutcliffe-type defence of diminished responsibility due to religious delusions, and the prosecution was happy to leave the question unanswered. The judge, Mr Justice Gross, nevertheless cited the 'macabre' positioning of Annette's and Anneli's bodies as an aggravating feature of the case, contributing to his decision to impose a whole-life sentence on Wright. In his summing up, he described their arrangement in detail: Anneli had her arms and her right leg outstretched, left leg flexed at the knee, and 'even her hair had been posed'. Annette, whose arms were also outstretched, had her hair arranged almost 'symmetrically straight up'.[20] Rather than parodies of the crucified Christ, the details about their hair suggest images of figures that are falling from a height, or suspended upside down, as found in some representations of the Hanged Man (who is not always male) in a deck of Tarot cards. Wright gave no appearance of being the sort of man to have any interest in such quasi-occult matters, but he did not give the impression of being a man to dress up in a wig and PVC

---

[19]Nick Allen and Gordon Rayner, 'Steve Wright "may have killed others"', *The Telegraph*, 21 February 2008 (see http://www.telegraph.co.uk/news/main.jhtml?xml=/news/2008/02/21/nsuffolk521.xml).
[20]Judge's summing up, 19 February 2008.

skirt either.[21] My patience with Tarot websites expired rapidly, but one of these described the Hanged Man card as sometimes 'representing the natural and normal function of disposing of something that no longer suits its purpose as well as its replacement will.'[22] Whatever image Wright was trying to convey in his positioning of these bodies, it seems possible that his methods of disposal did have a meaning which went beyond the basic necessity of getting rid of the corpses.

Before Wright's arrest, when swarms of journalists appointed themselves amateur detectives, searching for likely suspects, one was described as '"The Uncle", the mysterious man obsessed with Christianity who used to pick up prostitutes, talk to them about God and give them drugs'.[23] This does not sound like Wright, who was the 'normal, average punter', or merely 'Mondeo man', but one sex worker said he had helped her to buy drugs: 'He could see that I was withdrawing and wasn't well so he insisted on taking me to my dealer.'[24] Yet the prosecution do not seem to have utilised this woman's evidence. As the defence pointed out, there was 'no suggestion that Wright was a supplier and no suggestion he had anything to do with the women taking drugs,'[25] but if Wright did know where to find drug dealers as well as sex workers, it might account for the very high level of drugs in the bodies of his victims and the absence of signs of struggle. Whether or not he gave them drugs himself, he seems to have attacked when they were at their most incapacitated and in an extremely controlled fashion.

This level of control is at odds with various accounts of Wright's behaviour 20 years earlier, when he was alleged to have been violent to his ex-wife, Diane. A former neighbour said, 'Steve used to strangle Diane right in front of us .... He would pin her up against the wall and put both hands around her throat. There were at least three times when he did it in front of witnesses.'[26] The formerly high-profile sex

---

[21]The accuracy of assertions about Wright's cross-dressing has been questioned – see below.

[22]http://www.angelpaths.com/majors/hanged.html

[23]Mark Townsend and Anushka Asthana, 'The killer of Handford Road', *The Observer*, 17 December 2006.

[24]'Street girl felt comfortable with Wright', *Evening Star*, 22 February 2008; Harrison and Wilson (2008) also suggest Wright promoted his victims' drug use (2008: 65).

[25]Defence summing up, 14 February 2008.

[26]'Steve Wright found guilty of murdering five Ipswich prostitutes', *Times Online*, 21 February 2008 (see http://www.timesonline.co.uk/tol/news/uk/

worker Lindi St Clair claimed she was attacked by Wright in the 1980s, and that he lunged at her, trying to grab her throat.[27] Even if this was Wright, he does not seem to have lunged and grabbed at the Ipswich women; if he had, there would presumably have been marks on their bodies to show it. Accounts of his behaviour when he ran the Ferry Boat pub in the soliciting area of Norwich in the late 1980s are also difficult to reconcile with the man he had become by 2006. It was said that he used to cross-dress when soliciting women, and one sex worker claimed, 'If you didn't get in the car he would get naked and just sit there with the headlights on. He freaked me out. The police knew about him.' But none of the Ipswich women who knew him 20 years later had witnessed such bizarre behaviour, and the Norwich local paper could not corroborate these stories. Harrison and Wilson (2008) nevertheless imply that this account of Wright's behaviour during the 1980s applied to the time of the murders in 2006. Other accounts of Wright's time in Norwich are completely different, for example:

> During his time at the Ferry Boat, Wright did not pay for sex. He did, however, make friends with the women and welcome them into the pub. 'Some landlords are funny about prostitutes,' one girl said. 'But he was always friendly and, if you needed money, you knew you could go to him and he'd help you out.[28]

Wright's colourful past – steward aboard the QE2, Thailand, massive debts, suicide attempts – is in stark contrast to his quiet, tidy, low-key existence prior to the murders. He played golf, washed his car, had a drink at his local and paid for sex. His golfing chums said he was boring, his neighbours thought him decent, the landlady at his local thought him quiet and lacking in personality and sex workers thought him a nice bloke. One psychiatrist opined that Wright's history suggested a bipolar disorder, which might account for florid episodes in a normally unremarkable man.[29] Obviously the

---

crime/article3410456.ece); Nick Allen and Gordon Rayner, 'Steve Wright: a real Jekyll and Hyde', *The Telegraph*, 21 February 2008.

[27]'Wright "attacked ex-prostitute"', *BBC News*, 28 February 2008 (see http://news.bbc.co.uk/go/pr/fr/-/1/hi/england/hereford/worcs/7265501.stm).

[28]'Wright's city pub was girls' safe haven', *Evening News*, 22 February 2008; 'Street girl felt comfortable with Wright', *Evening Star*, 22 February 2008.

[29]'Steve Wright found guilty of murdering five Ipswich prostitutes', *Times*

prosecution would not welcome any suggestions of mental illness, raising the contentious spectre of 'diminished responsibility', and with Wright protesting his innocence neither could the defence make any, but some such explanation might account for his extraordinarily inconsistent behaviour.

However, the control that enabled Wright to kill four women leaving barely a mark on them, dispose of their bodies with ritualistic care and still find sex workers trusting enough to accept his business had evidently begun to slip with Paula Clennell. There were marks indicating struggle on her body, and he dumped her hurriedly, apparently taken by surprise to find police cordons around the area where he had laid out Annette Nicholls a few days before. A sex worker, who thought him 'nice' and 'trustworthy', went to Wright's house soon after Paula's body was discovered. She said he 'wasn't himself'; normally smart, he was scruffy and sweaty; normally gentle, he was 'nasty', and scared her by pinning her down in frustration when he couldn't maintain an erection – a problem he had not had with her before and one which would place Wright in a well-known class of violent punters and give him something in common with Sutcliffe.[30] Had this woman's testimony been heard in court, it would have been clear that Wright had lied on several matters: not picking up street sex workers prior to October 2006; not having sex with them in the bed he shared with his partner; removing condoms wearing gardening gloves; and not possessing a red blanket, fibres of which were found in his car and on the bodies.[31] Yet she does not seem to have been called as a witness.

Unheard voices

The exclusion of sex workers from the trial is disturbing. The police are said to have interviewed every known street worker in Ipswich

---

Online, 21 February 2008 (see http://www.timesonline.co.uk/tol/news/uk/crime/article3410456.ece).
[30]See Chapter 1, page 17; Chapter 5, pages 60–1; Chapter 12, page 155.
[31]Mark Bulstrode (Press Association), 'Wright: prostitute "saved by unexpected noise"', *The Independent*, 21 February 2008 (see http://www.independent.co.uk/news/uk/crime/wright-prostitute-saved-by-unexpected-noise-785174.html); Harrison and Wilson (2008) are the source for the suggestion of Wright's impotence.

before Wright was arrested,[32] but only two gave evidence in court, 'Miss F' who had been with Paula shortly before she disappeared, and 'Miss D' who knew Anneli but was vague about when she last saw her. Clearly, some would have been useless to the prosecution's case because they had only seen the 'good punter' side of Wright, but the defence did not call them either. There were others who did not appear in court, whom one would have thought had relevant testimony to give, who had a right to be heard, to be allowed to defend themselves, to confront the person who had so grievously changed their lives, or to ask how it was possible for Wright to carry on killing in a tiny area bristling with police officers. Wright's partner did not give evidence; her son, whose DNA was found on a cigarette butt in Wright's car, did not give evidence; Tom Stephens, whom the defence tried to implicate, and the prosecution did not exonerate, did not give evidence. Anneli's boyfriend did give evidence, but Gemma's boyfriend, Jon Simpson, did not.

Jon and Gemma had been together since they were teenagers. He always stayed close to her when she was working, keeping in touch by text messages. On the night Gemma disappeared, he sent her two texts between 12 and 1 a.m., but she replied to neither. His last text was sent minutes before Wright's car was captured on CCTV in Handford Road. Jon then drove around looking for her for two hours and reported her missing at 2.55 a.m.[33] Surely his evidence was relevant to the trial? But Gemma's body was not found for two weeks and it was not the police who found her. Jon was banned from Ipswich in January 2007 after 'assaulting a police officer', a fracas in which he (not the officer) sustained a broken wrist.[34] Is it possible that he felt the police had been slow to respond to her disappearance? If the CCTV images had been examined sooner, could lives have been saved? Is that why his role in reporting her missing was never mentioned in court? Was it better for everyone that he was not given a turn in the witness box?

[32] Mark Townsend and Anushka Asthana, 'The killer of Handford Road', The Observer, 17 December 2006.
[33] 'No sex assault on prostitute found dead', East Anglia News, 7 December 2006.
[34] Mark Townsend and Denis Campbell, 'Serial killer hunted after second woman found dead', The Observer, 10 December 2006; 'Gemma's boyfriend banned from town', Evening Star, 29 January 2007.

Policing and vulnerability

Sex workers believed that the low-key police response after both Tania and Gemma went missing had endangered the others,[35] and the exclusion of Jon Simpson from the trial suggests it was orchestrated to exclude any hint of responsibility on the part of police for failing to respond quickly enough to their disappearances. The role of the police before, during and after the murders, and the attitudes to street sex workers which pertained at the time, also received perfunctory or no attention during the trial, but the little that was said indicates how anti-street prostitution measures contributed to the women's vulnerability. The prosecution's opening statement accounted for the limited evidence from CCTV cameras by explaining that: 'The presence of close circuit television cameras often acts as a deterrent both to prostitutes and their clients. Accordingly, there is a tendency for these activities to be conducted out of sight of the close circuit television cameras and in circumstances in which their conduct cannot be captured on any particular medium.'[36] A policewoman testified that the introduction of CCTV in areas previously used for soliciting had moved the women into residential areas, which may have provoked more complaints and more hostile policing. However, it is not inevitable that sex workers avoid monitored areas. On the contrary, in places where they do not fear arrest, they often deliberately solicit in and take their clients to areas that are covered by cameras, knowing that it will be a deterrent to attackers and assist police enquiries if they go missing.[37]

A survey of Ipswich sex workers in 2004 found that 86 per cent said they would work in a monitored 'safety zone' – a policy option that had not then been rejected by the Home Office – proving that it was not the cameras that forced the women to hide but the way they were used. It also found that 60 per cent of the women feared being attacked when working; that they feared the dark streets and alleyways; that they knew their vulnerability was increased by having nowhere to take clients and no one knowing where they were when they went off in a stranger's car. The river bank in particular was

---

[35]Mark Townsend and Anushka Asthana, 'The killer of Handford Road', *The Observer*, 17 December 2006.
[36]Prosecution opening statement, 16 February 2008.
[37]See Chapter 6; 'Tackling prostitution in Ipswich', *BBC News*, 23 February 2007 (see http://news.bbc.co.uk/go/pr/fr/-/1/hi/england/suffolk/6385741. stm).

described as 'dark and scary' (Jones 2004).[38] The policewoman who gave evidence at the trial said it was normal for sex workers to take clients out of the area to do business, including to Belstead Brook where the bodies of Tania Nicol and Gemma Adams were found.[39] Was this the 'dark and scary' river bank that women had mentioned two years earlier, and did the police think it was acceptable for them to be frightened? After the murders, The Observer reported, 'All the dead women had complained that the police, rather than protect them, simply ushered them on or threatened them with ASBOs.'[40]

After the third victim, Anneli Alderton, had been found dead, the Assistant Chief Constable of Suffolk, Jacqui Cheer, could think of only one way for sex workers to stay safe, saying, 'Please stay off the streets, if you are out alone at night you are putting yourself in danger.'[41] Lower ranks showed more imagination: while the Ipswich investigation was underway, both Suffolk police and other forces around the country suspended their usual 'zero tolerance' approach and instead implemented 'safety first' strategies – text messaging, attack alarms, encouragement to report attackers – simple, sensible and cheap techniques which have been advocated by sex work projects for years. But once Wright was charged this shift of focus came to an abrupt halt.

Immediately after the murders, Sir Menzies Campbell[42] called for a review of prostitution policy to address the safety of sex workers; a Downing Street spokesman responded: 'This is a difficult issue. We're balancing different and conflicting needs,'[43] but by March 2007, it was clear whose needs were regarded as more important. Attitudes at Ipswich Borough Council had been barely dented by the tragedy that had happened on their watch. Despite having fostered the worst manifestation of sex workers' vulnerability for a generation, the Ipswich Crime and Disorder Reduction Partnership's street prostitution strategy, published in March 2007, explicitly excluded the

---

[38]Jones (2004) also reports that 57 per cent of the women were homeless, which underlines their vulnerability to persuasion to do business at a client's home, demonstrated as an increasing risk factor for homicide (pages 177–8).

[39]Trial evidence, 22 January 2008.

[40]Mark Townsend and Anushka Asthana, 'The killer of Handford Road', The Observer, 17 December 2006.

[41]'Fourth Suffolk prostitute missing', BBC News, 11 December 2006 (see http://news.bbc.co.uk/1/hi/england/suffolk/6168697.stm).

[42]Then the Liberal Democrat leader.

[43]'Tolerance zones plan in tatters', The Guardian, 14 December 2006.

'Ensuring Justice' element of the government's *Co-ordinated Strategy on Prostitution*, which was aimed at 'bringing to justice those who exploit individuals through prostitution and those who commit violent and sexual offences against those involved in prostitution' (Home Office 2006). Announcing a return to former policies of zero tolerance, the Leader of the Council, Liz Harsant, said:

> We have been taking a softly softly approach with the street workers because it is an ongoing inquiry and the police had to interview the girls to get information from them about the murders. But now that the main part of the inquiry has come to an end *we are taking a zero tolerance stance to the kerb crawlers and girls working the streets ... many of the residents there have had enough of the girls, the needles, the foul language and fights.* (Emphasis added)

A sex worker described the effect of this brutal attitude on the behaviour of the police towards them:

> Immediately after the murders happened they were really supportive towards us. They gave us a number we could text to tell them where we were going with a punter. But that number stopped working. A few weeks after that the police started arresting us again for soliciting and loitering, and some have been very abusive .... Some [women] have been carrying bricks and other weapons for protection.[44]

The intense anti-prostitution strategy adopted in Ipswich to get rid of street prostitution once and for all was given enthusiastic encouragement by the Home Office, and throughout the rest of 2007 the media regularly reported claims of its spectacular success, through addressing sex workers' needs for drug treatment, housing and other social care, as well as by cracking down on kerb-crawlers. By the time Wright was convicted, Liz Harsant claimed that where once there were 100 women there were now one or two, and had convinced herself that her views had always been non-judgemental. She said 'the community had not sought to judge the victims, instead sympathising with their desperate plight',[45] but other representatives

[44]Diane Taylor and Hugh Muir, 'Anti-prostitution strategy to offer counselling or court', *The Guardian*, 22 March 2007.
[45]'Pride over town's response to killings', *Evening Star*, 24 February 2008.

of the town were still having difficulty in their choice of language. On the day that Wright was convicted, the MP for Ipswich, Chris Mole, spoke on television about the need for the 'elimination of prostitutes', while Canon Graham Hedger said it had taken five murders to persuade the authorities to do anything to help sex workers. Could the murders therefore be considered a good thing? Is this what is needed to galvanise an effective level of intervention?

However, while it is clear that many of the Ipswich women have been helped to obtain the drug treatment and other services that should have been available to them before the murders, the claims that street prostitution has been almost removed from the town should be regarded with caution. As in other areas where there has been intense political pressure to declare anti-street work measures a total success, it appears that the 'before and after' comparisons made in Ipswich may not be comparing like with like.[46] In February 2008, a local resident compared seeing one woman soliciting on her street to seeing ten a year before, while an Ipswich sex worker recounted that she and Annette Nicholls were the only women out working on the night Annette disappeared.[47] Certainly, after three murders, sex workers may have been staying away from their usual beats, but this comment shows that 'one or two' on the streets of a night was not an unknown phenomenon before the anti-prostitution blitz was implemented. It is also clear that some of the reduction in visible prostitution was due to other factors. Displacement of street workers to Norwich was noted in February 2007, and some have remained there. It was also reported that the police encouraged women to move to indoor work. A massage parlour owner offered sex workers the chance to use her premises:

> She would tolerate drug users as long as there were no substances on site, and anyone who turned up to work 'smashed' would be sent home. Suffolk police community support officers were coming to the premises on a weekly basis to offer help and support and 'doing a good job'.[48]

---

[46]See pages 67–8.
[47]Lucy Bannerman, 'Sex still for sale, but more discreetly', *The Times*, 22 February 2008.
[48]'Scared vice girls move to city', *Evening News*, 27 February 2007, and personal communications; 'Tackling prostitution in Ipswich', *BBC News*, 23 February 2007 (see http://news.bbc.co.uk/go/pr/fr/-/1/hi/england/suffolk/6385741.stm).

Whether the efforts that have been made in Ipswich to address the drug-related needs of the street workers who survived Wright's slaughter will also prevent a new generation of drug-using women, or women who are impelled by other forms of economic desperation, from taking their places, has yet to be seen. What is not in doubt, however, is the continuing vulnerability of street workers: at least six more were murdered elsewhere in Britain between January 2007 and April 2008. Neither 'exit strategies' focused on drug problems nor anti-kerbcrawling measures have any protective effect on those women that continue, for whatever reason, to work in this way.

Chapter 17

Explanations and excuses

We will never know why you killed her, whether it was a disagreement over payment, or your anger which lacks self control, or out of shame or disgust or contempt that you had for the heroin addict prostitute you had just used.[1]

The convictions of Wright and Dixie[2] have, say police sources, underlined the role of drug addiction in many of society's most brutal crimes. All five of Wright's victims sold their bodies to buy heroin, an addiction the serial killer exploited to terrible effect. Dixie's crimes too were fuelled, partly at least, by drugs. (Townsend and Asthana 2008)

These two quotes illustrate contrasting approaches to trying to find explanations for homicide: focusing on the behaviour and motivations of the perpetrators, or on the vulnerabilities of victims. Wilson (2007) argues that the 'medico-psychological tradition' of ascribing vulnerability to the abnormal behaviour of the perpetrators is inadequate, that the focus should be on the outcast status of the victims and on the reasons why the state allows them to be victimised. However, he restricts his criticism of the state to police failures to investigate sex worker homicides competently, using the

---

[1]'Man jailed second time for murder', *BBC News*, 16 February 2001 (see http://news.bbc.co.uk/1/hi/scotland/1174285.stm).
[2]Mark Dixie, convicted in February 2008 of murdering a young woman in London.

Yorkshire Ripper case of the 1970s as a convenient example. He calls this 'creating vulnerability through policing', but he does not explore the failure of the criminal justice system to identify, monitor or restrain offenders who have a history of violence, a far more relevant criticism in contemporary Britain, where, as has been shown, success in solving sex worker homicides has improved greatly in the past ten years.[3] Neither does he address the way in which the state requires the police to enforce anti-prostitution laws which place sex workers in jeopardy, nor those laws themselves.

While I share Wilson's reluctance to feed the narcissism of murderers by making them the centre of attention (Wilson 2007) and agree that focusing on the psychopathology of killers does not contribute to practical strategies for protecting potential victims, blaming victims for being vulnerable is outrageous, and blaming misogyny does not help either. Wilson bows to the prevailing feminist orthodoxy that it is patriarchy and misogyny which make women vulnerable, but does not really explain how, except in the crudest sense, that women are less valued than men, and that men who kill them, hate them. Neither does misogyny explain why sex workers are disproportionately victimised. In the same week that Wright was convicted of the Ipswich murders, Levi Bellfield was convicted of two murders and several other attacks: all his victims were women, but none of his victims were sex workers. Bellfield's crimes were committed in several parts of west London, none of them street soliciting areas; his victims were, however, outdoors and alone when he attacked them.[4] Misogyny appears to have been an aspect of Bellfield's psychopathology, and the same might be said of many other killers, whether their victims are sex workers or not, but they attack in places where their victims are vulnerable, where no one is protecting them and where no one can intervene to prevent or reduce the violence.

The comment by Townsend and Asthana (2008) also betrays a major problem with the 'victim-centred' discourse. The perception that drug-dependence *caused* the Ipswich women to become victims has

---

[3]See Chapter 14; Wilson seriously misrepresents the current rate of success in solving sex worker homicides – see page 203.

[4]Bellfield has been granted leave to appeal against conviction and sentence; 'Killer Bellfield makes appeal bid', *BBC News*, 17 April 2008 (see http://news.bbc.co.uk/go/pr/fr/-/1/hi/england/london/7352634.stm); 'Stalker guilty of student murders', *BBC News*, 25 February 2008 (see http://news.bbc.co.uk/go/pr/fr/-/1/hi/england/london/7227830.stm).

surfaced in numerous other media reports and Internet discussions, but it is absurd. If drug-dependence inevitably attracted murder, drug users would be slaughtered on buses, in pubs, in social security offices, by anyone who perceived their impaired reactions and inability to resist. But by stressing the victims' drug use, the dangers inherent in street work need not be mentioned; by ignoring the fact that street prostitution was not dominated by drug users until very recently, blind optimism that addressing drug problems will eliminate street work and its dangers can be sustained. Imagining that the drug use of victims 'causes' violence and murder not only absolves society from addressing sex workers' environmental vulnerability or the aggression of perpetrators, it also implicates the victims as responsible for their own victimisation. By likening the Ipswich victims' drug use to that of the murdering necrophiliac Mark Dixie, Townsend and Asthana also imply that there is an equivalence between the culpability of victims and of perpetrators.

Victim-blaming has a long and ignoble history in the annals of violence against women, but these days we are usually more enlightened, except, it seems, when it comes to sex workers. At the National Vice Conference in July 2007, the ACPO[5] spokesman on prostitution, Dr Tim Brain, announced that young women on the streets or in massage parlours and saunas 'become magnets for serious violence and sexual crime and trafficking offences' (Brain 2007) – a classic example of the simplistic generalisations that impede progress in understanding and reducing violence in the sex industry. Not only are many of those victimised not young, some are not women, and risk of victimisation varies enormously for different types of crime and across different sex work settings. Even more disturbing, for a statement from someone with so much influence over policing strategies towards the sex industry, is the description of sex workers as 'magnets' drawing these crimes upon themselves.

The view that sex workers themselves generate the violence they suffer, their very existence provoking murderous rage and encouraging sadistic tendencies in men who would otherwise behave themselves, was stressed at Wright's trial. The prosecution claimed his behaviour was precipitated by his move into the soliciting area of Ipswich and his alleged switch from indoor to street sex workers, the implication being that it was the proximity of drug-using street workers, rather than the massage parlour workers he patronised previously which elicited his murderous response. The fact that Wright was a

[5]ACPO – Association of Chief Police Officers.

well-known street punter in both Ipswich and Norwich long before he moved house was never mentioned in court, but must have been known to the police, which suggests the prosecution intended to implicate the victims in their own fate. The judge, however, did not agree. Sentencing Wright, he said: 'Drugs and prostitution meant they were at risk. But neither drugs nor prostitution killed them. You did.'[6]

Which brings us back to perpetrators.

Although 118 homicides is a sad and shameful total, statistically speaking it is a very small number, especially as the cases are distributed over a 17-year period, and because the homicide suspects fall into several different sub-categories with few cases in each category, it could be argued that it is pointless trying to divine any overarching causation for their homicidal behaviour. It should also be remembered that 35 per cent of sex worker homicides (where suspects were identified) were not committed by 'clients', so the motivations of robbers, partners, acquaintances and others should not be ignored. However, the largest group of suspects are described as 'clients', although only 23 homicides (26 per cent) were committed by those known to have paid for sex. Thirty-one (35 per cent) were killed by men who also seem to have approached as clients, but there is no evidence that they had ever paid for sex, although two-thirds of these had a known history of violence towards sex workers or others.

To return to the quote which opened this chapter, from the trial of Brian Donnelly for the murder of Glasgow sex worker Margo Lafferty; prosecution counsel's suggestions for motive picked out several familiar themes: disagreement over payment, anger, lack of self-control, shame and disgust or contempt for the victim. It was also suggested in court that Donnelly was wreaking vengeance on Margo for having been rejected by a female work colleague earlier in the night. These themes were explored in relation to non-fatal violence,[7] but it is not entirely clear that suspects charged with homicide are comparable to those charged with non-fatal violence. Case inclusion in the analysis of non-fatal attacks was dependent on chance factors, whereas the number of homicide cases analysed is very similar to the official total.[8] The geographic distribution of the two datasets is

---

[6]Mr Justice Gross, sentencing Wright to a whole-life term, Ipswich Crown Court, 22 February 2008.
[7]See Chapter 5 and Chapter 12..
[8]See Chapter 13, page 163.

somewhat different and the demographic profiles of suspects also differ. Those charged with homicide appeared more likely to be white British than those charged with non-fatal violence, but there was so much missing data regarding ethnicity that it is unwise to speculate about the reasons for this. Age data was more comprehensive and showed clear differences: homicide suspects were half as likely to be in the 16 to 24 age group as those charged with non-fatal violence (19 per cent compared to 40 per cent), and 'client' homicide suspects were on average five years older (35) than 'clients' charged with non-fatal violence (30). This might be a cohort effect, perpetrators simply progressing to homicide after an earlier history of violence, but Brookman and Maguire (2003) point out that the age profile for homicide suspects in general is similar to that for violent offenders. The differences in age distribution might indicate a rather different spectrum of behaviours and characteristics involved in sex worker homicides as compared to non-fatal attacks, but the difficulties of establishing what has occurred immediately prior to a homicide, and suspects' tendency to deny involvement or to refuse to explain their actions, make this a problematic area to explore (Brewer *et al.* 2006).

Of the 47 'client' suspects, 31 (66 per cent) either denied the charges, offered no explanation, claimed the death was accidental or blamed their mental health problems. Brewer *et al.* (2006) mention various possible motives proffered either by perpetrators or commentators, including provocation by the victim through arguments over money or drugs, attempted robbery, verbal insults, etc., and factors which implicate the assailant, such as his misogyny, sadism, psychopathology or hatred of prostitutes. Brookman and Maguire (2003) refer to interpretations of homicide which distinguish between 'confrontational' homicide arising unplanned from 'honour' contests over minor disagreements and 'grudge/revenge killings' which were more purposeful, determined and often planned in advance. Common situations which appear to trigger and escalate violence in the context of sex work might be likened to 'honour contests' in which the terms of the sexual bargain are contested, with violence arising as a result of the assailant feeling his manhood (honour) was impugned by being expected to pay for sex as well as by failure to get an erection or ejaculate. Grudge/revenge factors are also sometimes made explicit, such as revenge for being robbed by another sex worker, or when 'collective liability' seems to be invoked and sex workers attacked by those seeking revenge for rejection by another woman.[9]

---

[9]The murder of Geraldine Brocklehurst by Shane Haynes would appear to

However, these models do not fully capture the distinct character of many attacks on sex workers, where the violence is intimately connected to rejection of the client role. Of the 16 British 'client' homicide suspects, where some trigger for their actions was either mentioned in court or can be inferred from their behaviour towards other sex workers, 13 became violent over money, suggesting that rejection of the client role was an important factor in the escalation of violence in these cases. As mentioned in the exploration of Steve Wright's motives, American serial sex worker killers, Hansen and Ridgway, both explicitly acknowledged that selecting sex workers *but not paying them* was fundamental to their homicidal behaviour.[10] They both also expressed contempt and hate of sex workers as a group, an attitude which seems to underlie cases where sex workers are targeted only because they are sex workers, without any pretence of client behaviour beforehand and without any prior dispute or confrontation.

It is difficult to comment on what is often referred to in court as 'a sexual motive', mainly because my information sources rarely mention anything too explicit regarding the sexual aspects of homicides. I suspect that a minority of homicides result from extreme sadism or from sexual arousal through killing, and those where such motivation seems likely, rarely have the appearance of preplanning. Killers such as Anthony Hardy, David Smith, George Naylor and Kenneth Valentine, who all had multiple victims and used torture and/or mutilation, nevertheless do not seem to have made sophisticated plans to evade detection. Smith discarded a victim's bloodstained possessions in the streets near his home; Naylor was caught driving around with one body in his car; Hardy and Valentine were also caught through their methods of disposing of their victims' bodies. Others who had killed in their own homes simply went on the run leaving the bodies to rot, some then returning to deal with the remains, others giving themselves up to the police, behaviour which does not suggest much forethought let alone 'cunning' or 'control'. Most killers appear to have acted in a completely disorganised way, in scenarios which suggest sudden rage, sometimes fuelled by alcohol or drugs, probably in fury at their own physical or social impotence, because they don't want to pay, because they are angry with women in general or at

---

have been of this kind. See Chapter 5, pages 64–5.
[10]Wilson and Seaman (2007); 'Defendant pleads guilty to 48 murders in Green River case', *New York Times*, 5 November 2003.

their own inadequacies, or because of mental disturbances of a more intractable kind.

Under one in ten of the homicide victims were killed by someone with a known serious psychiatric diagnosis, but all these cases illustrate the failure of mental health services to monitor, restrain or even identify potentially violent individuals. Mark Corner, Anthony Hardy, Paul Brumfitt, George Leighers and Peter Slack had eight victims between them; all had had extensive prior contact with mental health professionals; Brumfitt and Leighers had both killed before; explicit concerns were raised about the dangerousness of Hardy and Corner in the months before they killed, while Slack was considered so dangerous he appeared in court in shackles. Yet all were living independently in the community. The pathetic excuse offered by the Mental Health Trust in Hardy's case, that they could not be expected to realise he was dangerous (although several professionals were very concerned about the threat he posed to others) because Hardy 'did not declare his crimes', is a dreadful indictment of the limitations of psychiatric knowledge and mental health care procedures.[11] In Corner's case, the Mental Health Trust readily admitted its procedures had not been followed and had the grace to apologise, reporting the psychiatrist concerned, Eric Birchall, to the GMC. The GMC, however, declined even to give Birchall a warning, declaring that the catalogue of errors in Corner's case[12] resulting in the deaths, mutilation and dismemberment of two young women was 'a single error of judgement' and did not constitute 'incompetence or negligence of a high degree'.[13]

The responsibility of these and other state institutions, through placing sex workers in environments where they are vulnerable and through failure to restrain those known to be violent, appears to be of greater relevance in explaining sex workers' risk of homicide than the 'motives' of those who kill them.

---

[11]See Chapter 15, pages 221–3.
[12]See Chapter 15, pages 223–4.
[13]'Doctor in "murderer release" will not be struck off, GMC rules', *Liverpool Daily Post*, 17 April 2008.

Chapter 18

Shutting the stable door

Successful prosecutions against those who have attacked or killed sex workers bring relief that dangerous predators are no longer menacing the vulnerable, and they also appear to vindicate the criminal justice system, demonstrating society's competence to deal with malefactors. Nonetheless, not all prosecutions have satisfactory outcomes. Although the overall rate of acquittal in sex worker homicide cases is no different to those where the victim is not a sex worker, and proportionately fewer cases result in a manslaughter conviction,[1] there are sometimes aspects of the judicial process, even in successful prosecutions, which appear to exemplify institutional prejudice against sex workers, from milder charges being brought against perpetrators than might be thought warranted, to reduced Criminal Injuries Compensation payments to victims or their families. There are also numerous cases which demonstrate the ineffectiveness and incompetence of the criminal justice system in restraining those known to be dangerous. Previous chapters have shown that at least 25 per cent of those charged with non-fatal attacks on sex workers and 45 per cent of those charged with homicide, had previous convictions for violence, including homicide, for whom such monitoring systems as we have, proved entirely inadequate. Conviction and incarceration of the violent, except in those extremely rare cases where a whole-life sentence is imposed, is not the end of the matter. Many of those convicted since 1990 will have been released by now, into a society where sex workers are at least as vulnerable as when they

---

[1]See Chapter 14.

were convicted. These institutional failings are not addressed in the prosecution of individual offenders: one horse may be rounded up, but the stable door is still open.

Failure to prosecute

Thirty-six per cent of 'client' homicide suspects had a known history of violence against sex workers, only half of whom are known to have been prosecuted for such attacks, while 45 per cent of those charged with non-fatal attacks had multiple sex worker victims, suggesting that failure to prosecute inexorably leads to escalation in the number of offences, if not to murder. Failure to prosecute does not only occur because sex workers fail to report attacks:

- Stephen Tanner, convicted on three counts of rape in April 2008, had over 60 previous convictions, including convictions for sexual assaults on children, and had served 12 years in Broadmoor. Five years after his release in 2000, two sex workers made allegations of rape against him, but these cases were not prosecuted, allegedly because one victim was in custody for theft. Likewise Ron Castree, eventually convicted of murdering 11-year-old Lesley Molseed in 1975. He was only identified as her murderer when his DNA was taken after attacking a sex worker in October 2005, but he was not prosecuted for that attack. Neither was Castree charged with Lesley Molseed's murder until more than a year after his DNA was taken, raising questions over the level of priority given to processing forensic evidence in relation to attacks on sex workers. It is not known why Castree was not prosecuted for this attack.[2]

- Dahir Ibrahim, who raped street sex workers at knifepoint in Birmingham over a three-year period, was first reported in March 2003. The victim did not follow through her complaint because she had an ASBO and did not want to admit to police that she had been working. None of Ibrahim's other victims reported his attacks to police until September 2005 when he was arrested, but he was then released due to insufficient forensic evidence.

[2]Because Tanner and Castree's attacks on sex workers were not prosecuted, neither offender is included in the non-fatal attacks data (Chapter 11); 'Serial rapist kept victim prisoner for two days', Richard Smith, *The Mirror*, 12 April 2008; Paul Byrne and Patrick Mulchrone, 'Child sex fiend gets life in jail', *The Mirror*, 13 November 2007.

Outreach workers assisted the police in tracing other victims, while Birmingham City Council obtained an ASBO and a public nuisance injunction against him, banning him from the soliciting area. In 2006, the CPS finally decided that there was sufficient evidence to prosecute; he was convicted on three counts of rape and sentenced to ten years.[3]

Bail

Even when sex workers do report attacks and suspects are charged, granting bail can allow attacks to continue. James Aird Walker was convicted in 2001 for eleven offences against sex workers in Plymouth. Walker was charged with the indecent assault and false imprisonment of one woman in December 2000, but was then arrested a further *three* times before being remanded in custody. Had he been remanded in custody after the first arrest, his subsequent offences, including two rapes, three indecent assaults and three false imprisonments, would not have taken place.[4] The expectation that assailants will be granted bail may inhibit victims from reporting attacks for fear of reprisals and may allow offenders to escape justice. A man accused of raping two sex workers in Yorkshire in 2003 was granted bail, then went on the run; he was convicted in absentia, but had still not been apprehended four years later.[5] Questionable bail decisions were highlighted in January 2008 when a senior police officer accused of murdering his wife was granted bail, enabling him to also murder his mother-in-law and then kill himself. Subsequent investigations revealed that 13 per cent of current murder suspects had been granted bail and 85 per cent of those charged with manslaughter, suggesting that the prisons are now so desperately overcrowded even those charged with the most serious offences are likely to be bailed.[6]

---

[3]Sean O'Neill, 'Police powerless to arrest serial rapist terrorising a community', *The Times*, 15 October 2005; Sean O'Neill, 'Serial rapist was given ASBO to keep him off streets', *The Times*, 14 August 2006.
[4]'Evil: violent man who hated women faces a life behind bars', *Evening Herald*, 1 December 2001.
[5]'TV plea fails to trace rapist', *Doncaster Star*, 22 August 2007.
[6]Matthew Taylor, 'Bail rules inquiry after officer on murder charge kills himself and trial witness', *The Guardian*, 14 January 2008; Nicholas Watt, 'Demand for stricter bail after 60 on murder charges go free', *The Guardian*, 25 February 2008.

Charges brought

The decisions of the Crown Prosecution Service about what charges are brought sometimes appear inconsistent. One of the homicide cases concerns a sex worker who had been leaning through a car window arguing about payment with a client when he drove off. She died from hitting her head on the pavement and the driver was charged with manslaughter. He was acquitted, but the case had been tried as a homicide. In contrast, after Govind Jeshani killed a sex worker by driving over her in his lorry, he was initially charged with and convicted of causing death by dangerous driving. Jeshani claimed she had jumped into the cab offering him business, which he refused. She jumped back out, grabbing his mileage book. Witnesses stated that he then drove forward, crushing her beneath the wheels of his lorry, stopped, got out and calmly removed his mileage book from her hand. Nevertheless, when passing sentence the judge said, 'any culpability on your part was so slight it was scarcely existing', giving him an absolute discharge and six penalty points on his driving licence. On appeal, even this conviction was quashed completely and replaced with the lighter one of careless driving, with three penalty points on his licence, the same as for a minor speeding offence.[7] These cases have similarities with one of the non-fatal attacks which resulted in a prosecution, where the offender claimed he had inadvertently driven off with the sex worker's handbag in his car. She dived through the window to retrieve it and was dragged for 140 yards before she fell, breaking her leg. The suspect in this case was convicted of causing grievous bodily harm and given a 12-month prison sentence, whereas the other two drivers, both involved in a death, were not penalised at all.[8]

There are sometimes cases where it appears that sex worker homicides are dealt with more leniently than when non-sex workers are involved. For example, the homicide of lap-dancer Adelle Hamilton in 2001 and that of Mohamed Raheem in 2007 appear to have strong similarities. Both homicides were motivated by robbery; in both cases, a gang carried out the attack, stealing money, jewellery and other property. Both victims were gagged, left tied to their beds and died through suffocation. But the killers of Raheem were charged with murder, convicted and sentenced to between 23 and 30 years

---

[7]'Driver's three points for prostitute death', *Ham and High*, 4 February 2005; 'Prostitute's killer walks free', *Borehamwood & Elstree Times*, 20 May 2004.
[8]'Vice girl left hurt in road', *Liverpool Echo*, 1 November 2005.

imprisonment, while the gang who robbed Adelle Hamilton, leaving her to die, were charged with manslaughter; three were convicted, two got eight years, one ten years, but the fourth, Adelle's 'friend' who arranged the robbery, was convicted of conspiracy to rob only and got six years.[9]

Likewise the homicides of Susan Third, a sex worker in Aberdeen who died in February 2005, and Sally Anne Bowman, a non-sex worker from south London who died in September the same year. Susan Third was strangled by Joseph Harrison; the court heard there was a 70 per cent chance he then had sex with her dead body, but Harrison successfully pleaded diminished responsibility due to heavy use of recreational drugs, a row with his mother and, he claimed, 'hearing voices' – although the psychiatrists who assessed him declared him fit to serve his sentence in a normal prison. Harrison was convicted of culpable homicide and sentenced to six years. Sally Anne Bowman was stabbed seven times by Mark Dixie, who admitted having sex with her dead body and that he was intoxicated with alcohol and cocaine at the time. Dixie got 34 years for murder.[10]

Attitudes to sex workers

The attitudes to sex workers sometimes expressed by judges, barristers and professional witnesses indicate that hostile beliefs are not always confined to the people sitting in the dock. In 2005, when passing sentence on a man convicted of sexually assaulting a Bradford sex worker, Judge Roger Scott said:

> I think he's a really decent young man and I'm sorry that I have to sentence him today, but I have got my job to do ... I have no doubt that, thick skinned though you have to be as a prostitute working on the streets, she would have been scared and she

---

[9]'Three brothers jailed for murder', *BBC News*, 28 April 2008 (see http://news.bbc.co.uk/go/pr/fr/-/1/hi/england/london/7372098.stm); Chris Summers, 'Killed by greed and envy', *BBC News*, 31 March 2007 (see http://news.bbc.co.uk/1/hi/uk/6512847.stm).
[10]Tanya Thompson, 'Asking for it?', *The Scotsman*, 3 March 2007; Angela Balakrishnan and agencies, 'Ex-chef sentenced to 34 years for model's murder', *Guardian Online*, 22 February 2008 (see http://www.guardian.co.uk/uk/2008/feb/22/ukcrime3).

reported it to the authorities pretty quickly. Of its type this was quite a nasty offence.[11]

Defence counsel for one of a gang who had attacked several sex workers, in which women were raped, sexually assaulted, robbed and threatened with knives, thought it relevant to point out 'that the women would have been willing to have sex with them for money,'[12] and rapist Christopher Savill's defence counsel asserted 'no violence had been used against her and that she was uninjured afterwards.'[13] At the trial of Omar Jawanda for murdering his partner, Judge Frank Chapman said she had 'degraded herself' by earning £87,000 a year as an indoor sex worker. Judge Chapman redeemed himself (in my opinion) by acknowledging that she worked to provide a better lifestyle for her children and by describing Jawanda as a 'sponging parasite'.[14]

Thirty-one people testified against Martin Rogers, convicted of knifepoint attacks on four sex workers in Stoke-on-Trent in 2000 and 2001. At his trial it emerged that he 'had fantasies of raping and murdering vulnerable women', but one doctor nevertheless argued he 'did not pose a significant risk to women'.[15]

Sentencing

Even when a 'life' sentence is given, the minimum tariff may be less than the maximum five-year sentence for breaching an ASBO. Martin Rogers was sentenced to life imprisonment, but with a minimum tariff of only four years. As soon as his four years were up Rogers applied for parole or for transfer to open prison. Fortunately both requests were turned down. Andrew Humphris, convicted of attacking three women in one night in 2004 and biting off part of one victim's tongue, was given a 'life' sentence with a minimum tariff of five and a half years. He had previous convictions for sexual violence

---

[11]'"Decent" man jailed for prostitute attack', Bradford Telegraph & Argus, 22 December 2005.

[12]'Students jailed for prostitute attacks', Telegraph & Argus, 8 March 2005.

[13]'Man jailed for raping prostitute', The Herald, 17 April 2007 (see http://www.theherald.co.uk/misc/print.php?artid=1334345).

[14]Ron Warrilow, 'Evil parasite jailed for life', Birmingham Mail, 21 March 2007.

[15]'Rape files found after blunder', Brighton & Hove Argus, 5 April 2006.

going back to 1989.[16] Darren Scott was given a 'life' sentence in 2005, with a minimum tariff of five years, after being convicted of the rape and attempted rape of two sex workers in 2004; he had a previous conviction for raping a teenager in 1992.[17] Lee Butcher, who carried out a four-hour attack on a sex worker in 2005, was convicted of two offences of rape, assault by penetration and grievous bodily harm. Apart from the sexual assaults, he had put her hand on a hard surface and struck her fingers repeatedly with a hammer, hit her across the legs with a wheelbrace and flogged her with his belt. Butcher had 16 previous convictions which included dishonesty, burglary, criminal damage and driving offences, but not violence. He was given an indefinite sentence with a minimum tariff of six-and-a-half years.[18]

A MAN dubbed the Teesside Ripper was last night starting an indefinite prison sentence for an attack that left a prostitute fearing for her life. (April 2007)[19]

Indefinite sentences for public protection (IPPs), whereby prisoners only become eligible for release after completing courses to address their offending behaviour, were introduced in 2005 and have been used extensively. However, prison overcrowding and under-resourcing has meant such courses are not available to many on IPP sentences, so they are not able to meet the conditions necessary for their release. In February 2008, the Court of Appeal ruled that it was illegal to detain IPP prisoners who had served their minimum tariff, since it amounted to 'arbitrary detention'.[20] Unless the Justice Minister is able to pour sufficient resources into the prison system to make these rehabilitative courses available, a number of extremely violent men will be released after serving short sentences for attacks on sex workers. For example, the 'Teesside Ripper' referred to above was given a minimum tariff of three years. Frank Ormesher, who attacked two Bolton sex workers with an iron bar in 2005, was given a minimum tariff of three years and 59 days which he will have

---

[16]'Life for tongue-bite sex attacker', *Manchester Evening News*, 13 April 2005.
[17]'Evil sex fiend jailed for life', *The Star*, Sheffield, 14 March 2005.
[18]'Brutal attack on prostitute', *Newsquest Media Group*, 11 January 2006 (see http://archive.thisisthewestcountry.co.uk/2006/1/11/51172.html).
[19]'How they stopped another "Ripper"', *Northern Echo*, 17 April 2007.
[20]Clare Dyer, 'Court rulings to force parole and prison changes', *The Guardian*, 2 February 2008.

served by the time this book is published.[21] Some judges have been more cautious. Ardi Hila, convicted of two rapes and three robberies at massage parlours, was given an indefinite sentence in 2007. The judge said if it had not been for the IPP option, he would have jailed Hila for ten years, but stipulated a minimum of nine and a half years anyway.

IPPs are one of the factors contributing to prison overcrowding, which senior judges have insisted must be addressed by more selective use of custodial sentences and IPPs in particular.[22] However, there is no guarantee that more selectivity will ensure that prison is reserved for violent offenders. Numerous minor offences and forms of anti-social behaviour result in prison sentences; the cells are full of shoplifters, drug addicts, people with mental health problems and asylum seekers. The government has tried to reintroduce imprisonment for soliciting and may yet succeed; sex workers are already imprisoned for breaching ASBOs and radical feminists want men who pay for sex to be jailed.[23]

Monitoring of offenders after release

Without long detention or rehabilitation programmes when in custody, monitoring of offenders in the community remains the only option for restraining those known to be violent. Unfortunately, there is considerable evidence of the ineffectiveness and inadequacies of mechanisms for monitoring known offenders.

Electronic tagging was introduced in 1999 to allow the early release of offenders and less costly monitoring in the community. In 2006 the Home Office admitted that over 1,000 serious offences had been committed by tagged offenders since 1999, and in March 2007 faulty equipment was reportedly being used by one of the profit-making companies contracted to monitor those on tags. The same company was involved when, four months later, a 17-year-old who should

---

[21]'Life for prostitute attacks', *Manchester Evening News*, 13 December 2005.
[22]Alan Travis, 'Inmates left in limbo by failures in new sentences – judges', *The Guardian*, 1 August 2007; Alan Travis, 'Cut sentences to tackle jails crisis, judges are urged', *The Guardian*, 24 November 2007.
[23]'Sex industry in Scotland: MSP calls for crackdown on punters', *Daily Record*, 29 April 2008 (see http://www.dailyrecord.co.uk/news/special-reports/prostitution/).

have been tagged committed a murder.[24] Gary Allen was jailed for five and a half years in 2000 for attacks on sex workers in Plymouth which occurred within six weeks of his acquittal for the murder of a sex worker in Hull. Despite the judge's order that he should remain on licence for ten years and on the Sex Offenders Register indefinitely, by March 2004 Allen had been released on a home detention tagging scheme. He removed the tag and went on the run. Police warned that he was 'considered a "substantial" risk, particularly to women' and should not be approached, but it is not known whether he was ever traced. [25]

Multi-agency public protection arrangements (MAPPA) constitute the system intended to protect potential victims and prevent harm through the assessment and management of the risks posed by offenders. The police, prison service and probation are the principal agencies responsible, but electronic monitoring providers, social services, youth offending teams and housing and health authorities may also be involved. In a few areas, agencies working with sex workers are involved in MAPPA deliberations, and in others sex work projects report good liaison with police over offenders known to be violent towards sex workers. However, this level of liaison and information sharing appears to be very limited, which is disappointing, considering the extent of repeat and multiple offending amongst those who attack sex workers, and MAPPA's remit which specifically includes protection of those potentially at risk from known offenders.[26]

"When it comes to dealing with sex offenders it would be true to say resources don't match demand," said Chief Constable Terry Grange, the Association of Chief Police Officers' lead spokesman on violent crime.[27]

---

[24]'Home Office admits tagged offenders guilty of 1,000 serious crimes', *The Guardian*, 12 October 2006; 'Paedophiles "going unmonitored"', Press Association, 23 March, 2007 (see http://www.guardian.co.uk/uklatest/story/0,,-6502534,00.html); 'Killer "should have been tagged"', *BBC News*, 18 December 2007 (see http://news.bbc.co.uk/go/pr/fr/-/1/hi/england/sussex/7149978.stm).
[25]'Sex attack man goes on the run', *Yorkshire Post*, 11 March 2004.
[26]Home Office (2003) *Preventing Serious Harm: Managing Risks through MAPPA – Protecting Communities from Violent and Sexual Offenders*. London: Home Office.
[27]Amelia Hill, 'Police fears over sex crime risks', *The Observer*, 7 January 2007.

259

The under-resourcing of this element of the criminal justice system is appalling, given that there are nearly 50,000 people on the Violent and Sex Offenders Register, over 30,000 of them sex offenders, of whom at least 1,300 are deemed likely to reoffend within four weeks. In the year 2006/7, 83 known offenders were charged with further serious offences such as murder or rape.[28] Yet radical feminist groups are demanding that merely paying for sex should lead to classification as a sex offender, if not a prison sentence.[29] If these demands were heeded, the Sex Offenders Register would be swamped, and murderers, rapists and child abusers would be invisible among hundreds of thousands of non-violent clients.

[28] Alan Travis, 'Increase in serious crime by offenders on parole', *The Guardian*, 23 October 2007.
[29] 'Sex industry in Scotland: MSP calls for crackdown on punters', *Daily Record*, 29 April 2008 (see http://www.dailyrecord.co.uk/news/special-reports/prostitution/).

Chapter 19

Promoting violence

The continued exposure of sex workers to preventable violence is government policy. The *Co-ordinated Strategy on Prostitution* (Home Office 2006) had one positive proposal, to permit 'mini-brothels', recognising that indoor sex work is demonstrably safer than street work. This proposal has now been abandoned. The Strategy makes clear that warnings about anti-street prostitution enforcement exacerbating sex workers' vulnerability had been heard but not heeded. Instead, intensified enforcement was demanded, with great emphasis on using CCTV to catch kerb-crawlers. The results of this were seen in Ipswich and indirectly acknowledged at Wright's trial. While in many places street workers have clung to areas covered by CCTV because the cameras deter violence, in Ipswich they did not. Commenting on the Ipswich murders in December 2006, Deborah Orr criticised the government's 'abolitionist strategy, that concerns itself least with the welfare of the uncooperative people,' adding:

> Maybe it deters some, and of course that's not a bad thing. But for those who continue with this work, it is a perilous policy. It propels women into the darkest and least policed places, where there are no CCTV cameras to record them or their clients, and it propels them to make no report to the police when they are assaulted or when they have reason to believe that one of their clients might be a dangerous character.[1]

---

[1]Deborah Orr, 'Why these women are paying the price of a zero tolerance approach to street prostitution', *The Independent*, 13 December 2006.

This 'abolitionist strategy' remains in place, legitimated by a radical feminist ideology obsessed with the supposedly damaging effects of being paid for sex, which has completely replaced any sisterly or human impulse to protect sex workers from rape and murder. Their current demand is to criminalise paying for sex, but it is quite clear that sex workers are far more frequently attacked by those who *do not pay* for sex than by those who do. Most violence against indoor sex workers occurs in the course of robberies, and much violence against street sex workers comes from people who make no pretence of being clients. Violence from these sources will not be addressed by criminalising paying for sex. Neither will the violence that is commonly referred to as 'client violence'. Those who adopt the guise of 'clients' and then commit sexual or physical assaults are already very unlikely to be paying for sex. The London Ugly Mugs List shows that 75 per cent of attacks on street workers were committed by those who did not pay. Only 9 per cent reports made by indoor sex workers described a sexual assault by someone who had paid, and of those charged with non-fatal attacks on sex workers, 64 per cent were either not clients nor posing as clients, or posed as clients but then refused to pay and/or robbed their victims of all their money. Only 4 per cent were described as actually having paid. David Carruthers, convicted of attempted rape and other assaults on sex workers in Edinburgh in 2004[2] sought to excuse himself by saying the women had consented to sex but withdrew consent when he refused to pay. How will the courts deal with him if paying for sex is criminalised? Some murderers have even rationalised their aggression by claiming that they did not know their victim was a sex worker and that it was the request for payment which provoked rage. How will such rapists and murderers be treated by the courts if paying for sex is criminalised? Will the fact that they have *not* paid be regarded as a mitigating factor?

Those who advocate attacking the 'demand' for commercial sex argue that criminalising clients would 'send out a message' that paying for sex is socially unacceptable, but it is already socially unacceptable. Exposure of public figures as clients brings abject apologies or feeble denials, not preening and self-congratulation. It is argued that reducing demand would gradually reduce the numbers of women involved in sex work, so fewer are exposed to its dangers, but how long is this transformation of perhaps 10 per cent of the

---

[2] 'Ex-soldier attacked prostitutes', *BBC News*, 7 January 2004 (see http://news. bbc.co.uk/1/hi/scotland/3376177.stm).

adult male population likely to take? And what kind of a society regards physical assaults, rape and murder as useful deterrents against 'anti-social behaviour'?

Last word

I always intended to write a book that would be comprehensible to a wide audience and hoped that sex workers would be among those who read it. I don't know if I have achieved this, but to any who do, this is for you.

Not much of this will be news to any sex worker who has been in the business for any length of time: on the street, you are vulnerable to random violence from anyone who has a grudge against sex workers, against women in general, who is in a bad mood and feels like beating someone up for any reason at all, from anyone who is desperate for cash and assumes you have it – the list goes on and on.

For those of you working from parlours, sex flats or saunas, the main risk is robbery, often violent, often involving weapons, often involving gangs where one comes in first, maybe has a service, then lets in the others. However, in London the biggest rise in robbery up to 2005 was by single men using guns, and this change may be affecting other areas by now.

There are clients who think paying for sex entitles them to do anything they want, but violence, whether working indoors or outdoors, is far more likely to come from those who do not pay than from those who do, from the rapist who simply grabs a woman on the street, to the 'client' who has a service with no problems and then turns nasty, takes his money back and robs whatever else he can get.

What to do about it? There seems little chance that government policy will change from trying to eliminate the sex industry to trying to make it safer. Instead, it seems quite possible that perfectly decent clients will be classed as sex offenders, making the Sex Offenders Register even more useless, or even sent to prison, thus ensuring that more killers and rapists are bailed or let out early to make room for the clients.

So sex workers are going to have to carry on looking out for themselves, and for each other. All I can add to the usual advice on safety is: don't go to a punter's place for business and don't assume middle-aged white men are safe. And take care.

Hilary Kinnell

References

Addley, E. (2006) 'I've never done anything for less than £15. You can get a bag of heroin for £15', *The Guardian*, 14 December.

Agustín, L. (2007) *Sex at the Margins: Migration, Labour Markets and the Rescue Industry*. London: Zed Books.

Anderson, B. and O'Connell Davidson, J. (2003) *Is Trafficking in Human Beings Demand Driven? A Multi-Country Pilot Study*, IOM Migration Research Series No. 15. Geneva: International Organization for Migration.

Bains, B. and Klodawski, E. (2006) *DMAG Briefing 2006/22; November 2006; GLA 2005 Round Interim Ethnic Group Population Projections*. Data Management and Analysis Group, Greater London Authority.

Barnard, M., Hart, G. and Church, S. (2001) *Client Violence Against Prostitute Women Working from Street and Off-Street Locations: A Three City Comparison*. London: Economic & Social Research Council, Violence Research Programme.

Bilton, M. (1995) 'Footsteps of the Ripper', *The Sunday Times Magazine*, 17 September.

Bilton, M. (2006) *Wicked Beyond Belief: The Hunt for the Yorkshire Ripper*, revised edn. London: Harper Perennial; first published, 2003.

Bindel, J. (2006) *No Escape? An Investigation into London's Service Provision for Women Involved in the Commercial Sex Industry*. Published by the POPPY Project, c/o Eaves Housing, London.

Bindel, J. and Atkins, H. (2007) *Streets Apart: Outdoor Prostitution in London*. Published by the POPPY Project, c/o Eaves Housing, London.

Blackwood, S. and Williams, K. (1999) *Resistance! Client-led Self-defence Training with Women Sex Workers, 1994–1999*. Southampton Working With Prostitutes Project, Department of Genito-Urinary Medicine, Royal Hants Hospital, Southampton, SO14 0YG.

Bland, L. (1984) 'The case of the Yorkshire Ripper: mad, bad, beast or male?', reprinted in J. Radford and D. Russell (eds) (1992), *Femicide: The Politics of Woman Killing*. Buckingham: Open University Press.

Bloor, M. J., McKeganey, N. P., Finlay, A. and Barnard, M. A. (1992) 'The inappropriateness of psycho-social models of risk behaviour for understanding HIV-related risk practices among Glasgow male prostitutes', *AIDS Care*, 4 (2): 131–7.

Brewer, D.D., Dudek, J.A., Potterat, J.J., Muth, S.Q., Roberts, J.M. and Woodhouse, D.E. (2006) 'Extent, trends and perpetrators of prostitution-related homicide in the United States', *Journal of Forensic Science*, 51 (5): 1101–8.

Britton, P. (2001) *Picking Up the Pieces*. London: Corgi Books; first published Bantam Press, 2000.

Brookman, F. and Maguire, M. (2003) *Reducing Homicide: A Review of the Possibilities*, Home Office Online Report 01/03. See http://www.homeoffice.gov.uk/rds/pdfs2/rdsolr0103.pdf.

Brooks-Gordon, B. (2006) *The Price of Sex*. Cullompton: Willan.

Brussa, L. (ed.) (2000) *Health, Migration and Sex Work: Transnational AIDS/STD Prevention among Migrant Prostitutes in Europe*. Amsterdam: TAMPEP (Transnational AIDS/STD Prevention among Migrant Prostitutes in Europe Project), International Foundation.

Byford, L. (1981) *The Yorkshire Ripper Case: Review of the Police Investigation of the Case by Lawrence Byford, Esq., C.B.E., Q.P.M., Her Majesty's Inspector of Constabulary*. London: Home Office.

Campbell, R. (2002) *Working on the Street: An Evaluation of the Linx Project, 1998–2001*. Liverpool: Liverpool Hope University.

Campbell, R. (2007) *Critical Reflections on the National Strategy*. Paper presented at the 'Tackling Prostitution' Conference, 11 December, Capita Conferences, London.

Campbell, R. and Hancock, L. (1998) *Sex Work in the Climate of Zero Tolerance: Hearing Loud Voices and the Silencing of Dissent*. Presentation to the Sex Work Reassessed Conference, University of East London.

Church, S., Henderson, M. and Barnard, M. (2001) 'Violence by clients towards female prostitutes in different work settings: questionnaire survey', *British Medical Journal*, 322: 524–5.

Cohen, N. (2000) 'When self-help is not enough', *New Statesman*, 3 April.

Coleman, K. *et al.* (2007) *Homicides, Firearms Offences and Intimate Violence 2005/6*, Home Office Statistical Bulletin. London: Office of National Statistics.

Connell, J. and Hart, G. (2003) *An Overview of Male Sex Work in Edinburgh and Glasgow: The Male Sex Worker Perspective*, Occasional Paper 8. Glasgow: MRC Social & Public Health Sciences Unit.

Cooke, L. (1986) 'The Police versus the North Moseley Residents' Association Action Group'. Undergraduate sociology dissertation, University of Warwick.

Curren, E. and Sinclair, S. (1998) *Sexual Health Outreach Project Report*. Harbour Centre Alcohol and Drug Advisory Service, 9/10 Ermington Terrace, Mutley, Plymouth PL4 6QG.

Cusick, L. (1998) 'Female prostitution in Glasgow: drug use and occupational sector', *Addiction Research*, 6: 115–30.

Daniels, C. (2006) *Priceless*. London: Hodder & Stoughton.

Davis, J. (2004) *Off the Streets: Tackling Homelessness among Female Sex Workers*. London: Shelter.

Day, S., Ziersch, A., Casey, M. and Ward, H. (1996) 'Country report of UK', in R.P. Mak (ed.), *EUROPAP: European Project Aids Prevention for Prostitutes*. Ghent: Academia Press.

Dibb, R., Mitchell, T., Munro, G., Rough, E. and Emberson, M. (2006) *Substance Use and Health Related Needs of Migrant Sex Workers and Women Trafficked into Sexual Exploitation in the London Borough of Tower Hamlets and the City of London*. London: Salvation Army United Kingdom Territory with the Republic of Ireland.

Dorling, D. (2005) 'Prime suspect: murder in Britain', in P. Hillyard *et al.* (eds), *Criminal Obsessions*. London: Crime and Society Foundation.

Fairweather, E. (1979) 'Leeds: curfew on men', *Spare Rib*, 83, June; reprinted in M. Rowe (1982) *Spare Rib Reader*. Harmondsworth: Penguin.

Gaffney, J. (2006) *The Working Men Project Annual Review*, November 2006. London: St Mary's NHS Trust.

Gilbert, J. *et al.* (2007) *Thematic Review of Lesbian Gay Bisexual Transgender Related Murders*. London: LGBT Advisory Group to the Metropolitan Police.

Gottfredson, M.R. and Hirschi, T. (1990) *A General Theory of Crime*. Stanford, CA: Stanford University Press.

Green, A., Day, S. and Ward, H. (2000) 'Crack cocaine and prostitution in London in the 1990s', *Sociology of Health and Illness*, 22: 27–39.

Green, V. (1977) '"We're not criminals": prostitutes organize', *Spare Rib*, 56, March; reprinted in M. Rowe (ed.) (1982), *Spare Rib Reader*. Harmondsworth: Penguin.

Hanmer, J. and Saunders, S. (1984) *Well-Founded Fear*. London: Hutchinson.

Harrison, P. and Wilson, D. (2008) *Hunting Evil: Inside the Ipswich Serial Murders*. London: Sphere.

Hester, M. and Westmarland, N. (2004) *Tackling Street Prostitution: Towards a Holistic Approach*. London: Home Office Development and Statistics Directorate.

Hillyard, P. and Tombs, S. (2005) 'Beyond criminology?', in P. Hillyard *et al.* (eds), *Criminal Obsessions*. London: Crime and Society Foundation.

Hobbs, A. (2004) *Streetlink: Supporting Vulnerable Women on the Streets of Preston*, Project Report. Streetlink, The Foxton Centre, Knowsley Street, Preston PR1 3SA.

Hollway, W. (1981) '"I just wanted to kill a woman". Why? The Ripper and male sexuality', *Feminist Review*, 9: 33–40.

Home Office (2004) *Paying the Price: A Consultation Paper on Prostitution*. London: Home Office Communication Directorate.

Home Office (2006) *A Co-ordinated Prostitution Strategy*. London: Home Office Communication Directorate.

Hubbard, P. (1998) 'Community action and the displacement of street prostitution: evidence from British cities', *Geoforum*, 29 (3): 269–86.

Hubbard, P. and Sanders, T. (2003) 'Making space for sex work: female street prostitution and the production of urban space', *International Journal of Urban and Regional Research*, 27: 75–89.

Ibbitson, M. (2002) *Out of Sight, Out of Mind: An Assessment of the Health Needs of Women Off-street Sex Workers*. Bolton Specialist Health Promotion Service.

Jeffreys, S. (1980) 'Prostitution', in D. Rhodes and S. McNeill (eds) (1985), *Women Against Violence Against Women*. London: Onlywomen Press.

Jones, L. (2004) *Assessment of Service Provision Needs of Women who Work in the Sex Industry in Ipswich*. Ipswich Crime and Disorder Reduction Partnership, July.

Kinnell, H. (1995) 'Prostitutes' exposure to rape and other violence as an occupational hazard', in D. Friedrich and W. Heckman (eds), *AIDS in Europe – The Behavioural Aspect. Vol. 2: Risk Behaviour and Its Determinants*. Ergebnisse sozialwissenschaftlicher Aids-Forschung, Bd. 16.

Kinnell, H. (2001) 'Murderous clients and indifferent justice', *Research for Sex Work*, 4, June, Department of Health Care and Culture, Vrije Universiteit, Amsterdam (see http://www.med.vu.nl/hcc).

Kinnell, H. (2004) 'Violence and sex work in Britain', in S. Day and H. Ward (eds), *Sex Work, Mobility and Health in Europe*. London: Kegan Paul.

Kinnell, H. (2006a) 'Murder made easy: the final solution to prostitution?', in R. Campbell and M. O'Neill (eds), *Sex Work Now*. Cullompton: Willan.

Kinnell, H. (2006b) 'Clients of female sex workers: men or monsters?', in R. Campbell and M. O'Neill (eds), *Sex Work Now*. Cullompton: Willan.

Lean, M. (1996) *Red Lights Go Green in Birmingham*. Initiatives for Change, June/July (see http://www.forachange.co.uk/index.php?stoid=4).

Lees, S. (1992) 'Naggers, whores and libbers: provoking men to kill', in J. Radford and D. Russell (eds), *Femicide: The Politics of Woman Killing*. Buckingham: Open University Press.

Lowman, J. (2000) 'Violence and the outlaw status of (street) prostitution in Canada', in *Violence Against Women*, 6 (9): 987–1011.

McCann, R. (2004) *Just a Boy*. London: Ebury Press.

McKeganey, N. and Barnard, M. (1996) 'Dying for sex: prostitution and violence', in *Sex Work on the Streets*. Buckingham: Open University Press.

McKeganey, N., Barnard, M. and Bloor, M. (1992) *Researching Female Prostitution: Epidemiology out of Ethnography*. Paper presented at conference of Methodological Advances in Social Research on Aids, Harrogate.

McLeod, E. (1982) *Women Working: Prostitution Now*. London: Croom Helm.

Mak, R. P. (1996) *EUROPAP: European Project Aids Prevention for Prostitutes*. Ghent: Academia Press.

May, T., Harocopos, A. and Hough, M. (1999) *Street Business: The Links between Sex and Drug Markets*. London: Home Office.

May, T., Harocopos, A. and Hough, M. (2000) *For Love or Money: Pimps and the Management of Sex Work*. London: Home Office.

Miller, J. (1993) '"Your life is on the line every night you're on the streets": victimization and the resistance among street prostitutes', *Humanity and Society*, 17 (4): 422–46.

Miller, J. and Schwartz, M.D. (1995) 'Rape myths and violence against street prostitutes', *Deviant Behaviour: An Interdisciplinary Journal*, 16: 1–35.

Monto, M. and Hotaling, N. (2001) 'Predictors of rape myth acceptance among male clients of female street prostitutes', *Violence Against Women*, 7: 275–93

Newburn, T. and Rock, P. (2004) *Living In Fear: Violence and Victimisation in the Lives of Single Homeless People*. London: Mannheim Centre for Criminology, London School of Economics.

O'Connell Davidson, J. (1998) *Prostitution, Power and Freedom*. Cambridge: Polity Press.

O'Hara, M. (1980) 'Prostitution – towards a feminist analysis and strategy', in D. Rhodes and S. McNeill (eds) (1985), *Women Against Violence Against Women*. London: Onlywomen Press.

O'Kane, M. (2002) 'Mean streets', *The Guardian*, 16 September.

O'Neill, M. (1996) 'Researching prostitution and violence: towards a feminist praxis', in Hester, M. Radford, J. and Kelly, L. (eds), *Researching Male Violence*. Buckingham: Open University Press.

O'Neill, M. and Barbaret, R. (2000) 'Victimisation and the social organisation of prostitution in England and Spain', in R. Weitzer (ed.), *Sex for Sale*. London: Routledge.

Pateman, C. (1988) *The Sexual Contract*. Cambridge: Polity Press.

Penfold, C., Hunter, G., Campbell, R. and Barham, L. (2004) 'Tackling client violence in female street prostitution: inter-agency working between outreach agencies and the police', *Policing and Society*, 14 (4): 365–79.

Phal, S. (2002) *Survey on Police Human Rights Violations of Sex Workers in Toul Kork* (Phnom Penh, Cambodia), Cambodian Women's Development Association, August 2002.

Phoenix, J. (1999) *Making Sense of Prostitution*. Basingstoke: Macmillan Press.

Pitcher, J., Campbell, R., Hubbard, P., O'Neill, M. and Scoular, J. (2006) *Living and Working in Areas of Street Sex Work: From Conflict to Coexistence*. York: Joseph Rowntree Foundation and Bristol: Policy Press.

Plumridge, L. (2001) 'Rhetoric, reality and risk outcomes in sex work', *Health, Risk and Society*, 3 (2): 199–215.

Potterat, J.J., Brewer, D.D., Muth, S.Q., Rothenberg, R.B., Woodhouse, D.E., Muth, J.B., Stites, H. and Brody, S. (2004) 'Mortality in a long-term open cohort of prostitute women', *American Journal of Epidemiology*, 159 (8): 778–85.

Radford, J. (1984) 'Womanslaughter: "A license to kill? The killing of Jane Asher"', in P. Gordon and P. Scraton (eds), *Causes for Concern*. Harmondsworth: Penguin

Rhodes, D. and McNeill, S. (eds) (1985a) *Women Against Violence Against Women*, London: Onlywomen Press.

Rhodes, D. and McNeill, S. (1985b) 'Women, angry at male violence, say: "resist the curfew!"', reprinted in J. Radford and D. Russell (eds) (1992), *Femicide: The Politics of Woman Killing*. Buckingham: Open University Press.

Sagar, T. (2005) 'Street Watch: concept and practice', *British Journal of Criminology*, 45 (1): 98–112.

Sagar, T. (2007) 'Tackling on-street sex work: anti-social behaviour orders, sex workers and inclusive inter-agency initiatives', *Criminology and Criminal Justice*, 7: 153.

Sanders, T. (2001) 'Female street sex workers, sexual violence and protection strategies', *Journal of Sexual Aggression*, 7 (1): 5–18.

Sanders, T. (2005) *Sex Work: A Risky Business*. Cullompton: Willan.

Sanders, T. (2008) *Paying for Pleasure*. Cullompton: Willan.

Sanders, T. and Campbell, R. (2007) 'Designing out vulnerability, building in respect: violence, safety and sex work policy', *British Journal of Sociology*, 58 (1): 1–19.

SCOT-PEP (2004) *SCOT-PEP Ugly Mug Incidents Briefing Paper*, February. Edinburgh: Scottish Prostitutes Education Project.

Scoular, J., Pitcher, J., Campbell, R., Hubbard, P. and O'Neill, M. (2007) 'What's anti-social about sex work? The changing representation of prostitution's incivility', *Community Safety Journal*, 6 (1): 11–17.

Self, H. (2003) *Prostitution, Women and Misuse of the Law: The Fallen Daughters of Eve*. London: Frank Cass.

Shell, Y., Campbell, P. and Caren, I. (2001) *It's Not a Game: A Report on Hampshire Constabulary's Anti-Kerb Crawling Initiative*. Hampshire Constabulary.

Smith, J. (1989) *Misogynies*. London: Faber & Faber.

Smith, J. (2008) 'The same old story?', *The Guardian*, 22 February.

Spare Rib (1978) 'We will walk without fear', *Spare Rib*, 66, January; reprinted in M. Rowe (ed.) (1982), *Spare Rib Reader*. Harmondsworth: Penguin.

Stoops, S. and Campbell, R. (2008) *Responding to violence against sex workers in Liverpool: an analysis of the Armistead Street Ugly Mugs Scheme data & an overview of the Independent Sexual Violence Adviser role*. Armistead Project, Liverpool.

Thukral, J. and Ditmore, M. (2003) *Revolving Door: An Analysis of Street-Based Prostitution in New York City*. New York: Sex Worker Project, Urban Justice Center.

Townsend, M. and Asthana, A. (2008) 'How two brutal killers fuelled the DNA debate', *The Observer*, 24 February.

Toynbee, P. (1977) 'Prostitutes', *Observer Magazine*, 3 April.

UKNSWP (2007) *Good Practice Guidance: Ugly Mugs and Dodgy Punters*. London: UK Network of Sex Work Projects.

UKNSWP (2008) *Briefing Re: Criminal Justice and Immigration Bill & Review of Demand (Paying for Sexual Services)*. London: UK Network of Sex Work Projects.

Walkowitz, J. (1992) *City of Dreadful Delight. Narratives of Sexual Danger in Late-Victorian London*. London: Virago.

Ward, H. and Day, S. (2001) 'Violence in sex work extends to more than risks from clients', *British Medical Journal*, 323: 230.

Ward, H. and Day, S. (2006) 'What happens to women who sell sex? Report of a unique occupational cohort', *Sexually Transmitted Infections*, 82: 413–17.

Ward, H., Day, S. and Weber, J. (1999) 'Risky business: health and safety in the sex industry over a 9 year period', *Sexually Transmitted Infections*, 75 (5): 340–3.

Ward, H., Day, S., Green, A., Cooper, K. and Weber, J. (2004) 'Declining prevalence of STI in the London sex industry, 1985 to 2002', *Sexually Transmitted Infections*, 80: 374–8.

Watson, S. (1995) *Personal Safety and Prostitution*, report for Streetreach, Doncaster.

West Yorkshire Police Authority (2000) *The Kerb Crawlers Rehabilitation Programme: An Evaluation from the Police Perspective*, Appendix D. West Yorkshire Police Authority.

Whittaker, D. and Hart, G. (1996) 'Research note: managing risks: the social organization of indoor sex work', *Sociology of Health and Illness*, 18 (3): 399–414.

Whittaker, D., Hart, G., Mercey, D., Penny, N. and Johnson, A. (1996) *Satellite Clinics and Delivery of Sexual Health Services to the 'Hard to Reach': An Evaluation. Final Report to the North Thames Regional Health Authority*. Academic Department of STD, University College London Medical School and Central London Action on Street Health.

Wilson, C. and Seaman, D. (2007) *The Serial Killers: A Study in the Psychology of Violence*. London: Virgin Books; first published 1990.

Wilson, D. (2007) *Serial Killers: Hunting Britons and their victims*. Winchester: Waterside Press.

Yallop, D. A. (1981) *Deliver Us from Evil*. London: Macdonald Futura.

Index